AMERICA RISING

AMERICA RISING

power and political economy
in the first nation

David Felix

Transaction Publishers
New Brunswick (U.S.A.) and London (U.K.)

Library of Congress Catalog Number: 2008031104
ISBN: 978-1-4128-0811-8
Printed in the United States of America

Library of Congress Cataloging-in-Publication Data

Felix, David, 1921-
    America rising : power and political economy in the first nation / David
    Felix.
        p. cm.
    Includes bibliographical references and index.
    ISBN 978-1-4128-0811-8 (alk. paper)
    1. United States—Economic conditions—1918-1945. 2. United
States—Economic conditions—1945- 3. Economic history—1918-1945.
4. Economic history—1945- 5. International economic relations—History—20th century. 6. International economic relations. 7. Great powers.
8. Balance of power. 9. World politics—20th century. 10. World politics—1989- I. Title.

HC106.F45 2008
330.973—dc22   2008031104

For Georgette

Contents

Introduction

America Rising

The United States became a great power in the last quarter of the nineteenth century and a superpower during World War II without quite knowing it. Few Americans, even our experts, fully appreciate the fact today. How many persons know that in recent years we have had a quarter of a million troops on 700 bases throughout the world?[1] Consider our recent history of military operations in the Caribbean, East Asia, the Far East, Middle East, Southeast Asia, Africa, and the Balkans. At its imperial height Great Britain ruled a quarter of the earthly geography, but it never had the power given us by our massive economy as armored by nuclear and other modes of killing capability.

If we need a reminder that our own situation is not assured, Paul Kennedy's *Rise and Fall of the Great Powers*: *Economic Change and Military Conflict from 1500 to 2000* is eloquent. He begins by noting the superiority of Ming China (1368-1644) with a population of 100-130 million as compared to Europe's 50-55 million, China's descent into becoming a nineteenth-century victim of rising nations from the United States to Japan, and then China's rise,[2] thus my chapter 12, "China Rising." From 1500 we see the rises of France, Great Britain, Habsburg Spain and Austria, and Germany, and their various descents. We remember Edward Gibbon's *Decline and Fall of the Roman Empire*.

We got here tortuously but expeditiously. Great Britain was the richest income-receiver until 1901. Between 1900 and 1901 the United States began to outstrip her, going from $4,091 to $4,464 in per capita gross domestic product (GDP), while she went down from $4.492 to $4,450 (in 1990 dollars).[3] The gap increased considerably through the century. While it is no grounds for self-congratulation, it expresses the real nature of our positive qualities. In 1800 the country had a population of 5.3 million;

in 1900, 76 million, and today close to 300 million. At the turn of the twenty-first century the American GDP was $8 trillion out of the world total of $37 trillion (in 1990 dollars or $9.8 and $46 trillion in current dollars), the American people, some 5 percent of the world population, dominating, if not quite ruling, the rest of the world's six billions: super-power.[4] No wonder we are enthusiastically and existentially hated.

We take for granted the extraordinary increases in wealth. In the twentieth century the average real per capita income of the advanced nations increased by a multiple of seven, America slightly more, and the average of a dozen Western European nations slightly less. (Italy, starting lower and ending higher, was at no less than 11.) That means enjoying automobiles, movies, television, air travel, computer networking, Asian vacations, other delectations—and also medical methods providing for more life, longevity in the advanced nations increasing more than 50 percent in the century. The class war and commercial rivalries might have been fought less passionately if the contenders had waited more patiently for the wealth increases.

One central fact of the rise of America was the intensely energizing interaction between polity and economy. The nation began with a political order and administration, as Alexis de Tocqueville noted, which derived from our British origins and enabled our pragmatic culture to take best advantage of the vast wealth of the near-virgin continent. Political and economic freedom were paired, authority yielding to both freedoms. Our farmers, unlike European peasants, were commerce-minded; our businessmen were dreamers, John D. Rockefeller, Andrew Carnegie, J. P. Morgan, Henry Ford, and, lately, Bill Gates, manufacturing realities out of those dreams. They were all workers. The nation had mastered the economics of Adam Smith, as he himself recognized, better than his British countrymen. This account makes a point of the economics in its second chapter as an anvil on which to hammer out a sharper sense of the economic content of our existence.

A corollary of the great increases of American wealth was economic instability. In its greater freedom, with fewer restrictions and safeguards, our economy was looser and more subject to sudden, deep depressions. Indeed the period 1877-97 was known as the Great Depression before the greater Great Depression of the 1930s. While Europe experienced a depression at that time, it was not nearly so severe, no European nation suffering through anything like the 15 percent to 20 percent unemployment rate of the United States in 1893-94. The Great Depression of the nineteenth century pointed the way to the disaster of the 1930s.

Absently taking advantage of the rich economy, President Woodrow Wilson significantly reduced the lag in the nation's consciousness of its role in the world. He knew and felt that the United States was a great power, and instructed the Old World in this new wisdom. In the course of the first world war (ten million dead) he correctly associated the United States with the fates of Great Britain and France, and their representative governments, as closer in spirit to us. Scamping the economic side of the American responsibility, however, he attempted to create an international comity essentially on a political and administrative basis. He also trusted in the vague "collective security" of the League of Nations in place of the balance of power, a denial of the realities of American and national power generally. It would take another generation to overleap the ensuing disasters and began to make up for them.

The American Congress and people, reacting to all the unsolved problems, turned their backs on Wilson's League of Nations. If it had helped save Europe, the United States now made Europe's condition infinitely worse by disclaiming its world responsibilities. It went on to cause great hurt economically by demanding payment of the war debts and keeping our tariffs high. The last element meant a long-enduring and deep imbalance in the international economy. The war-impoverished Allies, defending themselves against the American bill-collector, demanded high reparation payments from Germany. One effect was the German hyperinflation. Out of all these political and economic strains came Communism, fascism, Nazism, and with the help of the Great Depression, World War II. With our greater economic power, wielding 40 percent of the world's industrial production, we had imposed our economic law on Europe and the world. The Great Depression, another instance of American economic instability, was an effect of our economic nonchalance. Perversely, this train of causes and effects, by way of World War II, promoted the United States to superpower level.

In ascribing heavy responsibility to the United States, this study does not exonerate the European people and leadership. France punished a pacific Germany and, with this country, created an environment supportive of Hitler. Great Britain, clinging to the archaic gold standard, depressed its economy and generalized a damaging deflation further. An unintegrated Soviet Union worsened a general sense of international discomfort and insecurity. The sum slowed an economic process that was trying to create more wealth. The Thirties slumped into dismal economics, ferocious politics, and war.

No one, particularly the economists, quite understood the economics of the period. Franklin Delano Roosevelt, however, mastered the politics and suffering. His optimism and experiments saved the nation's economic society and slipped, by trial and error, into the effective solution of modest inflation combined with active governmental management of the economy. This domestic success permitted him to accept the nation's global responsibilities. It could then join Great Britain (and Soviet Russia) in saving the more (or less) democratic world.

We pass through the unimaginable hell of World War II: 50 million dead, the Holocaust, the agonies, and the projection of more horrors into the future. But we see an equally incredible turnabout despite the Cold War and its mortal threat. The United States becomes an effective, generous, tactful leader of the free world. It successfully contains a Communism, which joins exaltation with a strongly engineered structure to threaten a free world made vulnerable by depression and unemployment. The economics lesson is well, if not completely, learned: free enterprise and socialistic leadership at the top and social welfare for the economically handicapped. Free Europe prospers. France enjoys her "thirty glorious years" while West Germany her "golden years" into which the old East Germany will be eventually introduced. The world, including the poorer parts of it to some extent, resumes the expansion of its wealth. In all this the United States plays a positive role, sometimes, however, as sneakily acted out by the Central Intelligence Agency, while the envious and the perverse denounce its dirty hands.

The *entr'acte* of the Sixties interrupts and satirizes the solemn order of events as if it had been a tale told by Polonius. An American outburst, led by university students, rejects all structures, including Communism. Oddly or not, such actions as university seizures, trashings of a political convention, and denunciations of the Pentagon had their enlivening and constructive effects. One is our hastened departure from the war in Vietnam. Another, encouraged by the idealism of the Sixties, is the great action by blacks, which achieved equal civil rights and dignity for them (at least morally and legally) and raised millions to the level of the middle class. The result is a more just, resilient, and efficient society and economy, one more capable of winning the Cold War.

The dénouement is gentle. The United States becomes the greatest power in all world history. A monster nation disappears. The image of another great power begins to appear. At the same time little devils crawl through the cracks in a flawed world. The United States betrays its common and pragmatic sense. One might trust that, drawing upon its deep resources, it will correct its absences of thought and continue as *the* superpower.

Notes

1. Michael H. Hunt, *The American Ascendancy* (Chapel Hill: University of North Carolina Press, 2007), 282.
2. New York, Random House, 4-9.
3. Angus Maddison, *The World Economy: Historical Statistics* (Paris: Organization of Economic Cooperation and Development, 2003), tables, 61, 88.
4. *Ibid.*, tables, 82, 83, 88, 89, 60, 64, 65, U. S. Bureau of Economic Research (*bea. gov*). In current dollars the American GDP rose to $14 trillion in 2007.

1

Critical Mass

During the last third of the nineteenth century the United States, becoming truly united following upon the Civil War, gathered itself into the critical mass that made it even then the world's greatest economic power. According to the law of lag effect, neither the nation nor the world quite recognized it.

The period was much traduced in its time and later for corrupt and meretricious behavior, in this sense suggestively libeled by Mark Twain and his forgotten collaborator, Charles Dudley Warner, in the title of their novel *The Gilded Age*. Yet the authors, more satirical than indignant, also gave credit for its exuberant energy and ultimate success to its virtuous heroes and heroines. Others have called it no less accurately the Age of Confidence, Cynicism, Energy, Enterprise, Excess, Negation, Reform, or The Robber Barons.[1] Granting that the balance remains debatable, under the gilt and the gross luxury of the age's robber barons, one could find quality steel and morally negotiable gold.

Americans who thought politically thought in near-isolation about such domestic preoccupations, besides corruption, as mortgage rates and the greed of the factory, railroad, oil, and general corporate interests, or defending these productive agencies against post-Luddite wreckers. The nation had a tiny army barely capable of killing Indians, as Native Americans were still called, and a navy that just begun to emerge from sub-mediocrity in the 1880s. And if the American economy was pouring out a widening and deepening stream of desirable products, it was still a debtor enjoying the patronage of British, French, Dutch, and other European investors. Of course a few signs, besides the production and trade figures, spoke differently. In 1898, a year before the British began to undergo the embarrassments of the Boer War, the Americans, bullying and bloodying the Spaniards, had collected an absurd little empire of their own. Its power inevitably asserting itself, United States had reentered world affairs.

Overt events like wars and elections were the epiphenomena of the massive factors upon which American power was building. The beginning was the vision of the discoverers and founders, who correctly saw vast potentials. The extraordinary generation of founders began with strong foundations from their English past. They had demanded and won freedom as Englishmen already schooled in freedom and responsibility as expressed in their town meetings, colonial legislatures, and economic lives. Their political culture drew upon the administrative techniques established by the Norman Conquest, the growth of local authorities and the judiciary as well as Parliament, the Magna Carta as first formal limit on royal power, the grinding down of the English nobility in the War of the Roses, the Puritan Revolution with its Civil War and regicide, and a resolution permitting Parliament to expand its powers and representation gradually while the sovereign was being elevated into figurehead and the aristocracy limited by the demands of the middle class. More palpably, the Americans could exploit their continent's enormous wealth. The republic was no historical accident.

Alexis de Tocqueville saw it well in Andrew Jackson's America of the early 1830s. Despite the centrality of the South and the accelerating potentials of the West, he found in the North the "main ideas which now constitute the basis of the social theory of the United States...." These ideas were, he specified, the people's involvement in public affairs, the free voting of taxes, the responsibility of the agents of power, personal liberty, and trial by jury: "They now extend their influence ... over the whole American world. The civilization of New England has been like a beacon lit upon the hill." It was a dynamic civilization or culture. In what is certainly an idealized image, Tocqueville saw: "Everything is in motion around you; here the people of one quarter of the town are met to decide upon the building of the church; there, the election of a representative is going on; a little farther, the delegates of the district are posting to the town in order to consult [on] some local improvement; in another place, the laborers of the village quit their plows to deliberate upon the subject of a road or public school." Yet America paid the price in its thinking or lack of it: "In no country in the civilized world is less attention paid to philosophy than the United States." There was democratic method in the apparent mindlessness. The Americans were able "[t]o evade the bondage of system and family-maxims [and] class opinion ... to aim at the substance through the form.... America is therefore one of the countries where the precepts of Descartes are least studied, and are best applied." Furthermore the dynamic was at work. No one allowed himself or herself to be "reduced to the mere material cares of life...." The American "multitude [will] begin to take an interest in the labors of the mind.... The number of those who cultivate science, letters, and the arts becomes immense." If Tocqueville saw other negatives, like slavery and the "petty ... insipid ... anti-poetic life of a man in the United States," he balanced that by attributing "the singular prosperity and growing strength of that people ... [t]o the superiority of their women."[2] On balance he was willing to join in American optimism.

Tocqueville had found America at a low point after its separation from the immediacy of English experience and the creation of its own culture. The men who had made the American revolution were an Enlightenment elite conversant in Greek and Latin with Plato and Cicero, and fertile with such expressions of the period as the Declaration of Independence and the Constitution, grounded as they were in philosophy, law, and administration. The next generation was exemplified by Andrew Jackson, the first Western president (1829-37), who appealed to the common man and his tastes. Obedient to Tocqueville's prophecy and led by New England, however, American culture presently made up some of its lost altitude.

We need a bifocal lens. We return to Mark Twain. In *The Gilded Age* he had diluted, if not falsified, his genius with a mediocre collaborator. Mark Twain saw America more truly, more variously, more profoundly in his other writings, his classics, most relevantly in his *Adventures of Huckleberry Finn* and *Life on the Mississippi*: life in the regularly beating heart of the nation. The books were written from 1876 to 1884 about pre-Civil War life in the United States.[3]

During the Jackson period, Huck Finn, a free soul escaping from a brutal drunkard of a father, joins up with Jim, an escaping slave, to float down the Mississippi on a raft. They join temporarily with the self-anointed King and Duke, two grifters mulcting innocents in the spirit of American free enterprise. Huck also encounters a Mississippi Romeo-and-Juliet romance leading to a murderous Mississippi Montague-and-Capulet blood feud: classic epic and American violence. More to the point, reflecting the conscience of its emancipated Southern author, Huck strains against the immorality of aiding an escaped slave, but cannot bring himself to inform on Jim: friendship and humanity before the received standards—and a portent of the historical emancipation.

Life could be a poem on the Mississippi: "Two or three days ... swum by ... slid along so quiet and smooth and lovely. Then we set out the lines ... take some fish off ... and cook up a hot breakfast. And afterward we would watch the lonesomeness of the river, and kind of lazy along,

by and by lazying off to sleep." Or it could be god-awful: "[L]oafers ...
whittling ... with their Barlow knives; and chawing tobacco and gaping
and yawning and stretching—a mighty ornery lot. All the streets was just
mud ... as black as tar, and about a foot deep." What to do after coming
home and finding that Jim had been freed and Aunt Sally was "going to
help me and sivilize me and I can't stand it? I been there before." Huck
had his American solution: "I reckon I got to light out for the Territory."
The frontier would not be declared closed before 1890.[4]

Life on the Mississippi was constructed more historically and auto-
biographically around Mark Twain's experiences as a young steamboat
pilot. It communicates a sense of the terrific labors and skills Americans
applied to their ever-new country. A tremendous and perverse river swept
its exploiters along to prosperity, but also, perversely, to deception and
danger, its course always shifting and its dangers sometimes destroying
its magnificent steamboats and proud pilots. The pilot Samuel Clem-
ens—Mark Twain—while escaping being blown up with the boilers of the
steamer *Pennsylvania*, learned every bend of more than twelve hundred
miles of river, left and right bank, upstream and downstream. But then,
in a swift American rhythm of expansion, contraction, and expansion,
railroads and other factors, beginning with the Civil War, killed steam-
boating as Twain knew it: "So I became a silver-miner in Nevada; next
a newspaper reporter ... and finally a scribbler of books."[5]

Mark Twain was vastly more than a reporter: general and economic
and business historian, and sociologist, his research deriving from an
imaginative genius producing wonderful stories and overimaginative
businesses ventures, the latter betting extravagantly, for example, on
a typesetting machine subject to irreparable breakdowns. Here, in the
Mississippi River book, is the economic observer: "The Natchez Cotton
Mills Company began operations four years ago in a two-story building
of 50 x 190 feet, with 4000 spindles and 128 looms; capital $105,000....
Two years later ... 10,300 spindles and 304 looms." He concedes that he
was not expecting to see "Natchez and the other river towns becom[ing]
manufacturing strongholds and railway-centers." The United States was
outrunning his imagination and becoming a great industrial nation.

The sociologist Twain reports on wealth and taste in "The House Beau-
tiful": "The engraving 'Washington Crossing the Delaware' ... other works
of art, conceived and committed by the young ladies ... solitary sailboat,
petrified clouds, geological trees ... persons all fresh, raw, red—appar-
ently skinned," a multitude of objects: plaster fruit painted incompetently,
sentimental music books, a guitar, photographs of grandparents and

simpering female grandchildren, and so on for four more pages.[6] With these solecisms and extravagances, as Tocqueville saw it, the American trader, Mark Twain joining him, would conquer the world.

One significant stage in recreating America was the Cambridge meetings of the Metaphysical Club in the early 1870s. It is typical of the national contradictions that the group excogitated an American pragmatism while using metaphysics to seize the angular facts of American existence. The contradictions did not disturb the group. Among its members were the two founding pragmatists Charles S. Peirce and William James. Other members included the lawyer and future Supreme Court justice, Oliver Wendell Holmes, Jr., other lawyers, a historian, and other scholars and intellectuals. The writings of the Vermonter John Dewey converged with those of Peirce and James and proceeded much further.

Both Peirce, whom James credited with inventing pragmatism, and James himself mixed the metaphysical with the psychological into their pragmatics. It was by way of his personal idealism that Peirce arrived at his trial-and-error experimentalism, his variant of pragmatism, where the truth emerged from the real world as laboratory. Leaning heavily on psychology, especially its own, James found the truth of an idea not inherent in it but upon his encounter with it. His "will to believe," thus, overcame an otherwise uncompromising determinism and provided the freedom to make decisions. Dewey added a populist variant of pragmatism in his instrumentalism, which tried to show how philosophical ideas worked in everyday life. Changing all the while, his logic adapted itself to need and circumstance. This led the Harvard idealist George Santayana to remark, "Insofar as thought is instrumental, it is not worth having."[7]

Upon such shifting grounds the philosophy of pragmatism made its New England compromise with the practical, non-thinking aspect of American life—rationalized it. Dewey brought his philosophy into education, in 1896 creating a school at the University of Chicago, which emphasized activities over formal curricula. This was a "dumbing down" of education, as it would later be characterized, diluting its context but exposing badly prepared school children to some of it, at least. With its deceptions pragmatism made sense.[8] One had to be patient to let Tocqueville's logic work itself out toward its hopeful horizons.

The physical frame for the development of the American ethos began small, however big with promise. At Jefferson's inauguration in 1801, the 13 states had a population of 5.3 million, including more than a million slaves, but not counting 600,000 Native Americans (down from an estimated 5 million as a result of disease and other American effects). At President William McKinley's inauguration, a century later, the census counted 77 million Americans, including the former slaves and their descendants, and also the Native Americans at their nadir of 250,000, in 45 states.

In the early years agriculture made up nearly all the American economy except for the requisite trading and small crafts. At the time of the American Revolution 75 percent to 90 percent of the Americans were farmers. Of the first three presidents, George Washington and Thomas Jefferson were great landowners (and notoriously, also, slaveholders) and John Adams, who came between them in chronological order, maintained a working farm all his adult life, his spirited wife, Abigail, doing the greater share of the working.[9] In 1900, 60 percent of the nation still lived on farms; at the end of the twentieth century the agricultural population was below 2 percent. In 1900 the American farmer fed himself and one other person. At the end of the century he was feeding more than two dozen others.[10] The export figures paralleled these numbers. In 1901 agriculture provided 65 percent of American exports, the totals falling to 32 percent in 1917, but rising under the effects of World War I to 51 percent in 1919, then falling again to 32 percent in 1930, holding in the 30 percent range to 1936, then dropping below 20 percent in the 1960s and below 10 percent in 1997.[11] Yet even in relative decline compared with industry, American agriculture was a leading global exporter[12] while contributing substantially to the nation's annual Gross Domestic Product of $10 trillion by the turn of the twenty-first century. Equipped by science and technology, more Americans were feeding more Americans *and* foreigners.

In the nineteenth century, wielding their substantial numbers, American farmers had been a powerful constituency. To serve them the Department of Agriculture was created during the Civil War, on May 15, 1862. Actually this would have happened earlier but for an entanglement in the dispute on slavery. The department was first limited to research and education, but, as time went on, it entered into regulatory operations and, later, into direct assistance to farmers. Meanwhile, five days following the department's creation, the Homestead Act granted 160 acres free to settlers—effectively licensing them to rape land reserved for Native Americans. (Before he became president in 1829, Andrew Jackson had been a major force in driving them from the Southeast.) Also in 1862, on July 7, the Morrell Land-Grant College Act more constructively gave land to the states for agricultural colleges, the beginnings of the great state universities. For the farmers all this was not enough.

Of course American farmers had their monumental problems. The inexorable improvements in productive efficiency, on the land as well as in the factories, were making most of them redundant. Nature disobliged with droughts and winter freezes. Business downswings, particularly the depression of 1893-97, resulted in widespread distress and foreclosures of overextended farmers. In response they demanded or attempted a series of reforms and panaceas: government price supports, cooperatives, revival of wartime paper money or, at least, silver-based currency, and support of a populist third party. In 1896 the populists actually captured the Democratic Party and achieved the failed candidacy of William Jennings Bryan as champion of silver.[13] While their more ambitious demands were frustrated, the farmers would win many concessions, thus price supports and government aid, in the years ahead. Meanwhile they could enjoy two comparatively prosperous decades in the recovery from the 1890s depression, which was followed by the increased demand for food products caused by World War I.

The relation of agriculture and industry was closer and more mutually helpful than their politics would suggest. With industry providing much of the means, from 1860 to 1915 the production of corn almost quadrupled and that of wheat more than quintupled as unit costs fell. From 1900 to 1910 prices of farm products rose 50 percent; between 1910 and 1920 farmland quadrupled in value.[14] One sees the early signs of the agribusiness of the later twentieth century.

In their political demands American farmers continued to see themselves as simple toilers on the land beset by the urban instruments of exploitation. Yet their agriculture had been more explicitly commercial than that of other countries: "[C]ommercial gain . . . has dominated the thoughts, goals, and endeavors of most American farmers throughout the nation's history,"[15] as the agricultural historian cited above put it. Technology allied itself with profit-seeking. In the later years of the nineteenth century the farmers began using commercial fertilizers, the cream separator, the steel plow, the grain drill, reaper, binder, thresher, and combine, and the steam tractor, and more widely, the gasoline-powered tractor. The life and works of Henry Ford fused farming, technology, and commerce. At the age of fourteen he left his father's farm and went to work in a Detroit machine shop—to return to the farm at nineteen and spend more than a decade as a farmer. He was, however, also augmenting his income by repairing farm machinery. Then, intrigued by the gasoline engine and the attractions of profits, he returned to Detroit and industry.[16] The result became an important chapter in the economic and industrial history of the United States and the world.

The American farmers diverged widely from the patterns of the European peasants. Society and economy in the United States were fluid, Americans moving much more easily from occupation to occupation and class to class. One began as an immigrant pioneer and moved on to farmer, prospector, teacher, lawyer, politician, or merchant. The European peasantry, obsessed with its property boundaries and attached to ramified relationships deriving from feudal times, could hardly imagine a different existence. The innumerable possibilities of the American economy expanded the imagination of the American agricultural community.

The unalloyed success of the American economy, led by such masters as Rockefeller, Carnegie, Morgan, and Ford, was not equaled by its management of foreign trade. Tariffs accreted into being an important, if rarely read, chapter in the economic history of the United States. Alexander Hamilton's 1793 Report on Manufactures recommended bounties for manufacturers and protective tariffs against the expected flood of British goods, but the Congress refused to approve action upon it at the time. In 1816, however, President James Madison was able to support and sign a moderate tariff bill when the British goods did indeed appear. At the time of the Civil War the government of Lincoln, beginning with the Morrell Tariff of 1861 and again in 1862 and 1864, drastically increased tariffs from about 18 percent to the 40 percent level. There they remained subject to still more increases into the 1890s. The earlier tariffs had been rationalized, with some excuse, as revenue measures, but the special interests they created or succored were demanding protection when it was no longer needed, a self-indulgence that was a massive element in the world's political economy into the mid-twentieth century.[17]

Whether or not protection helped, American industry, naturally efficient, ruthless, alert, and drawing on rich resources, developed fast, often precipitously. One early example of many was the enterprise of Francis Cabot Lowell. After spending 1810 to 1812 spying out power-loom secrets in England, he brought in partners and founded two hugely successful cotton mills in Massachusetts beginning in 1814.[18] A year later the Springfield Armory, an example of public action in the spirit of private enterprise, established another major precedent. Operating with meticulous inspection and controlling expenses by equally meticulous bookkeeping, an enterprising colonel developed the technique of manufacturing its weapons with interchangeable parts. Thus any firing pin or trigger, for example, would fit into any revolver of the same make and caliber. It was "the prototype of the modern factory," and by the late 1840s and 1850s private companies, including: Colt Patent Firearms;

Remington, the forerunner of the Winchester Arms Company; and the Pratt and Whitney Company, a future manufacturer of aircraft engines, would generalize the Armory's methods.[19] With coal mining, railroad construction, and the telegraph (invented 1844) all vigorously operative before the Civil War, American industry was ready to explode into a vast expansion afterward.

As soon as the Civil War ended, entrepreneurs laid railroad tracks across the breadth of the land. Among the other anticipatory economic measures during the war, Lincoln had signed the Pacific Railroad Act in 1862 authorizing land grants to support the Central Pacific, building eastward from Sacramento, and the Union Pacific, westward from the Missouri River. They met at Ogden, Utah, on May 10, 1869. Three other transcontinental lines were completed, two in 1883, and the last in 1893. The country went from 35,000 miles of tracks in 1865 to 193,000 miles in 1900.[20] "The tremendous railroad construction ... gave basic industries a national market," as seen in one perspective.[21] In another: "For several decades the consolidated railroad systems remained the largest business enterprises in the world."[22] Industry and agriculture—the nation—grew with the trackage.

American industry could draw upon the American genius for invention, now showing itself variously. In May 1876 Philadelphia held its Centennial Exposition, the heart of which was the fourteen-acre Machinery Hall. Among the exhibits were Thomas Alva Edison's quadruplex telegraph (a further development of an Englishman's 1844 invention), Alexander Graham Bell's telephone (which Edison would improve), the six-story-high Corliss steam engine and many other smaller steam engines; blowers and lathes; sewing, knitting, and paper cutting machines; and cotton and printing presses. A French observer wrote, "The Americans possess the genius of invention to the highest degree." A German professor called his country's products "cheap and bad" compared to the American's, and Adolph Hitler, a later commentator, remarked with characteristic vulgarity that the Philadelphia exposition had been a salutary "kick in the pants" for German industry and invention.[23]

Other inventions and adaptations of the era included Edison's incandescent lamp of the 1880s and his almost immediate creation of lighting systems to bring the lamp and electric power to everyone; his phonograph of 1877 and his moving pictures from 1896; the swift development of the motor car by Henry Ford and others in the 1890s; Marconi's radio of 1898 (exploiting radio waves Edison had discovered but failed to pursue), and the Wright brothers' airplane of 1903. To produce all these, American industry swiftly adapted the Bessemer and the open hearth steel-making processes, invented, respectively, by an Englishman in 1856 and a German in 1860. The terrific promise of expanding territory, population, and wealth drove American industry into continually multiplying the numbers and variations of its products: a mostly metallic cornucopia.

American industry was overtaking and outstripping all its rivals. From 1840 to 1880 its output grew at an annual rate of 4.03 percent, and for the next 40 years, at 3.52 percent. Compared with that, Great Britain grew in virtually the same periods at, respectively, 2.4 percent and 1.77 percent, while Germany had an impressive annual rate of 3.09 percent for 1871-75 to 1917. (One country, however, had a somewhat better record than the United States; Japan, building from a small base, grew at 4.14 percent annually from 1878-82 to1918-22.) Per capita output showed the United States accelerating much faster than Great Britain, which grew at a per capita rate of 1.33 percent, compared with the American rate of 1.26 percent for the first period, but then fell back to .86 percent, compared with America's 1.61 percent for the second. Having multiplied by five from 1860 to 1900, American industrial production surpassed the individual production of Great Britain, Germany, and France by 1890, and their combined production by 1900.[24] In 1913, by another measure indexing American per capita production at 100, Great Britain's per capita production was at 90, Germany's at 64, and France's at 46.[25] Except militarily, the United States was a world power, indeed a superpower.

Among the American innovations the refinement of factory management, more broadly, economic administration, was of first importance. It amounted to the use of common-sense principles, as in the case of the prototypical Springfield Armory, in managing the whole range of industrial and agricultural operations. The Americans had the advantage of operating on a virtual and vast tabula rasa, without the impediments of established customs and laws, thus ancient inheritances and regulations, guilds, and other inhibitions of enterprise. Nor could peoples like the Native Americans interpose their different rhythm; they were simply swept away. American firms were constructed of strangers, coolly selected for efficiency or discarded for lacking it, while Europe's family firms, developed over generations, could take advantage of inherited talent but too often would qualify their judgment with more human factors. Fish-blooded management monopolized the rewards.

The common-sense principles of the American managers were really common and ordinary. The interchangeability of parts implied the maximal standardization, thus the track gauges of the railroads and even time:

the railroads inevitably forced the various regions to agreed on common hours so that train schedules were true at any point on the track length. Another banal principle was reducing costs, but it was a prime element in the management of those great industrialists, John Davison Rockefeller and Andrew Carnegie. Both insistently pressed for economies at every stage in production and marketing. During the crucial years 1862-85 Rockefeller's Standard Oil was establishing itself as a great power in the industry by cutting the average cost of producing a gallon of refined oil to a third, from 1.5 cents to 0.5 cents.[26] In the same years Carnegie was building up his steel-making business. "Costs would always be Carnegie's obsession in business.... 'Carnegie never wanted to know the profits,' one of his partners said. He always wanted to know the cost." The principle was: watch the costs and the profits will take care of themselves.[27]

A few other elements characterized American managerial techniques. One was scale: the inevitable aim of successful enterprise was to become as big as possible and enjoy the maximal economies of size. Production was continuous so that no time was lost: the various raw materials entered at one end of the plant and the finished product emerged as the other without interruption. Production was integrated. Thus Rockefeller began with refining oil, later controlled the oil wells producing it, the pipelines delivering it, and the distribution system to sell it and its by-products. Carnegie captured the richest iron ore field in the world. Actually he got it at a fair price from Rockefeller, who had fallen into it first—and created a fleet to ship it across Lake Superior. A great railroad man like J. Edgar Thomson of the Pennsylvania Railroad and financiers like Jay Gould and William Vanderbilt managed and financed the great railroads. Other examples of integration and expansion abounded.

Consumer products were being manufactured and marketed similarly. In 1885 James Buchanan Duke bought the rights to the Bonsack cigarette machine, which produced a continuous tube of tobacco to be wrapped in paper and sliced into individual cigarettes, which were then packaged mechanically. As important, he developed a mass distribution network placing the cigarette packages into consumer hands as conveniently and lethally as possible. In 1881 Gustavus F. Swift had a refrigerator car designed to carry meat. He was followed into the long-distance shipment of refrigerated meat by Philip D. Armour and the Cudahy Brothers, among others. The leading firms added stockyards to control supply, developed a carefully subdivided system of butchering on moving "disassemblying lines" and national marketing operations. Similarly, and almost simultaneously, brewers set up distribution networks to enter the national market.[28]

In a work published in 1990, following his study of the managerial structure of American enterprise noted above, the business historian Alfred Chandler compared it with the business organization of other leading nations. Picking 1973 as one baseline, he denoted the specifics of American predominance among the world's largest industrial corporations. Of 401 firms with more than 20,000 employees, 211 or 52.6 percent were American; 50 or 12.5 percent, British, while Germany had 29 such firms, Japan, 28, and France, 24, these latter, thus, at about 7 percent. In other references going beyond 1973 into the 1980s, he found the United States much further advanced than Britain or Germany into managerial capitalism as opposed to the older familial type, Germany ahead of Britain.[29] (He failed, however, to discuss Japan, not a comparative magnitude but an innovator in managerial techniques.) Peering beyond Chandler's works into the twenty-first century, we can see that the United States, astride its bulk and nurturing its inventiveness, thus in the field of computers, inter alia, continues to maintain its global entrepreneurial leadership.

The United States was extending the marvelous achievements of the Industrial Revolution, which sprang out of Great Britain from 1760, and the promise of laissez-faire as conceived by Adam Smith in his *Wealth of Nations*. No nation was better equipped to realize Smith's sensible, roomy view than this country. He saw America as growing rich the fastest, with "much higher" wages than England, and went on to "compare the slow progress of : . . European conditions with the rapid advances of our North American colonies."[30] Untrammeled with the numerous restrictions accreted over time in the older countries, brushing past the Native Americans and mobilizing the slaves and indentured servants, America could use its economic freedom and license to experiment widely upon the national resources as found. An examination of that economy's potentials and limits should lead to a better sense of the theory and practice of economics. No country, the United States appearing at just the right time, could better embody the sense and—and the disappointments—of the new science.

The negative side of such tremendous increases in productivity and wealth produced by the American economy was their inherent instability. All of the advanced nations experienced it, the 1873-97 period being known as the Great Depression for all of them, surely an exaggeration before the true Great Depression of the 1930s. The United States, however, experienced greater swings upward and downward because of its looser economy and more casual regulations. Nor was unemployment a major problem for most nations at the time, except for the American experience of 1893-97. A later estimate found "savage" joblessness, at a maximum of 15 percent to 20 percent, in 1893-94, but "partial" recovery by 1895 reduced the savagery by interposing brevity.[31] Otherwise all reports elsewhere emphasized production and price falls, with reduced revenues and bankruptcies, as the major depression features. In the United States, with no formal state or local aid, private charity could do little to alleviate the suffering of the unemployed. This was the condign price of American good fortune.

Free-form and formal politics dramatized the unemployment issue. On March 25, 1894 a group of a hundred unemployed left Massillon, Ohio, to bring their protest to Washington. Led by the businessman Jacob S. Coxey, the group had gathered some 500 members by the time it arrived. Trusting in an inflationary cure, Coxey's Army, as it was called, was demanding $500 million in paper money to finance road construction. On May 1, with a few lieutenants, Coxey was arrested for trespassing on the Capitol lawn and his army disintegrated. More effective protests followed.

The hard times emboldened the Democratic supporters of a bimetallic currency system, another inflationary solution, and won William Jennings Bryan's nomination in 1896. Their effort failed at that point, however, and William McKinley, the Republican nominee, would find his administration helped by the discovery of gold and the resumption of economic expansion. The 1893-97 depression remained a dire suggestion.

The insecurities emphasized a great absence in the American economy, that of a central bank, a contemporary of the Bank of England, the Banque de France, and the German Reichsbank. The United States had had one and lost it to popular prejudices. The First Bank of the United States, founded in 1791 and designed by the financial and administrative genius of Alexander Hamilton, was superbly effective, but its prudent management of credit antagonized many as catering to elitist interests. Responding to these objections and to the principle of states' rights, President Andrew Jackson effectively ended the life of the Second Bank of the United States by 1836. Without a central bank, the nation made do with insecure state banks and ad hoc solutions to the inevitable financial and economic problems. If this was a regressive move, it nevertheless reflected the federal character of the union and accorded with the burgeoning experimentation of the American economy, or rather, political economy.

The insecurities were only opportunities for the great entrepreneurs. Uninhibited by regulations, able to maneuver among the various local, state, and federal authorities, they could direct themselves toward great objectives, which only they could see or see first. At the same time they kept in mind second and third goals to be advanced upon without pause when the first ones had been reached. They took advantage of situations that defeated others, thus depressions, when Andrew Carnegie bought up steel plants and Rockefeller, oil refineries. They could do it cheaply with carefully saved reserves, while other firms starved for funds and were forced to sell. The great banker J. P. Morgan, effectively the nation's central banker, gave the government critical assistance in overcoming financial crises and grew richer.

After a three-month business course, the sixteen-year-old John D. Rockefeller (1839-1937), son of a presently disappearing salesman of fake cures, got a job with a commission merchant in Cleveland in 1855. At eighteen he became a partner in a produce merchandising firm. At twenty-four, prospering, he joined an expert in oil, discovered nearby in northwest Pennsylvania in 1859, in building a refinery, and in 1865 bought out his partners to wager on the great possibility. By 1870, at thirty, Rockefeller had enlisted talented new partners, some with more capital, and, easily maintaining his ascendancy, organized the Standard Oil Co. (Ohio). In 1872 Standard Oil was powerful enough to join with the powerful Pennsylvania Railroad in an arrangement providing for such special advantages for participants as rebates for large shippers, a business practice then widely denounced. Resistance and indignation were so great that the new operation was dissolved in two months, but the threat frightened twenty-two of Standard Oil's twenty-six Cleveland competitors into letting Rockefeller buy them out. Assisting him was his store of cash reserves, which easily financed purchases of those weakened by the 1873-79 depression. By 1879, at forty, Rockefeller was one of the twenty richest men in the United States and Standard Oil was a huge firm expanding hugely. In the 1890s it had 100,000 employees.

The continually mounting resistance and indignation validated and bonified Rockefeller's success. The Sherman Anti-Trust Act of 1890, inspired by a wave of mergers Standard Oil exemplified, caused its scission into thirty-four new companies in 1911. As the largest share-holder, Rockefeller, however, saw his portfolio triple in value from $300 million to $900 million, shrewd financial observers, placing their buy orders, translating every Rockefeller defeat into victory. Of the new firms three became members of the Seven Sisters dominating the world's oil establishment into the twenty-first century: Exxon (Standard Oil of New Jersey), Mobil (New York), and Chevron (California).[32] In his later years, after delegating more and more responsibility, Rockefeller devoted himself as creatively to philanthropies.

Andrew Carnegie (1835-1919), becoming the leading steel producer as Rockefeller became the greatest oil producer, anticipated most of the broad lines of his actions. Son of a Scottish weaver, Carnegie began precociously, moved swiftly from one objective to a higher one, picked talented associates, linked a series of processes into an integrated operation, cut costs, and drove out or bought out competitors. He enriched himself by offering the consumer the lowest prices and best quality. He spent his last years responsibly and self-congratulatingly giving away his money.[33]

A generation later, Henry Ford (1863-1947) replicated the functional characteristics of both Rockefeller and Carnegie crudely but no less effectively. With his Model T Ford, first produced in 1908, he magically matched the industry's lowest prices with the highest wages by making the cars identical and selling so many. The price went from $825 to $345 by 1916. He was paying the competitive wage of $2.50 a day in 1913, when he decided to reduce turnover by raising it to a five-dollar minimum for an eight-hour shift; great crowds of applicants rioted to accept. Also, in 1913, Ford established the first moving assembly line, another tremendous advance to be emulated everywhere. Earlier Ford had proposed: "The proper system ... is to get the car to the multitude" at the multitude's wages. By the end of World War I almost half of the world's automobiles were Model Ts. By 1937, however, General Motors, adopting sophisticated management techniques, had overtaken him, its Chevrolet outselling the Ford at a lower price, while its range of four more costly models attracted choicer sectors of the multitude. In these later years, Ford had grown rigid and dictatorial, firing his best managers and persisting too long in old practices, but he had been the great initiator.[34]

Thomas Alva Edison (1847-1931), governing a modest plant but creating new products, occupied as important a position as the grand entrepreneurs. His contribution precisely validated the prophecy of Tocqueville that Americans would move from the practical to the scientific. A self-taught master of technology, possessor of 1,093 patents, more than any other person,[35] he had abjured a command of science: "I do not regard myself as a pure scientist.... I do not study science ... simply for the purpose of learning truth. I am only a professional inventor."[36] Yet he could not have functioned as he did it without an intuitive command of science's laws.

Edison's ultimate laboratory, in West Orange, NJ, was an "invention factory ": he had invented not merely a series of technological wonders but the *scientific* process of inventing endlessly. (The Bell Laboratories, creator of the transistor, are one of the many imitative invention factories.) On his own Edison invented the light bulb, "the whole basis for the modern system of power distribution, including sockets, switches, fuses, fixtures, [and] meters." Besides creating the phonograph, he contributed enormously to the telegraph, the telephone (making it practical for general use with the carbon transmitter), typewriter, microphone, motion picture camera and film, storage battery, the electric railway, synthetic chemicals and rubber, and mining machinery, wax paper, Portland cement, mimeograph, and the dynamo. He was the "father of the electrical age."[37]

The techniques of production were given sharper point by Frederick Winslow Taylor (1856-1915), who propounded the philosophy of scientific management.[38] His tool was a stopwatch and his method little more than the elimination of waste motion. Of course it was simplistic, but a disciplined emphasis of simple principles could improve efficiency significantly. Henry Ford's assembly line and industry generally applied "Taylorism," the United States Army Ordinance mobilizing it in World War I and Lenin and Stalin yearning toward it. Communists and capitalists knew that efficiency was essential in operating an economy.

Sympathetic to their employees' needs as they professed to be and actually were most of the time, Rockefeller, Carnegie, and Ford found themselves in bitter conflict with them. Their humanity yielded to efficiency, the first condition for their success, to the point of violence. The economic philosopher Adam Smith might have questioned union activity as organizing monopoly in restraint of trade, but the moral philosopher Adam Smith, abhorring violence as regression to medieval practices, would have sought a compromise permitting maximum peaceable expression to all contending parties. This might be demanding too much. In economics, as in civilization, progress, or better said, "progress," remains irreducibly ambiguous.

Absolutely anti-union, Rockefeller kept Standard Oil union-free. In 1903, in one instructive instance, that of the corporation's refinery in Bayonne, NJ, he used persuasion and deftly broke a strike for union recognition. This easy resolution, however, was followed by an extraordinarily bloody and protracted strike at a mining and steel production company Rockefeller had acquired as a separate investment in 1900. This was the Colorado Steel and Iron Company, the state's largest employer; his manager, in line with Rockefeller's explicit wish, spent fifteen months resisting a strike of 9,000 workers for union recognition, begun in September 1913. One result of Rockefeller's policy, in April 1914, was the shooting deaths of several strikers by drunken National Guardsmen and the accompanying deaths by asphyxiation of two women and eleven children huddling for safety in an inadequately protected bunker of the strikers' tent colony. Rockefeller's manager went on to break the strike by December. Only later, profoundly affected by the deadly violence and public outcry, did John D. Rockefeller, Jr., who assumed responsibility as his father retreated from it, change the company's policy. Eventually, the union was granted recognition, but not until 1933.[39]

Compared to Rockefeller Sr., Andrew Carnegie was a towering hypocrite on unions. Son of a local Chartist leader in Scotland, Carnegie tried to unite the radical and egalitarian philosophy of his childhood with the demands of efficiency. Efficiency won. Yet he published magazine articles defending unions in 1886. At issue was a contract with the Amalgamated Association of Iron and Steel Workers, a craft union, in his Homestead plant near Pittsburgh. The union had 800 members in the workforce, otherwise not organized, of 3,800. Carnegie agreed with his partner, the intensely principled Henry Clay Frick (an art lover and a founder of the Frick Museum in New York City), that the contract should not be revived on the terminal date of June 30, 1892. Giving Frick carte blanche, Carnegie thereupon went on his annual vacation in Scotland, where he disappeared, evidently purposefully. Frick particularly objected to the union's traditional work rules, which interfered with effective management. He offered the union terms so bad that they were clearly unacceptable, effectively shut down operations, and had 300 strikebreakers, provided by the notorious Pinkerton detective agency, towed up the Monongahela River on barges. Along with town inhabitants, 3,000 nonunion workers, all paid a third less than the Amalgamated men, supported the union. They attacked the invading fleet and conquered the strikebreakers in a pitched battle on July 6. Seven workers and three strikebreakers were killed, one of the latter clubbed to death as he walked a gantlet in town after surrendering, and sixty persons were wounded, some fatally. Although the Pinkerton men had retreated in Homestead, the workers had only won a Pyrrhic victory. No one has clearly explained why these nonunion workers and town dwellers risked and lost lives and jobs for the elite union's privileged position. Frick survived two bullet and three stab wounds administered by a demonstrative anarchist two weeks later, and went on grimly to break the union. After the fact the consistently hypocritical Carnegie, more sensitive to opinion than the Coriolanan Frick, blamed him for undiplomatically brutal action and, by 1899, broke with him. The Carnegie operations finished the decade with huge profits.[40]

Henry Ford, operating into a later era, had been as obdurately anti-union as Rockefeller, Harry Bennett, his notorious, strong-arming labor relations director, incorporating his policy. In the late 1930s the organizing drive of the United Automobile Workers, encouraged by Franklin Delano Roosevelt's administration and the spirit of the times, persuaded two of the three great automobile firms, General Motors and Chrysler, to be reasonable and negotiate union contracts. Ford was less reasonable, his minions emphasizing his judgment by bloodying four union leaders, who were distributing union pamphlets, in a famously photographed encounter at the Ford plant on May 26, 1937. The photographs recorded the anti-union enforcers approaching them, and the assault itself on Richard Frankenstein, who had his coat pulled over his head, and the bloodied faces of Frankenstein and Walter P. Reuther, the UAW president. The back of one of the other men was broken and the fourth also spent several days in the hospital. The terrific public reaction had its effect on Ford and Bennett after more struggles and a strike in 1941, when the employees voted overwhelmingly for UAW representation. Ford was shocked into seeing himself in a strange world and "never the same after that." Outraging other industrial leaders, the Byzantine Bennett then negotiated a surprisingly and extraordinarily generous union contract in a vain effort to put the union in his debt.[41]

One must go beyond and above industrial enterprises to identify the era's critical figure. He was John Pierpont Morgan (1837-1913), manager of the purest expression of economic value, money, or as the twentieth century's greatest economist, John Maynard Keynes, liked to call it illustratively, liquidity. Rockefeller meant oil, Carnegie steel, Ford automobiles, Edison inventions, Taylor scientific management, but Morgan meant almost everything of economic value: steel, if not directly oil and automobiles, railroads, local transit, an oceanic fleet, electricity, communications generally, iron ore mining, agricultural machines, federal and city government, and books and newspaper publishing. Illustrating the ubiquity of his liquidity, some of his concerns, like the last pair, were modest, while others were historic. At the end of his career Morgan and his partners held 72 directorships in 122 of the nation's biggest companies, while his bank's corporate issues in 1902-12 were valued at $1.95 billion.[42]

Junius Spencer Morgan, John Pierpont's masterful father, had established himself as a banker in London in 1854. The son, carefully schooled in banking, began operating as New York agent for the London bank in the 1860s. Presently the Morgans became the most important conduit of European capital financing American industrial expansion, particularly in its railroads. A promising investment, the United States was the great international debtor of the period. This began to change in the 1890s when the wealthier American classes had amassed enough profits and began to invest overseas themselves.[43] Junius remained a strong force until he died in 1890, while John Pierpont was seeing his independent power rising upon the rising American wealth. If he was not completely independent until 1890, the younger Morgan had long demonstrated his pure genius as a banker—his ability to enter creatively and powerfully into a great range of profitable enterprises.

A master of calculations but inarticulate, unable to explain how he arrived at his swift decisions, John Pierpont Morgan had a feeling for character and for what worked in the economy. Applying himself to railroads, an instinctive Taylorite, he financed, reorganized, and/or consolidated many, reducing charges and management staff, imposing better accounting controls, and ruthlessly disposing of weaker affiliates. He mediated the peace between William H. Vanderbilt's New York Central and the equally powerful Pennsylvania Railroad when their battle threatened both with bankruptcy.[44] At the turn of the century Morgan found himself, assisted by the enduring Henry Clay Frick, in an uneasy, temporary association with John D. Rockefeller, in completing the life work of Andrew Carnegie for Carnegie and achieving another, greater triumph for himself. Out of this entanglement of personalities and enterprises Morgan created, perhaps to his own surprise as to everyone else's, the United States Steel Corporation, another corporate trust and the first billion-dollar company.

The various elements of United States Steel included the 120-mile long Mesabi Range of Minnesota, the greatest iron ore mine in North America, where the ore was in the convenient form of a grainy powder conveniently placed on or near the surface. The mine, which Andrew Carnegie had failed to buy when first given the opportunity, would have given him an essential piece to his steel empire. At the same time he was plotting to build another transcontinental railroad, an enterprise clashing with Morgan's various railroad interests. Yet, although his old momentum was carrying him forward, Carnegie was tiring of business and cherishing other ambitions. Rockefeller, having fallen upon the Mesabi Range as an investment, had got his value out of it and also had concerns beyond business. Morgan found himself too deep in the steel fabrication business, having backed an associate in organizing the Federal Steel and National Tube Company, vulnerable to Carnegie's vaster steel operations. In this unstable compound Charles Schwab, a brilliant protégé of Carnegie's, played catalyst. Competent enough to function as president of Carnegie Steel, Schwab had the vision to see a new order. He proposed that Morgan buy the sum of Carnegie's operations from Carnegie and the Mesabi Range (including Rockefeller's iron ore fleet) from Rockefeller, and build around Carnegie Steel and Federal Steel. Rockefeller was happy to take away a substantial profit of $55 million on the original price of $85.5 million for the ore field. Carnegie demanded (and was happy to get) his price of $480 million for all his operations instantly from Morgan, who never haggled over a few score millions if the proportions were right. Schwab's idea had provided an extraordinarily satisfactory resolution of the desires of the three major players. Thus the United States Steel Corporation, created on March 3, 1901 and capitalized at $1.4 billion.[45]

Morgan himself was rising to the level of an independent government, however generously he might assist his own government. In 1890 the nation got itself absurdly into deep trouble. William McKinley, then chairman of the House Ways and Means Committee, reported out a bill raising the tariff level close to 50 percent, an historic high. Becoming law, the bill reduced trade and hence tariff revenues abruptly over the next years. With trade in deficit, gold flowed out of the country.

Two interlocking examples of two great American economic errors, tariff and financial policy, were leading to many short-run troubles and greater, indeed catastrophic, long-run disasters. The nation's high tariffs inevitably reduced the income of its foreign customers, who had to limit their purchases of American exports. This was not quite self-evident under the din of the demands for protection. At home, under the effects of self-defeating financial populism, American finances revolved around the hollow center of the non-existent central bank eliminated by Andrew Jackson and the need for emergency support in the inevitable crises. In its pragmatic way the nation had made do with the necessarily public-spirited help of the great New York bankers, J. P. Morgan in chief.

In 1895 the United States Treasury called upon Morgan. To avoid the need for congressional approval of a loan, Morgan proposed to acquire gold coin and trade it to the Treasury for U. S. bonds. The transaction provided $62.3 million and stabilized the situation temporarily. Morgan then had to continue providing funds well into 1896, President Cleveland, meanwhile, destabilizing the situation politically and financially by his intervention in a British-Venezuelan border dispute. In the end Morgan had collected $262.3 million for the government in three years. Many persons suspected falsely that he was taking advantage of the situation to win huge profits and the New York *World* darkly saw a Wall Street conspiracy. Of course he would have been blamed had he taken no action. The Democrat Cleveland defended Morgan: "He was not looking for a bargain, but to avert peril ... in a severe and trying crisis."[46] Morgan himself "always considered the Treasury rescue the proudest accomplishment of his life."[47]

Another crisis, the Panic of 1907, was graver, a matter of the national economy and not simply an international payments problem. The overexpanded American economy was faltering after a heady rise from the depression of the 1890s, the stock market dropping off in March and collapsing more emphatically in October. Morgan, returning from an Episcopal Church convention on October 20 (he was its leading layman) spent two weeks contending with the crisis, which brought with it a burst of bankruptcies and unemployment. Under threat were major New York banks, the New York Stock Exchange, and New York City itself, which could not pay its employees. All risking their institutions' funds, Morgan breveted two New York bankers as his lieutenants, also calling upon Rockefeller's aid to match his own. In the final episode Morgan commanded the presidents of other New York banks to his library on Sunday, October 3, to extort from them a final loan of $25 million. Part of his efforts included a merciless triage to decide which banks were viable enough to be saved.[48] Although he was cooperating with a grateful U.S. Treasury, Morgan's success got him into deep trouble with the administration and public opinion.

If his help in the 1895 crisis aroused irresponsible suspicions, Morgan's newer action was so important—so *national*—that it raised serious, objective questions. He had been acting like the head of the missing central bank. Indeed another cause of the crisis was a lack of liquidity, which that bank could have provided. Even if he was not making an illegitimate profit, Morgan was indubitably carrying out a major governmental function.

Morgan was, moreover, the organizer of great corporate trusts quite possibly violating the Sherman Anti-Trust Act. Indeed in 1902 President Theodore Roosevelt's government had instituted a suit under that act, which had long been dormant, against the Northern Securities holding company, organized by Morgan. The company had attempted to control rail transportation in the Northwest, and the Supreme Court dissolved it the next year. This was one of the mergers, which had, according to one count, consolidated 4,277 firms into 257 around the turn of the century.[49] Yet also in 1902 Roosevelt had gratefully accepted Morgan's cooperation in settling a great coal mine strike, and later tried to control the great corporations instead of breaking them up.[50] Morgan, meanwhile, had to answer to the government he had so masterfully aided.

The Panic of 1907, making it shockingly clear that no authority occupied the directing center of the nation's banking operations, led to the creation of the initially inadequate Federal Reserve System. Under way, however, the House Banking and Currency Committee set up a subcommittee to investigate financial abuses and the "money trust," as personified particularly by Morgan. Committee Counsel Samuel Untermeyer suggested that the New York banks cooperating in the 1907 financial rescue had monopolized sales of prime issues and otherwise stifled competition. On December 18-19, 1912, Morgan, characteristically inarticulate but unable to tergiversate, endured this cross-examination:

> Untermeyer: You are an advocate of coordination and cooperation as against competition, are you not?
> Morgan: Yes, cooperation, I should favor.
> Untermeyer: Combination as against competition?
> Morgan: I do not object to competition, either. I like a little competition.[51]

Morgan had been to so honest that he confessed to more of an advocacy, if not an active imposition, of a limit to competition. Actually, as he expressed it, American business was troubled by the frantic competition of too many small, inefficient firms, and he had responsibly encouraged consolidation, efficiency, and stability. Powerful as he was, he thought he had more power that he actually had, and his efforts had left much undone. Certainly the great corporations, while wielding their economies of scale and other advantages, were still vulnerable to even more efficient firms or to chance and chaos. The study of mergers between 1895 and 1904, noted above, studied 93 consolidations and reported that 1800 firms had "disappeared" in that period.[52] Most of those surviving 93 corporations have themselves disappeared since then, thus American Bicycle, Amalgamated Copper, Massachusetts Breweries, Continental Tobacco, among others. More than a half century later the American economy remained sufficiently open for a vast number of independent companies to appear, leading to a repetition of the earlier events. Alfred Chandler reported in his 1990 study, also mentioned above: "By the late 1960s the drive for growth through acquisitions and mergers had almost become a mania."

The number of consolidations had risen from 2,000 to 6,000 between 1965 and 1969.[53] Morgan had liked a little competition.

Morgan suffered a series of strokes, and, three months after testifying in Washington, died March 30, 1913.[54] The Federal Reserve bill became law on December 23, and the banking system could function more or less safely without him. Yet, requiring more ad hoc makeshifts, the nation remained tentative about central banking for another two decades before the Federal Reserve System could become truly effective.

The public and social element was important, even central, in the lives of exemplars of private enterprise like Morgan et al. However harsh in business, they were all exemplars of efficient service to humanity.

It was the individual spirit of enterprise driving these entrepreneurs to their economic vision that generated their equally individualistic bene- factions. One irreducible element in their creativity was that individual character. No government, church, or committee had the personal and psychic freedom and method to think and act so imaginatively. Suggest- ing the limits to social and socialist strivings, these business leaders were operating on a higher functional level of social giving. This was a unique American initiative, another element in the nation's productive superior- ity. Each of these four titans of the economic world found a peculiarly fitting manner of giving, both for themselves and for society.

John D. Rockefeller began at the age of fourteen when he joined a poor Baptist Church in Cleveland, becoming volunteer janitor, minute- taking board secretary, Sunday school teacher, and minister's deputy. Out of his income as a merchant's clerk he tithed the fifty dollars of his three-month starting wages. He went on to beg donations from the poor congregation, himself contributing, to pay off the church's enormous debt of $2,000. Beginning with the Atlanta Baptist Female Seminary for black women, later Spelman College, he went on to generalize his aid to black education in the modestly named General Education Board. Beyond that he created the great University of Chicago in 1892, the Rockefeller Institute (later University) for Medical Research, and the Rockefeller Foundation. He gave away more than $1.5 billion in much less inflated dollars than today's.[55]

Andrew Carnegie gave $50 million for 2,800 free libraries, built the Carnegie Institute of Technology (today's Carnegie-Mellon University), and founded the Carnegie Endowment to seek world peace, the latter raising the Palace of Peace in The Hague.[56]

As member of an Episcopal church near his home, J. P. Morgan sup- ported its social action and brought into his own firm a partner with experience in dealing with social and political problems.[57] While enjoying a substantial yacht, he funded the construction of the Cathedral Church of St. John the Divine in New York's Morningside Heights, aided Columbia University's move to that area, presided over the Metropolitan Museum while contributing to its collections, and through his son gave 7000 *objets d'art* worth $80 million to the museum. The younger Morgan also gave his father's library to New York City, a small wonder comparable to the Frick Collection.[58]

Besides doubling the pay of his automotive workers, Henry Ford pioneered in the active employment of blacks, women, physically-challenged persons, and convicts. He was naïve enough to try to stop World War I with the famous Peace Ship of 1915. He was also malevolent enough to publish anti-Semitic material in the local Dearborn newspaper, an initiative he dropped when, stubbornly naïve, he entertained presidential ambitions. More constructively, he founded the Dearborn Museum exhibiting artifacts, which represented the transition from agriculture to industry. More grandly civic while avoiding huge taxes, he then helped fund the Ford Foundation in 1936 "for scientific, educational, and charitable programs, all for the public welfare." Much richer than the Rockefeller Foundation, it had spent some $8 billion by 1994, some of its programs swerving to the left under his grandson-successor, perhaps not in violation of the founder's populist principles.[59]

The operations of these entrepreneurs, public as well as private, were a central part of the period's greatness. For these years, historians, oriented toward the political, related complex narratives of the Reconstruction agony, the old struggle against corruption, and the unavailing efforts to do something, anything, about the absurd tariffs. Between Lincoln and Theodore Roosevelt, from 1865 to 1901, while Congress wrangled loudly, the president remained at a modest elevation of competence and effectiveness. Andrew Johnson, attempting to moderate the radical Republicans' virtuous bullying of the impoverished white South, was impeached, while the radicals themselves failed to moderate its neglect or brutalization of blacks. Ulysses S. Grant was embarrassed by scandals. Later, Grover Cleveland, a sensible reformer, governed sensibly (except for the gratuitous quarrel with Great Britain), but was embarrassed by the tariffs and the depression of 1893-97. The elected leaders lost themselves too often among the shadows of the economic realities managed by the Rockefellers, Carnegies, Fords, Morgans, et al.

The exuberantly political Theodore Roosevelt began the process of taking back the country's leadership from the economic giants. (Recall that he found it politic to cooperate with J. P. Morgan as well as frustrate him.) Woodrow Wilson would strengthen the newer political command, and if the next three presidents would regress, Franklin Delano Roosevelt would reaffirm it all the more forcefully.

Son of a Lincoln Republican and reformer, Theodore Roosevelt rose precociously from New York State legislator to civil service commissioner, president of the New York City Police Commission, assistant Navy secretary, governor of New York State, vice president, and president in 1901. He assisted his ascension to the presidency by resigning from the Navy Department to recruit his volunteer regiment of Rough Riders and lead them in the 113-day Spanish-American War of 1898. He met his destiny when President McKinley died of an anarchist assassin's bullet on September 14, 1901. By then Roosevelt had established himself both as a reformer and imperialist. This was the age of the New Imperialism, a friendly context.

Rudyard Kipling's "Take up the white man's burden," was published in February 1899. In 1904 Roosevelt proposed his so-called Corollary to the Monroe Doctrine, giving "some civilized nation," thus the United States, the right to correct "chronic wrongdoing" committed by a self-evidently less civilized nation. In that spirit, already in 1902, Congress and Roosevelt launched themselves toward the Panama Canal project (with the assistance of J. P. Morgan as master of liquidity), Congress authorizing the president to buy the rights of the canal stockholders. The next year the legislature of Colombia, seeking more compensation for its command over the area, balked, and an impatient Roosevelt encouraged and defended a rebellion creating an independent Panama, that is, independent of Colombia and dependent on the United States. Roosevelt later boasted, "I took the Canal Zone."[60] In those years, besides seizing the Philippines and Puerto Rico and assuming protectorates over Cuba and Hawaii, the United States took upon itself to send the Marines into the Dominican Republic, Haiti, and Nicaragua to civilize their finances and governments.

The acquisition of the strategically exposed Philippines led to a concern with Asia. In 1899 and 1900 Secretary of State John Hay issued his Open Door notes affirming the principle of equal trading rights for all in a prostrate China. In 1900 the United States had joined other foreign powers in repressing the Boxer Rebellion, an early reaction against the imperialism they were practicing there. In 1905, demonstrating America's power along with its good opinion of peace, Roosevelt intervened in the Russo-Japanese War and mediated the treaty ending it. He got the Nobel

Peace Prize for his trouble. In December 1907 he showed American power more bluntly by sending a fleet of sixteen battleships on a fifteen-month world voyage. Roosevelt had established America's presence in Asia and international affairs.

Woodrow Wilson thereupon conquered Europe, at least temporarily.

Notes

1. Introduction, Louis J. Budd, Mark Twain, and Charles Dudley Warner, *The Gilded Age: A Tale of Today* (New York, Penguin Putnam, 2001); 21st ed.: 1873), xiv.
2. Alexis de Tocqueville, *Democracy in America*, ed. Richard D. Heffner (New York: New American Library, 1956; original French eds.: 1835, 1840), 246, 42, 46, 42, 108, 143,162, 181.
3. Mark Twain, *Adventures of Huckleberry Finn* (Berkeley: University of California Press, 2002, revised ed.: 2002; 1st ed.: 1884); *Life on the Mississippi*, 1st ed.: 1883, *The Favorite Works of Mark Twain* (Garden City, NY: Garden City Publishing Company, 1935).
4. *Adventures of Huckleberry Finn*, 156-57, 181, 183, 362.
5. Twain, *Life on the Mississippi*, 98-102; quotation, 102.
6. *Ibid.*, 175-76, 170-73.
7. Quoted, "Pragmatism," *Dictionary of the History of Ideas.*
8. As rationalized in the widely read Henry Steele Commager, *The American Mind: An Interpretation of American Thought since the 1880s* (New Haven: Yale University Press, 1950), which is better as reflection of its time than interpretation of the selected period. While it conscientiously addressed all the aspects one might reasonably demand, it failed to study pragmatism adequately and remains blurred by tactful generalities. It ends contemplating the atomic bomb: "They [the Americans] made the atomic bomb; would they use it for purposes of civilization or destruction?" (443). This is still an America contemplating not much more than itself.
9. R. Douglas Hurt, *American Agriculture: A Brief History* (Ames, IA: Iowa State University Press, 1994), 33; David McCullough, *John Adams* (New York: Simon & Schuster, 2001), passim.
10. Bureau of the Census, *Statistical Abstract of the United States: 1930, 1990*, p. 619: table 578; p. 637: table 1098.
11. Bureau of the Census, *Historical Statistics of the United States: Colonial Times to 1970, Part I*, 482; Bureau of the Census, *Statistical Abstract of the United States, 1999*, 684: table 1121.
12. Hurt, *American Agriculture*, 391.
13. See Gretchen Ritter, *Goldbugs and Greenbacks: The Antimonopoly Tradition and the Politics of Finance in America* (Cambridge: Cambridge University Press, 1997).
14. Thomas C. Reeves, *Twentieth Century America: A Brief History* (New York: Oxford University Press, 2000), 6; Samuel Eliot Morison and Henry Steele Commager, *The Growth of the American Republic*, vol. 2 (New York: Oxford University Press, 1962 [5th ed.], 302-7.
15. Hurt, *American Agriculture,* ix.
16. Robert Lacey, *Ford: The Men and the Machine* (Boston: Little Brown, 1986), 24-41.

17. See Frank W. Taussig, *The Tariff History of the United States* (New York: Johnson Reprint, 1966; 1st ed.: G. P. Putnam, 1931).

18. Walter Licht, *Industrializing America: The Nineteenth Century* (Baltimore: Johns Hopkins University Press, 1975), 26-30.

19. Alfred D. Chandler, Jr., *The Visible Hand: The Managerial Revolution in American Business* (Cambridge, MA: Belknap/Harvard University Press, 1973), 72 ("prototype")-77.

20. Sean Dennis Cashman, *America in the Gilded Age* (New York. New York University Press, 1993: 3rd ed.), 23-30; John F. Stover, *American Railroads* (Chicago, University of Chicago Press, 1961).

21. Harold U. Faulkner, *Politics, Reform, and Expansion 1890-1900* (New York: Harper & Brothers, 1959), 74.

22. Chandler, *The Visible Hand*, 88.

23. Recorded and cited, Robert Kanigel, *The One Best Way: Frederick Winslow Taylor and the Enigma of Efficiency* (New York: Viking, 1997), 125-30 ("genius of invention," "cheap and bad," "kick in the pants").

24. Harold G. Vatter, *The Drive to Industrial Maturity: The United States Economy, 1860-1914* (Westport, CT: Greenwood, 1975), table, 68.

25. Licht, *Industrializing America*, 102; Cashman, *America in the Gilded Age*, 8.

26. Chandler, *The Visible Hand*, 324.

27. Joseph Frazier Wall, *Andrew Carnegie* (New York: Oxford University Press, 1970), 337.

28. Chandler, *The Visible Hand*, 382-91, 299-302.

29. Alfred Chandler, Jr., *Scale and Scope: The Dynamics of Industrial Capitalism* (Cambridge, MA: Belknap/Harvard University Press, 1990), 20, 234-94, 397-427.

30. Adam Smith, *The Wealth of Nations*, ed., Andrew Skinner (Baltimore: Penguin Books, 1970; 1st ed.: 1776), 172 (Book I, ch. 8), 516 (Book III, ch. 4).

31. Douglas Steeples and David O. Whittaker, *Democracy in Desperation: The Depression of 1893* (Westport, CT: Greenwood, 1998), 50. See also S. B. Saul, *The Myth of the Great Depression* (London: Macmillan, 1969) and J. T. Walton Newbold, "The Beginnings of the World Crisis, 1873-96," *Economic History*, supplement of *Economic Journal* 2, no. 7 (January 1932), 425-41.

32. Ron Chernow, *Titan: The Life of John D. Rockefeller, Sr.* (New York: Random House, 1998), 44-45, 63-65, 77-85, 129-60, 217, 537-59.

33. Wall, *Andrew Carnegie*, passim.

34. Lacey, *Ford*, 93-95, 117-31, 108, 84 ("The proper system . . ."), 97, 298.

35. Wyn Wachhorst, *Thomas Alva Edison: An American Myth* (Cambridge, MA: MIT Press, 1981), 4.

36. Ronald W. Clark, *Edison: The Man Who Made the Future* (London: Macdonald & Jane's, 1977), 67, 153.

37. Wachhorst, *Edison*, quoted, 4, 22.

38. See Kanigel, *The One Best Way*.

39. Chernow, *Titan*, 571-90.

40. Wall, *Carnegie*, 537-82, 714-64; Samuel A. Schreiner, Jr., *Henry Clay Frick: The Gospel of Greed* (New York: St. Martin's Press, 1995), 69-85.

41. Lacey, *Ford*, photographs between 364-65; account, xviii, 355-57, 368-74, 384; contract terms and "never the same," according to a Ford executive, 377.

42. Vincent P. Carosso, *The Morgans: Private International Bankers 1854-1913* (Cambridge, MA: Harvard University Press, 1987), 634. Morgan saved Harper & Brothers from bankruptcy, *ibid.*, 295-96, and helped finance Adolph Ochs's pur-

chase of *The New York Times* in 1896, Jean Strouse, *Morgan: American Financier* (New York: Random House, 1999), 356-57.

43. This earlier period, Carosso, *The Morgans*, 1-174 passim; the 1890s, *ibid.*, 397.
44. *Ibid.*, 363-83, 254-57, 259-67.
45. Carosso, *The Morgans*, 466-74; Strouse, *Morgan*, 391-415; Wall, *Andrew Carnegie*, 765-93; Chernow, *Titan*, 382-93.
46. Strouse, *Morgan*, 339-49; Carosso, *The Morgans*, 311-51, quotation, 336; Henry F. Bedford, Trevor Colbourn, and James H. Madison, *The Americans: A Brief History* (New York: Harcourt, Brace, Jovanovich, 1972, 4th ed.), 365.
47. Carosso, *The Morgans*, 337.
48. The episode, Strouse, *Morgan*, 575-94; Carosso, *The Morgans*, 528-49.
49. Strouse, *Morgan*, 396. See also Naomi R. Lamoreaux, *The Great Merger Movement in American Business, 1895-1904* (Cambridge, Cambridge University Press, 1985).
50. Reeves, *Twentieth Century America*, 35-36, 45-46.
51. Carosso, *The Morgans*, 724-47; testimony quoted, 632.
52. Lamoreaux, *The Great Mergers*, 1-42; "disappeared," 2.
53. Chandler, *Scale and Scope*, 622.
54. Strouse, *Morgan*, 674-80.
55. Chernow, *Titan*, 51-57, 481-500, 302-29, 493-97, 472-79, 562-70.
56. Wall, *Andrew Carnegie*, 866-69, 828-940.
57. Strouse, *Morgan*, 218-22, 415.
58. *Ibid.*, 275, 494-508, 687-89.
59. Lacey, *Ford*, 117, 194-219, 104-5.
60. Bedford et al., *The Americans*, 399 (I took. . . .")-400; J. P. Morgan's financial role, Reeves, *Twentieth Century America*, 38.

2

Economics Lesson for Economists and Others

Understanding America's rise as the dominating economic power of the twentieth century requires a sense of its economics. While one must plunge into economic theory, even into its depths, it is less difficult than it appears. One can avoid the rebarbative mathematics and specialized language economists like to employ today. Plain English is enough, as shown by Adam Smith, moral philosopher and founder of classical economics. Moreover, of the three great theorists of its completion as neoclassical economics, only one used mathematics in his discussion, but he accompanied it with comprehensible verbal analysis. Economics addresses the elemental needs of existence: every person is a practicing economist and possesses the practical experience and capacity to think about his or her economic actions.

As much as politics, economics expresses the major elements in history. To set economic history on an equal level with it is not to denigrate political history; the one makes the other more meaningful. While concentrated studies of either continue to give great value, a balanced examination of the two together can have its unique value. The material force of economic ideas is also central. A history of economic theory is an account, indeed a bookkeeping account, of the substance of history and life. We pursue reality when we study the labor (or cost) theory of value, marginal utility, division of labor, supply and demand curves, and the price of silver and gold.

Economics became more complex when the Commercial Revolution, expanding with the opening of the New World, began to lift the European heartland out of the simple agricultural economy of medieval times. The Industrial Revolution, beginning about 1760, added a new dimension of complexity, with its great range of new wealth in production facilities and consumption products, and the swings up and down of economic activity imposing their hardships and confusions on the global culture.

While remaining comprehensible, economics has required a continually widening and deepening of thinking about those changes. Lags in that thinking had been particularly deceptive. We have seen them in the case of the United States, thus its rejection of a central bank and, along with that, adequate central management of an economy continually expanding into regions of the unknown. Of course the Europeans have sinned in their fashion.

We can profitably look backward. The Greeks *thought* economics very well indeed. Plato (427-347 BCE), contemplating the division of labor, proposed an ideal stationary state managed by an elite in a communist order. Aristotle (384-322 BCE) defended private property as developing a spirit of responsibility, and examined distribution and exchange. On the latter he distinguished use value from exchange value, a distinction becoming a preoccupation of Adam Smith, David Ricardo, Thomas Malthus, John Stuart Mill, and Karl Marx. Aristotle made another contribution, this one of mischievous effect, when he called the charging of interest an evil as the unfair use of money to produce money. This logical-seeming thought, taken up by Christian theology as expressed in the reproving word *usury*, has pained bankers and interfered with business practices over the ages.

We begin properly with Adam Smith (1723-1790), professor of moral philosophy at Glasgow University, who established economics as a science within a large philosophical frame. While he necessarily missed much, he sensed most of what has been added to economics since his time. Naturally he knew Plato and Aristotle, and, in the course of a slow tour of France, personally experienced the Physiocrats, who had developed a sophisticated economic science of their own. He appropriated from them the ideal of laissez-faire but rejected their designation of agriculture as the sole source of wealth. He got to his *Inquiry into the Natural Causes of the Wealth of Nations*, published in the vintage year 1776, through his *Theory of the Moral Sentiments* (1759) and never lost his concern for morality. This softened the edge of his celebration of the "invisible hand," enlightened self-interest, which many called a cover for greed. But, with his moral and intellectual balance, he could counter that a free economy with free competition best served the interests of the commonality. His economic system expressed that sense in its various workings.

Smith enriched his economics by setting it in the context of philosophy and history. He proposed one of the two models of economic inquiry, the general as against the concentrated specifics, the widely inductive as against the rigorously deductive. Since his time economists have shuttled between the two, but increased professionalism has led toward the specialized and deductive, an inevitable and not necessarily wrong turning. That nevertheless made Smith all the more valuable to economists, who needed to communicate with laymen.

The philosopher Smith had a powerful grasp of the reality of industry and the making of *things*. Early in *The Wealth of Nations*, to illustrate the division of labor, he describes the manufacture of pins: "One man draws out the wire, another straights it, a third cuts it, a fourth grinds it . . . and the important business of making a pin is ... divided into about 18 distinct operations. . . ." He calculates that the individual could not have made "the two hundredth and fortieth ... perhaps not the four thousand, eight hundredth part" of what the team could produce.[1] He had got the sense of the Industrial Revolution. Going far beyond the use of machines, it was the purposeful organization of various activities in a *process* of multiplying production and consumption, thus wealth.

Smith could relate the advances he observed more appropriately to America. Compared with England, it was "much more thriving, and advancing with much greater rapidity to the further acquisition of riches." He could, moreover, compare all of Europe invidiously with America in the section "Inequalities Occasioned by the Policy of Europe." Among many other limits to free enterprise in Europe, he noted that guild privileges restricted competition for jobs.[2] America, he saw, had become the most hospitable locale for his economics.

Smith had less success with that essence of economics: value. He saw labor as its origin, hence the labor (or cost) theory of value: "The real price of every thing is the trouble of acquiring it."[3] Nature's contribution, he held, was free. Yet he had to explain the variance of prices for equal amounts of labor. He solved the problem verbally by seeing that "the word *value* has to two different meanings...." Following Aristotle, he distinguished use from exchange value, water being eminently useful but valueless in exchange while diamonds were hardly useful but hugely valuable in exchange. Thus the market price could vary widely from the "true" price, the value created by labor and expressed in its "true cost." Again and again he returned to what he could not fail to see was a paradox. Thus the increased/decreased supply of gold and silver meant decreases/increases in their exchange value. Similarly, as a history of the Black Plague recorded, an epidemic reducing the population of workers caused pay increases despite royal wage controls. Symmetrically, plentiful Argentine beef meant lower meat prices. Smith concluded: "Abundance, therefore, renders provisions cheap."[4] This was one step away from the determination of price by the interaction of supply and demand, but he had to leave that to a later generation (see below). He had contributed an enormous wealth to thought.

For good and ill Ricardo (1772-1823) led economics toward purity rather than comprehensiveness and deduction over induction. A stock broker of Dutch-Jewish parentage who had developed a passion for pure economic theory, he quickly amassed a fortune that permitted the leisure and comfort to pursue it for the last decade of his life. If he could not advance the *knowledge* of economics much beyond Smith, he recreated Smith's broad, humanistic social science into an instrument of analysis. Seeing the economy as divided into rent, profit, and wage sectors, he constructed a thought machine and set it to work through time inexorably grinding out a difficult and dismal future.

Ricardo's friend, Thomas Malthus, had set the dismal direction in his *Essay on the Principle of Population* (1798). Malthus posited a geometric population increase fed by planting land capable of being expanded only arithmetically, a mechanism which would require poorer and poorer soil. The resultant shortfalls would impoverish existence for all while killing off the marginal population, a thesis Ricardo's logic accepted. But the logical method is itself impoverished. At the same time that population was increasing, economic efficiency driven by the Industrial Revolution and the older Commercial Revolution, was disproportionately improving the agricultural as well as general productivity, hence well-being. This is one illustration of the limits of Ricardo's theorizing (although a margin of the dying would persist with a greater population). In order to make his logical machine work, Ricardo had to exclude too much of reality. Indeed all economists and practitioners of the other sciences as well make the same error, inevitable in the deductive method.

The quandary was incorporated in the good friends Ricardo and Malthus. The pitiless logic of his own theory was too much for Malthus himself, who also preferred induction as his method. He rewrote the essay in a series of six increasingly expanded book editions from 1803 to 1826, each successively softening its harsh thesis. While Malthus slipped into a gentler induction in the friends' always amiable and fruitful debates, Ricardo kept to his deductions. In the main the new profession of economists followed, although generally without his pessimistic conclusions.

Another example of the rigor—and the limits—of Ricardo's thought was his wrestling with Adam Smith's labor (cost) theory of value. Complaining that Smith had failed to analyze the effects of capital accumulation, he sought an "invariable standard" with which to measure value. In the end, however, he had to admit that "we have no knowledge" of that standard. Yet he insisted that "we may hypothetically argue and talk about it, as if we had; and may improve our knowledge of the science, by showing distinctly the absolute inapplicability of all standards which have hitherto been adopted." The best we could do, he was admitting, was to define his economist's ignorance more precisely. Sometimes, however, his rigor denied reality. Thus he defended Smith for failing to credit the contribution of the natural resources to value, arguing that "they perform their work gratuitously ... add[ing] nothing of value in exchange."[5] In this instance Ricardo's solution was metaphysical, his teachings remaining problematic.

The political philosopher and general thinker John Stuart Mill (1806-1873) attempted to consolidate the ideas of Smith, Ricardo, Malthus, and the Frenchman Jean-Baptiste Say (popularizer of the idea that supply creates an equal demand). Mill's *Principles of Political Economy*, first appearing in 1848, with newer editions in 1849 and 1852, established itself as Britain's dominant economic textbook for the rest of the century. While he speculated about supply and demand, he passed on his predecessors' arguments with little fundamental change and the complacent assurance that all the major economic problems had been solved. A new generation of economists, however, disagreed. These comprised the neoclassical group, as it was later categorized, while Smith and Ricardo were celebrated and corrected as the classicals. The neoclassicals were the English William Stanley Jevons, the Austrian Carl Menger, and the French, but Swiss-employed, Léon Walras. If they produced an eminently satisfactory new economic logic, however, one must continue to recognize the distance between the logic of economists and reality.

All three neoclassicals agreed absolutely on the general equilibrium system constructed around the intersection of supply and demand; and marginal utility, the last fraction of perceived usefulness of a commodity or service in impelling the exchange between seller and buyer in the "market." The market is any place where sellers and buyers meet, a "farmer's" market meeting physically once a week in a town locale or the global market of the financial services transmitting prices and quantity instantly. Jevons seems to have placed more emphasis on marginal utility, while Walras developed his vision of general equilibrium more elaborately, but both, like Menger, who kept uncanny balance between them, regarded the two elements as essential.

Walras put it justly for all three in his foreword to a later edition of his great work: "[T]he theory of exchange based on the proportionality of prices to *intensities of last wants satisfied* (i.e., *to final degrees of utility* ...)—this view evolved almost simultaneously by Jevons, Menger, and myself, constitutes the very foundation of the whole edifice of economics. . . ."[6] Jevons, having published an article with his conception in 1866, had temporal priority, but his *Theory of Political Economy* and Menger's *Principles of Economics* were both published in 1871. Walras wrote that he first saw the Jevons book when his own first edition was being printed in 1874.[7] Yet the independent thought *and* agreement of the three great thinkers is established beyond doubt. In his massive and erudite *History of Economic Analysis* (1954), Joseph A. Schumpeter of Harvard University, an immensely erudite Austrian economist schooled in the Menger tradition, called Walras "the greatest of all economists."

Milton Friedman, a virtuoso economist himself, found Schumpeter's opinion "extravagant," but he himself said of Walras: "His general equilibrium system gives a bird's eye view of the economic system as a whole, which has not only an extraordinary aesthetic appeal as a beautifully articulated abstraction but also a utilitarian appeal as providing relevant, meaningful, and mutually exhaustive categories."[8] The Walras book propounds its theory with "primitive mathematics" and "crabbed prose," according to William Jaffé, his superbly competent economist-translator. Yet Jaffé agrees with Friedman that the Walras explication was indeed aesthetically appealing. The same is even truer of the Jevons and Menger books, successively examples of electrically charged English and remarkably pellucid German prose.[9]

Despite attacks on it from within and without, and the ambiguities radiating from John Maynard Keynes's glosses, neoclassical economics still provides the most completely accepted way of studying the whole range of economic existence. More specifically to our purpose, it is the best approach to an understanding of economic reality and, perhaps more to the point, the American experience. We would do well to examine the general equilibrium system and its specification in marginal utility. The essence of it is simple but slippery. To assist understanding and its retention, we draw a picture or graph of the "market" as do the textbooks:

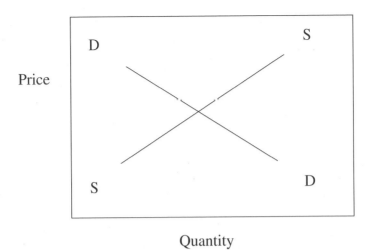

Quantity

Price is measured vertically and quantity, horizontally. The whole field is the market for a given commodity (or service) or all of such together, with the vertical expressing price and the horizontal, quantity. The two curves (or lines) represent supply and demand. While the curves are abstractions, they nevertheless represent reality—buyers and sellers and their intentions.

In any market we should the think of the demand (D-D) curve, falling from northwest to southeast, as representing increasing quantities of the commodity (or service) desired as the price falls. Symmetrically, the supply (S-S) curve, rising from southwest to northeast, represents increasing quantities of the commodity (or service) offered as the price increases. The intersection point is *the* point of the exercise. There, buyers and sellers agree on both price and quantity. If the suppliers demanded a price higher than the intersection, thus tried to climb the supply curve beyond that point, the buyers would begin to fall away and the sellers would either depart with unsold stocks or, rationally, slide back down the supply curve toward the intersection and reduce the price demanded. Similarly, if the buyers wanted a lower price than the intersection indicated, the shortage of supplies would leave them frustrated or drive them back up the supply curve. Thus the market satisfies all participants within the limits of reality and realistic desire.

The power of this abstraction can be demonstrated by the operation of price controls. In wartime the authorities use them to try to resist inflation, thus forcing sellers to sell at a point below the intersection. The resultant gap between demand and supply curves leaves some consumers unsatisfied at that level:

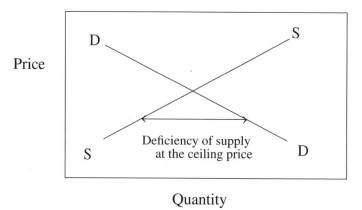

Price

Quantity

But the authorities cannot control desires, and consumers try to satisfy themselves by offering more than the officially sanctioned price. This is the origin of the black market, which appears in any price-control situation. Americans experienced this to a modest extent in World War II. The state power in Soviet Russia had attempted to deny the workings of supply and demand, thus creating the ubiquitous black market to satisfy all the potential buyers, in effect, everyone. More generally, efforts to resist the economic laws will cause such distortions and frustrations. A major governmental aim might well justify such actions, but at a price.

The idea of marginal utility as a measure of value seems banal to us. Indeed Milton Friedman abruptly minimized its analysis as "dated,"[10] but it was essential to arrive at exchange. In the well-known example the value of each successive unit of water gets smaller until the last unit—the marginal unit—falls to zero. While water was essential to life, the consumer eventually preferred to do without it. Thus Jevons could conclude, "Value" was purely relative, "not an object at all," and Menger, "[V]alue does not exist outside the consciousness of men."[11] In the free market, price was the social expression of value and the distinction between the two, the question that absorbed the classical economists, was nonexistent. Thus marginal utility and the general equilibrium system.

Jevons and Menger both approached marginal utility (or value) and exchange in a remarkably similar, logical way—to the point of similarly numbered chapters on each. Jevons proceeded from his Chapter 3, "Theory of Utility," to Chapter 4, "Theory of Exchange"; Menger from *his* Chapter 3, "The Theory of Value," to Chapter 4, "The Theory of Exchange." Jevons used graphic columns to illustrate descending series of marginal utility or value; Menger, descending columns in the form of tables of figures. The sense is identical, although Jevons went one step further by drawing a curve joining the tips of his columns.[12] Both went yet another step further, each on a different point. Jevons expanded the use of his graphics to two horizontal curves, but variously so, permitting them to intersect. This illustrated the relative value or utility of two commodities, one of which could be money.[13] Economic science needed only to take one step more to arrive at the textbooks' supply-and-demand intersection (above). Menger, for his part, used columns of descending and rising tables of figures to illustrate the balanced sense of supply and demand.[14]

Jevons joined Walras in emphasizing the usefulness of mathematics in economics. Walras's use of it in his classic work was so exhaustive and wearying that no one translated the book into English until the 1977 translation cited here.[15] While Jevons's marvelously clear prose avoided heavy use of mathematics, the introduction to his great work argued that since economics "deals with quantities, it must be a mathematical science in matter if not in language."[16] Menger, however, avoided figures except for the simple tables of figures as illustrations. He wrote Walras in 1883 that market phenomena should be traced back to the ultimate genetic determinants of man's nature, something he argued that mathematics could not do.[17] Yet Menger himself commanded mathematics well and his son became a noted mathematician.[18] The economists' profession has since redundantly agreed with Jevons and Walras on mathematics.

As perhaps the clearest argument for their greatness as thinkers, all three neoclassicals agreed on the limits of their vision. The supply-and-demand system promised perfection: any disturbance to equilibrium was self-correcting. An unexpected excess of supply would dissolve with price reductions; a shortage would be corrected through price increases encouraging production of more of the demanded goods. It was a perfect resolution—in the face of the painful ills of the free-enterprise system.

Unlike Ricardo, however, the three neoclassicals were willing to look beyond the pure economy. They accepted that politics and society could drastically disturb their economic abstraction. Jevons speculated imaginatively about the effects of sunspots, which could alter agricultural, hence economic, conditions and cause depressions and booms. Walras's father was both an economist and a socialist, and Walras *fils* remained taken with socialism and its promise of alleviating the workers' lot. He was sufficiently concerned to write another extended work paralleling his neoclassical book. His *Études d'économie sociale* proposed the nationalization of the land, the income from it to substitute for taxes, which the workers would be excused from paying. The drastic proposals of his social economy could not, however, be integrated into the abstract operations of his political economy and, denying its laissez-faire character, remained an expression of filial feeling more than economic logic.[19] As for Menger, his comment to Walras on using mathematics suggests why he could not follow up his great work, which was aphoristic and brief rather than exhaustive, and published when he was only thirty-one. He continued his researches energetically, first planning a revision, but he remained dissatisfied with its beginnings. Meanwhile he permitted a sharp struggle with German economists to divert him, but he returned to his economics as expanded into a treatise on the social sciences broadly viewed. His letter to Walras suggests an ambition impossible to satisfy. Dying at eighty-one in 1921, he left behind "voluminous and disordered notes."[20] Like his neoclassical colleagues, he had failed to integrate his economics completely into the human condition. He had sense enough not to try.

All three neoclassicals, unable to accomplish the impossible, failed quite to integrate economic theory and economic reality. The problem was that reality could arrange itself in a manner that would escape all purely economic theory, a lesson taught by history and illustrated most dramatically by the Great Depression of the 1930s. As we shall see, the United States would possess some 40 percent of the world's industrial establishment by the 1920s. With that power its mistaken economic actions would be so massive that they would throw off the delicate balance of global supply and demand, the self-adjustments of the economic mechanism being too slight to halt the plunge. And yet the resiliency of the system would begin to correct the imbalance at a lower level and prevent its complete self-destruction. In a second movement supply and demand, assisted by more reasonable policies, would then work toward recovery.

Departing from Ricardo, another great economist pursued a path that was radically different but no less logical. Karl Marx was dismissed by Paul A. Samuelson, a first-rate economist and author of the immensely influential Keynesian textbook *Economics*, as a "minor post-Ricardian." He is pedantically correct. Samuelson rejected the efforts of later Marxists to repair Marx's labor theory of value as a "detour ... and an unnecessary one for understanding the behavior of competitive capitalism." Marx's economics, Samuelson concluded, was a failure. Except for a few resistant Marxists, contemporary economists have agreed. But Samuelson had begun by qualifying that he "dealt with Marx the economist, not Marx the philosopher of history and revolution."[21] Consistent with that thought, Samuelson had to accept the fact that Marx was not attempting to understand "competitive capitalism," but was trying to annihilate it. Thus he did recognize the character of Marx as active revolutionary and leader, statesman of revolution. It is only by addressing these elements that one can best appreciate Marx as economist.

Marx proposed to build upon the French Revolution by extending its violent egalitarian ambitions from politics to economics. Maximilien Robespierre (1758-1794), its leader during the most extreme period, had stopped at the political, the guillotine as his leveler. A follower in spirit, Gracchus Babeuf (1760-1797), was executed after he had entered economics sufficiently to plot to socialize the land, distribute food equally, and execute the naysayers. Marx, indulging his fondness for revolutionary violence, found Smith's labor theory of value a great justification for any measure useful in expropriating capitalists and presenting the whole reward of work to the workers. The words were the argument. Yet Marx had been too intelligent to believe his own argument. We can see this in his masterpiece *Capital*, when he temporarily let the capitalist speak for himself: "'Have I myself not worked? Have I not performed the labor of superintendence and overlooking the spinner?...'" Marx then spoke for himself: "Though he chanted to us the whole creed of the economists [the capitalist] would not give a brass farthing for it. He leaves this and all such as subterfuges and puzzling tricks to the professors of political economy.... He himself is a practical man...." Thereupon, launching his restatement of the labor theory of value, the practical Marx marched the capitalist, his question unanswered, out of his book.[22] When not burying them under mountains of scorn, this was how Marx dealt with inconvenient theoretical problems.

This said, one must rescue Marx the economist from Samuelson's dismissal. *Capital*'s chaotic, 150-page chapter, "Machinery and Industry," was a great history of industrial production from the age of the individual craftsman through the period of small workshops to the big industry of his period.[23] Wassily Leontieff, the creator of input-output economics, has written that Marx's "rational theories ... do not hold water," but credited him with a "great feeling for social structure and the social order—what the capitalist system is."[24] If the theorist Marx had refused to recognize the character of exchange as the essence of an economy, the great institutional economist grasped the production complex like an instinctive capitalist.

Here we have paused to study the political Marx, who built upon his massive institutional economics to inspire both democratic socialist and revolutionary communist movements. We shall see how the first developed in the advanced societies of the West, where it lost its extreme character while, for a period, professing an idealized revolution. The second could use its apocalyptic promises more effectively in two huge, underdeveloped areas resistant to change: unqualified revolution, certainly more in Marx's spirit. We might also note, as these developments work themselves out, a more and more emphatically defined sense of the interaction of politics and economics.

In the advanced societies conflict was expressed verbally for the most part. We return to the Austro-German quarrel, the sufficiently furious *Methodenstreit* (Battle of Methods) initiated by Carl Menger. This will bring us back to neoclassical theory and the United States. At issue was the command, in theory and in administrative fact, of the great new powers economic and industrial progress had released. Wielded by Britain originally, they were being learned by Germany, Western Europe generally, and, more massively, by the United States.

Like the Americans, but with an acute appreciation of the refinements of theory, the Germans adopted a pragmatic approach. They had found Ricardo's theorizing too strained to accept and, reasonably enough, John Stuart Mill's *Principles of Political Economy* unconvincing. Questioning Ricardian theory, the German Historical School, adding up examples from history, went on to doubt all economic theory. It wanted to confront the new economic and social ills directly by an active governmental policy, which would be, reminiscent of Plato's ideas, both socialistic and elitist. This resulted in the founding of the Verein für Socialpolitik in 1872. The Germans, meanwhile, were ignoring or rejecting Carl Menger's *Principles of Economics*. A major new work of his, *Problems of Economics and Sociology* (1883), thereupon defended the new theory and lustily attacked German social pragmatism. Winning the debate in Austria, Menger inspired a generation of talented economists, who produced subtle variations of neoclassical theory. These economists included such personages as the long-lived Friedrich von Hayek (1899-1992) and Ludwig von Mises (1881-1973) as well as Joseph Schumpeter—all settling in the United States. The Germans, however, smothered theory at home until the age of Keynes.[25] As a rising *Kulturland*, Germany also captured the minds of a generation or two of leading American economists.

John Bates Clark (1847-1938) and Richard T. Ely (1854-1943) both studied at Heidelberg and translated the socialistic and pragmatic suggestions of the Verein für Socialpolitik and the German Historical School into their institutional economics. Clark's son, John Maurice (1884-1963), developed institutional economics variously, applying it to anti-trust laws, business cycles, and the economic costs of war. While the senior Clark also flirted with the neoclassicals' marginal utility, Richard Ely remained true to the social faith in the sense of American Progressives and employed politics and laws to achieve social action. He did not directly address the economic laws discovered by the neoclassicals, but tried to prevent their unhappy effects in poverty and unemployment. At the University of Wisconsin he headed the Department of Economics, Political Science, and History while helping shape labor laws and agricultural laws and public-utility pricing policy as adviser of Robert La Follette, the progressive governor. Also, in 1885, with other advocates of institutional economics, Ely organized the American Economic Association. But neoclassical theory began to win more and more adherents to its rational explanations of economic behavior. By the 1890s the AEA had become the neutral professional organization of American economists professing varied beliefs but dominated by later generations of neoclassicals.

The pragmatic arguments of institutional economists nevertheless continued to find supporters like Thorstein Veblen (1857-1929), with his populist outbursts, but also the sober Wesley C. Mitchell (1874-1948), who founded the still active National Bureau of Economic Research in 1920 to study business cycles. Mitchell was a great compiler of statistics, an approach mercilessly characterized as "measurement without theory." A few even severer critics have questioned his assumption of the existence of the cycles themselves. The institutional economists would experience a later blooming in the time of the New Deal. These theoretical and pragmatic divagations should help us further in grasping the factuality of the American and world economic experience.

Notes

1.   Adam Smith, *The Wealth of Nations*, ed., Andrew Skinner (Baltimore: Penguin Books, 1970; 1st ed.: 1776), book 1, ch. 1.
2.   *Ibid.*, book 1, chs. 8, 10.

3. *Ibid.*, book 1, ch. 4.
4. *Ibid.*, book 1, chs. 5, 8, 9; book 3, ch. 3.
5. David Ricardo, *On the Principles of Political Economy and Taxation* (Georgetown, DC: Joseph Milligan, 1819: 1st American ed.), 21, 286, 294.
6. Preface to 4th ed. (1906), Léon Walras, *Elements of Pure Economics or The Theory of Social Wealth,* tr., William Jaffé (Fairfield, NJ: Augustus M. Kelly, 1977; 1st [half] ed., 1874), 44.
7. *Ibid.*, 36.
8. Milton Friedman, quoting Schumpeter as well, "Léon Walras and his Economic System," in Léon Walras, *Léon Walras, 1834-1910,* ed. Mark Blaug (Aldershot: Elgar, 1992), 86, 92.
9. W. Stanley Jevons, *The Theory of Political Economy* (New York: Kelly & Millman, 1957; 5th ed.); Carl Menger, *Principles of Economics*, tr. James Dingwall and Bert F. Hoselitz (New York: New York University Press, 1981).
10. Friedman, op. cit., 86.
11. Jevons, *The Theory of Political Economy*, 77; Menger, *Principles of Economics*, 121.
12. Jevons, *The Theory of Political Economy*, 37-166; columns: 46, curve: 49; Menger, *Principles of Economics*, 114-90; columns of figures: 127.
13. Jevons, *The Theory of Political Economy*, 97.
14. Menger, *Principles of Economics*, 183-86.
15. William Jaffé, foreword, Walras, *Elements of Pure Economics*, 7-8.
16. Jevons, *The Theory of Political Economy*, vi.
17. Jaffé, "Menger, Jevons, and Walras De-homogenized," in *Léon Walras: Critical Assessments*, 2: *Walrasian Economics*, ed. John Cunningham Wood (London: Routledge, 1993), 67; article: 59-72.
18. Friedrich A. Hayek, introduction, Menger, *Principles of Economics*, 15.
19. Discussion, Renato Cirillo, "The 'Socialism' of Léon Walras and His Economic Thinking," in *Léon Walras: Critical Assessments*, 2: *Walrasian Economics*, 209-17.
20. Hayek, op. cit., 33.
21. Paul A. Samuelson, "Wages and Interest: A Modern Dissection of Marxian Economic Models," *AER* 47 (December 1957): 911, 890-92, 911; the article, 884-912.
22. Karl Marx, *Capital*, tr. Samuel Moore and Edward Aveling (New York: International Publishers, 1947; reprint of edition of 1889), vol. 1: 174. See his discussion on use and exchange value, labor and labor power, variable and constant capital, etc., 145-213.
23. *Ibid.*, 365-515.
24. Quoted, Leonard Silk, *The Economists* (New York: Basic Books, 1976), 166.
25. Hayek, op. cit., 22-25.

3

The Political Economy of World Power

The foregoing told how the United States, exploiting its great natural wealth, became a great economic power in obedience to Adam Smith's prescriptions as emendated by the neoclassical economists. The following will begin to show how it wielded—and failed to wield—its new strength.

"European political and economic power reached its zenith in the last quarter of the 19th century and the years before the first World War," the economic historian James Foreman-Peck noted not long ago. "The rise of Germany, challenging Britain's ... economic supremacy and displacing France from the political leadership of continental Europe, was the most fundamental power shift." Summarizing the world situation succinctly although somewhat inaccurately, he decided: "The United States's now massive economic strength impacted less on the world economy...." In fact the United States was affecting the world economy and polity more than the nation or the other powers realized. On second thought, Foreman-Peck, shifting from the adjective "less," modulated more aptly that the United States did indeed have "considerable impact on the international economy."[1]

The near-contradiction in act and interpretation can be resolved if one sees the United States as influencing other nations while not trying to do so. Self-centered, happy to escape the dangerous complications of world politics, it inquired little about foreign reactions to its actions. Yet its economic policies were imposing dangerous complications on the world outside: "With no central bank the United States was becoming an unpredictable bellows fanning but also dramatically cooling the world's trading system," another historian put it.[2] Events would force the United States and the world to rethink its international role, including its German relations.

Meanwhile, the European powers assumed America's non-participation and strained amongst themselves to win or keep world power, an objective very far from the American imagination. This was the period of the "new imperialism" superimposed upon a nationalism that was almost as new. One can date that nationalism from the period of the French Revolution, the revolutionary spirit then spread even more widely by Napoleon's armies. In the course of the nineteenth century nationalism produced a united Germany and Italy, both intensely nationalistic with representative governments, the first in a conservative structure with a military elite, and the second balancing a conservative Catholic society with secular liberalism. Both nations, particularly the larger, more powerful Germany, disturbed the old European equilibrium. From about 1870 until 1914 the nationalist drive expanded into the new imperialism, ultimately into World War I.

A doubled struggle characterized the imperialism of the period, the colonizing powers threateningly amongst themselves and, much less overtly, the colonized peoples themselves against their imperial masters.

"During the score of years the competition in the acquisition of territory and the struggle for influence and control was the most important factor in the international relations of Europe."[3] In purely geographical terms the returns from the imperialistic thrust were tremendous: between 1824 and 1870 the Europeans added 5 million square miles of territory, including India (effectively dominated earlier), the north and south of Africa, Australia, New Zealand, South Vietnam, and the Chinese treaty ports. Joined by the quick learner Japan in the period of the new imperialism, they added 8.6 million square miles by 1914, one sixth of the world's surface: almost all the rest of Africa, more of southeast Asia, and substantial parts of China. Of this the British Empire had taken 4.25 million square miles with a population of some 66 million and commanded a total of 400 million subjects by 1914. By 1914 France had 55 million colonial subjects; Germany, 12.3 million; and Japan, 19 million. Russia claimed 33 million subjects in its overland empire.[4] A few years later, among the arrangements of the Paris Peace Conference, a number of anachronistic annexes, called "mandates," would be built upon this imperial structure. Within the next fifty years virtually all of these empires would be gone with the "wind of change."[5] These were the words of Prime Minister Harold Macmillan in Cape Town, South Africa, on February 3, 1960. As imperial chief executive he was telling South African leaders and the world that the days of empire, at least as they knew it, were ending. What had been the sense of it all?

Great nations and empires, in the scholarly view of the economist Joseph Schumpeter, arose out of "'objectless' tendencies toward forcible expansion, without definite, utilitarian limits—that is, non-rational and irrational, purely instinctual inclinations toward war and conquest, play a very large role in the history of mankind...." The origins lay in an "activism [which] molded peoples and classes as warriors ... surviving features from earlier ages [and Schumpeter disputing with Karl Marx] arising from past rather than present relations of production." Thus, "numberless wars ... have been waged without adequate 'reason'...."[6] A parallel view was expressed by Sigmund Freud: in each individual the rapacious id, however mediated by ego and inhibited by superego, demands all at all costs and, as history records, gets its way much, if not most, of the time. If it does not, the frustrated id revenges itself by inflicting neuroses and other pains on the virtuous.[7]

The new century called upon the United States, despite the considerable costs, to participate more actively and responsibly in world affairs. It acted reluctantly, its exercise in the new imperialism notwithstanding, thus the Spanish-American War, the Panama episode, and the accompanying patriotic outbursts. Its new empire, deplored by Mark Twain and Andrew Carnegie, inter alia, was risibly trivial, while the distant and vulnerable Philippines provided a moral as well as strategic embarrassment, requiring the pacification, i.e., killing of independence-minded Filipinos. If the nation had indeed expanded its power in the Western Hemisphere, it had little intention of going beyond that, it virtuously insisted. Thus the construction (by 1914) and sober administration of the Panama Canal could be regarded as a service to the world economic community. With so many of its domestic resources remaining to be exploited, the country could still concentrate on getting richer. But all this had tremendous economic impact on the world. Without any colonies worth mentioning, this "unpredictable bellows" had ignorantly and irresponsibly become a great international power.

If the United States was a powerful but unrecognized factor in European and world affairs, the same could be said for Marxian socialism. Since Karl Marx's death in 1883 his influence was expanding through his classic *Capital* (1st vol.: 1867) and the effects of his leadership of the First International (1864-76) of radicals and labor groups. In Germany Marx's influence became more palpable and even respectable in the form of the German Social Democratic Party of 1875 (uniting two Marx-inspired parties of the 1860s). Remaining a minority representation, the Social Democrats could not make the revolution Marx had wanted but they became strong enough to become the largest party in the Reichstag, the German legislature, by 1890. Some Social Democrats still yearned toward revolution and the party provided fraternal help to revolutionary Marxist parties in other countries, thus Russia. The Social Democrats also took a leading role in the Second International of the Socialist parties, founded in 1889 as a revival of the spirit of the First International. With hindsight we shall be able to evaluate the importance of the United States and Marxism.

While the United States wielded its economic superiority diffidently, Germany used its economic power to maximum international effect. "The German Empire of Bismarck and William II awed the world with its military might but also with its phenomenal economic growth. By 1900 Germany had become the greatest industrial power in Europe." This is an accurate statement by the distinguished German émigré historian Hajo Holborn but only by innocently consigning the industrial leader Great Britain to non-European geography.[8] More realistically the economic historian Paul Bairoch, calculating per capita industrial levels in 1900 and using British production as an index figure of 100, put the German figure at 52 and the American at 69. The British figure was rising moderately from 87 in 1880 and going beyond 1900's 100 to 115 in 1913, while the German index figure rose steeply from 25 in 1880 to a competitive but still inferior 85 in 1913. The United States kept ahead of Germany in industrial level and rate of increase, rising to 126 (thus exceeding Great Britain's figure as well) in 1913. (Of the other countries, France began higher than Germany at 28 in 1880, but fell behind at 39 in 1900, and more so in the succeeding years; Russia beginning at 10, achieved 20 in 1913).[9] Another measure, pig iron for 1890 and steel thereafter emphasizes modern over traditional industry. While Great Britain produced 8 million tons in 1890, she fell to 5 million tons in 1900, and struggled to 7.7 million tons in 1913. The United States, already ahead with 9.3 million tons in 1890, achieved more than twice the British production in 1900 and 31.8 million tons in 1913. Germany, while lower in 1890 at 4.1 million tons, had already exceeded Great Britain's production in 1900 with 6.3 million tons and rose to 17.6 million tons in 1913. (Of the others, the Russian figures were modest, and France's, well behind Germany's.)[10] In the prewar period Germany was threatening Great Britain in industrial level and exceeding her in steel production. But the United States was affirming its position on another level as *the* dominant industrial power while also maintaining its concomitant agricultural strength.

Like all Europe Germany failed to *see* American power and potential. An isolated thought about the United States had been indeed expressed by the German bankers Bernhard Dernburg and Max Warburg, who were sent to the United States at the beginning of the war on a special mission.

In 1915 and again in 1916 they argued, emphasizing its power, "America … could, if challenged and convinced that it was fighting in a good cause, develop energies which would put into the shade anything experienced in Europe."[11] But these were well-traveled sophisticates who saw reality more truly than the self-reflecting German leadership. As it happened a generation later, the German leadership, fatally Eurocentric, failed to give the United States more than distracted, after-the-fact attention.

Always stipulating American primacy, one can nevertheless say that Germany had become a world leader in the production of chemicals, dyes, electrical power and equipment, coal, and steel. She was vigorously expanding her merchant marine. She had developed a strong banking system supporting industry and commerce fluently, while these operated with increasing sophistication. Like the contemporary monopolies in the United States, if less spectacularly, well-financed German cartels were integrating industry vertically and horizontally. Arthur von Gwinner, director of the Deutsche Bank, and the industrialist Walther Rathenau, titular ahead of the AEG (initials for the German words "General Electric Company"), were in an "intimate relationship" with Chancellor Theobald von Bethmann-Hollweg. Rathenau, an author of intellectually ambitious books, also had a number of interviews with the emperor to expatiate on industry and economy.[12] Upon a burst of prosperity from 1895, with per-capita income doubling in a generation, "the greatest change was the formation of a class of well-to-do and wealthy people." Yet the bankers and industrialists, however useful to imperial purposes, "recognized the pre-eminence of the *Junker* class."[13] Traditionally, absurdly, like Gewinner and Rathenau, they put themselves under the patronizing command of the emperor and his aristocratic and military elite.

With her new economic power, what did Germany want? *The world.* At least *world power* in a movement to seize it as affirmed in the German title of the book by the remarkably objective German scholar Fritz Fischer, *Griff nach der Weltmacht* (literally *Thrust toward World Power*), translated more anodynely as *Germany's Aims in the First World War*, as cited above. This was a Germany as led by her aristocracy and military, the latter created in the process of achieving the nation's unification in three surgical wars. In those circumstances too many of the middle class and even members of the working class, despite their Social Democratic leaders, let these wielders of grander power think and act for them.[14] But the English middle class and even workers had let Disraeli's empire with its Empress Victoria (of India) lead them into jingoism. As Schumpeter and Freud suggest, the fault was more general than German.

In her special situation, however, Germany veered further out of reality than did the other nations. She was also promiscuous in her imperial lust, wanting more on the continent *and* in the world outside. The thinking was institutionalized in a half-dozen nationalistic organizations, which flourished from the 1880s: the Navy, Defense, Pan-German, Colonial, and Eastern Marches Leagues, and, plainly, Germandom Abroad. The Navy League, founded in 1898 and achieving a membership of 371,500 by 1914, was a powerful pressure group organized by the Central Union of German Industrialists, as powerfully influenced by the Krupp munitions firm, and serving the aggressive purposes of Navy Minister Friedrich von Tirpitz. There was a German Peace Society.[15]

A dangerously irrational situation was inexorably becoming even less rational, every nation contributing to it. What was the sense of the old and new imperialism? What was the sense of Germany's competing with the naval power Great Britain for world empire? What was the sense of her simultaneously competing for continental power with France and Russia? Without forgetting the madness of the doubled and competing ambitions, what profit an empire? Consider the model case of Great Britain in 1914, commanding a quarter of the world's geography and people. One million persons were necessary to manage, hold, and finance Britain.[16] No one has, however, attempted to measure the returns or the costs, a problem compounded by such imponderables as wars caused or avoided, lives lost or saved, and the bankable nature of an empire itself. But then Britain could do well with or without empire, her income rising inexorably as the colonies were being added and then as they, led by India, fell away.[17] British industry and management would remain as resources.

If the British Empire's material gains were becoming questionable, other empires were plainly generators of losses. In 1911 one economist, British, it is true, found France's vast African possessions producing 10 times as many losses as profits.[18] Germany plunged into colonies and losses as emphatically. Beginning in 1884 she quickly acquired four African colonies and, in the Pacific, the northeast corner of New Guinea as well as the New Britain and Bismarck Archipelagos and the Marshall Islands.[19] The German Social Democrats, drawing upon their government's *Statistical Yearbooks*, could denounce its colonial policy along with rampant capitalism. They found the financial record for 1903-6 showing colonial costs of 562 million Reichmarks ($180 million at four marks to the dollar) and revenues of 53 million RM, with the imperial grants of 247 million RM to make up some of the difference. The record for 1909-13 was 138 million RM in deficit.[20] And yet, "The cry for raw materials was louder than ever. Great banks like the Deutsche Bank... invested millions in Turkey, the Far East, and South America...."[21] But Great Britain had imposed its free trade on the world; Germany could buy the raw materials at good prices. Chancellor Otto von Bismarck himself had no desire for colonial ventures, but was forced to support them in view of the general sentiment. As he realized, the important word here is "sentiment," *mindless* sentiment.

Moreover, the colonial peoples themselves were announcing their opinions. In 1882, just before Germany began to acquire African colonies, a rebellion of Egyptian junior officers led to a British naval bombardment of Alexandria. Ending their long presence there, the French found it politic to withdraw, but the British, concerned about the Suez Canal and their route to India, stayed for a long while. In 1885 the Indian National Congress was organized to demand more rights and authority at first, but presently unqualified independence. The All-India Muslim League paralleled it. In 1900 the Boxers, a nationalist secret society, killed 200 foreigners in Peking before they were put down by foreign powers led by Germany and including the United States, who punished the weak Manchu government. Before then, in 1896, Ethiopians made their statement, slaughtering an Italian army, which had invaded the country from Eritrea, on the Red Sea, occupied by Italy since 1890. In the sub-Saharan area, in the future Malawi, the religious leader John Chilembwe organized the African Christian Union for political rights in 1897. In 1916, he led 200 men in an attack on white settlers, killing a few before he was tracked down and hanged.[22] But, except for slightly increasing imperial vigilance, the sense of these signals was ignored.

By the second decade of the new century the new imperialism suggested another problem. Colonial expansion had absorbed much aggression. Now, with few more territories to be shared out, it was vindicating Freudian psychology and Schumpeterian historiography by returning to Europe.

A colonial empire needed a navy to defend it, but then it justified the existence of a navy in the first place: circular logic beginning in midair. Here is where German megalomania grew to an extreme as incorporated in Navy Secretary Alfred von Tirpitz, a master of elite German politics. Tirpitz manipulated the Navy League, the sympathetic German press, and the German leadership, beginning with Emperor William II. His first construction program, beginning in 1898, proposed to add 7 battleships, 2 heavy cruisers, and 7 light cruisers to a navy of 12 battleships, 10 heavy cruisers, and 23 light cruisers. If this did not quite match the British navy with its 54 battleships, the new naval bill, in 1909, doubled the estimates of the first bill. By 1917 Germany would have 38 battleships, 16 heavy cruisers, and 39 light cruisers. This was a direct threat to the British Empire, dependent on its navy to protect the home islands and maintain its colonies. It was also bad theory as the war proved. Germany was limited to a short shoreline on the North Sea and a useless one on the inland lake of the Baltic Sea, and the British fleet, remaining larger, bottled up and so effectively canceled the value of Tirpitz's fleet.

The German leadership had given a great technician his head. With little sense of what he was doing he had made state policy for emperor, ministers, politicians, businessmen, bankers, and voters. Naturally Britain had to react and, in 1903, began a new building program calling for four capital ships yearly, including a new class of battleships, the more heavily armed dreadnoughts. In 1904, Great Britain and France agreed to their Entente Cordiale. It was not an alliance, since Britain had not emerged totally from her insular position and did not want to encourage French imprudence and *revanche*. But the Entente would steadily become one in response to the German danger.

Germany was too much represented by William II, emperor in 1888 at the age of 29. Found "inexperienced, immature, and presumptuous" by his father two years earlier,[23] he reproduced in himself dangerous defects in the empire's mind and body politic. In March 1890 he worked the dismissal of Bismarck, an archaic monument of himself. William found the opportunities for continental and imperial intimidation intoxicating.

In early February 1912 War Secretary Richard Haldane came to Berlin to negotiate a slowing of the naval race. Excluding the more conciliatory Chancellor Theodor von Bethmann-Hollweg, the emperor and the navy secretary received Lord Haldane after a new supplementary naval vote was announced. Emperor and admiral wanted a promise of neutrality in a continental war involving France and let Haldane see their ambitions to create a *Mitteleuropa* dominated by German economy and arms. Haldane did not need to think hard and departed. The Reichstag voted the new naval estimates.[24]

By 1907 the Triple Alliance of Germany, Austria-Hungary, and Italy, and the Triple Entente of Britain, France, and Russia faced each other. The actions of William notwithstanding, both systems could be seen as rationally founded upon concerns of security and not necessarily aggression on either side. The demands of five of the six, however dangerous potentially, could be accommodated peacefully for the moment. Imperial Russia dreamed of winning Constantinople and entering the Mediterranean, but defeat in the Russo-Japanese war had enforced common sense on her. France wanted Alsace-Lorraine back, but, similarly, was too sane to start a war for it. Britain had much to defend and Italy was too small to act on her own. A wilder element was Serbia, whose leadership wanted to destroy Austria-Hungary and create a greater Balkan state. In this volatile situation, as expressed in the imperial faux pas of William, a powerful Germany was thrusting beyond rational limits. If the Serbs were the fuse, the Germans were the explosive.

We need not waste thought on the heavily belabored legalistic-moralistic question of war guilt, which has seized too much attention.[25] Every nation was responsible for causing the war, but Germany was the *active* destabilizing force. The point was not criminal but irrational intent. She had demanded world power, as Fritz Fischer has argued, in a blatant manner that doubled the presumption. Actually as she failed to realize, she *had* it by 1900. She needed to do absolutely nothing more to exercise it. All she had to do was go on manufacturing, banking, and marketing with demonstrated efficiency. "The great [German] capitalists were winning mastery in Europe without war: the industries of southern Russia, the iron-fields of Lorraine and Normandy, were already largely under their control," A. J. P. Taylor wrote.[26] A year before the war, Hugo Stinnes, president of a great coal-mining and shipping company and the rare exception among German business leaders, told the head of the Pan German League: "Give us three or four more years of peace and Germany will be unchallenged master of Europe."[27] Instead, yielding to the instinct toward aggression, the country's leaders went whoring after a tinsel imperium.

German war guilt was acted out after the fact. *L'appétit vient en mangeant*: once the war started, heartened into more megalomania by two great victories over the Russians in East Prussia, at Tannenberg in late August and the Masurian Lakes in early September 1914, the Germans planned on more. On September 9, just before the second battle, the erstwhile moderate Bethmann-Hollweg officially developed his ideas in his September program: "France must be so weakened as to make her revival as a great power impossible for all time." He also wanted a war indemnity imposed on her high enough to inhibit her armament spending for "the next 18-20 years."[28] The Pan-German League wanted more: all of Belgium, the part of France contiguous to Belgium as far as the Somme River, and the French Mediterranean port of Toulon. To that August Thyssen, head of the great Thyssen steel manufacturing company, added a swatch of Russia: the Don basin, Odessa, the Crimea, and the

Caucasus, *and* Asia Minor and Persia (Iran)—the latter meant to loosen Great Britain's hold on India and Egypt.[29] In the Peace of Brest-Litovsk of March 1918, before her final failed offensive on the Western Front, Germany took from Bolshevik Russia her Polish territories and the Baltic provinces, the Ukraine, Finland, and farther east, most of the Caucasus. In Germany's leadership the thinking of Hugo Stinnes had been the great exception—and he had been optimistic to expect a *peaceful* German domination of Europe. Indeed German tactlessness, often displayed in the course of the war, would almost certainly have provoked a war under the Stinnes plan as well.

The great imbalance in the international power situation may be condensed simply: Germany was egregiously presuming too much on the basis of her immediate and potential power. Furthermore, the United States was shrinking too much, given the magnitude of its present and potential power. Both nations had acted falsely. Peace would have been less endangered if the United States, balancing German aggressiveness with its own, had added its great power to the power struggle, as it would be obliged to do after the war had begun. The imbalance, affecting all of the major powers, had meant war—world war. Indeed, when we note that it would release even more nationalism and the Bolshevik variant of Marxism, we see that it meant not one but two world wars.

We need not repeat the weary story of the outbreak of the war as it resulted from the assassination of the Austrian Archduke by a Serb nationalist. While their alliance systems were indeed rational in origin, the great powers had also been acting rationally in the immediacy of 1914—up to a point. Austria, backed by Germany, wanted to quash the threat to her multinational existence in the form of an ambitious Serbia, Russia could not abandon her Slav brethren in the Balkans, Germany had to defend herself against the great Russian armies poised to invade from the East while anticipating French *revanche* in the West, and Great Britain had to defend France and her own coastline. Even Italy could justify entering the war the next year but on the Allied side, where her interests lay, in order to be able to participate in the peace negotiations. Right reason, among other factors, would at last persuade the United States to enter the war in its own time.

President Woodrow Wilson (1856-1924), a legally trained political scientist who had been a college president and a New Jersey governor, was as perfectly fitted for his role as was Emperor William II. He began office as a progressive despite a southerner's unconcern about black rights, and reluctantly but genially turned to foreign affairs. Upon excusable impulsions, he had twice sent American forces into Mexico (the first time to keep out German arms) and intervened bloodily in the Caribbean. Embarrassed, he was happy to accept Latin American mediation and withdrew from Mexico as soon as possible (but not the Caribbean). In the cause of Britain and France, educating himself and the nation in responsibility, he fluently implemented American sympathy and interest. Great Britain, meanwhile, was receiving an increasing stream of material from the United States financed by American credit, the J. P. Morgan bank providing $500 million in October 1915. The United States sent $508,269,245 in munitions to the Allies from August 1914 to December 1915, and more than $2 billion worth from January 1916 to March 1917.[30] Wilson's policy vis-à-vis Britain rubbed in the unfairness.

Britain was the only European country Wilson knew. He had obsessively admired Prime Minister William Gladstone, preferred the British parliamentary system to the raucous democracy of his country, and had strained destructively and vainly to transform Princeton University into an imitation of the Cambridge-and-Oxford college system.

Blockading the German coast, the British navy was violating international law. It was stopping neutral vessels that might be helpful to Germany while the German navy was helpless against the larger British surface fleet. In the Battle of Jutland, in May 1916, the Germans sallied out with 101 against 151 warships. They performed excellently, sinking more than being sunk, but had to turn back to home port and stay there to avoid inexorable annihilation. On February 4 Germany announced a submarine blockade of the British isles, and on May 7, a submarine sank the great British ship *Lusitania*; 1200 persons, including 128 Americans, drowned. The dramatic horror of it, even against a background of the horrors of the trenches on the Western Front, shocked the United States into its early movement toward war. More sinkings and the resultant indignation persuaded the Germans to restrict submarine action from March 1916. The decision, incidentally, led to the resignation of Tirpitz, who thus lost control of his splendid, useless instrument, and vanished from history. On January 31, 1917 the return to unrestricted submarine warfare by a desperate German leadership swiftly moved the United States to its war declaration on April 6.

Against his own pacifistic prejudices Wilson had subtly and masterfully, if unconsciously, led the nation to war. On one level he cleverly manipulated legalisms to keep Great Britain in the right and Germany in the wrong. On another level he obeyed his empathy for England. Even deeper, perhaps, he was Machiavellian enough to recognize the insatiable

German lust for world power, and refused to endure a German-dominated world. The only solution was domination by the United States. He was right although he would never admit his intention.

The country mobilized its spirit in a manner appreciated by Tocqueville and its resources in the pattern of Rockefeller, Carnegie, Ford, Frederick Winslow Taylor, and J. P. Morgan, and as understood by Adam Smith and the neoclassicals. Beginning in May 1917 it drafted 3 million men, accepted 2 million volunteers, sending 2 million men to France by the time of the Armistice in November 1918. In the late summer a quarter of a million fresh Americans helped bring the Germans to surrender, but the earlier money and munitions had been more important.[31] Maintaining a balance of private initiative and public order, a series of ad hoc boards led chiefly by businessmen had coordinated the various parts of the economy. The United States won another economic triumph.

After a last desperate offensive Germany had to sue for peace in that summer of 1918. Suddenly she had vanished as a great power and United States had replaced her as an unrecognized (also by itself) superpower.

Mounted on America's terrific economic and military establishment, Wilson had vast power to impose his will on the Allies. Claiming innocence of the power-seeking and vengefulness of the Allies, the United States could present itself as an unprejudiced broker of peace. Here was an extraordinary coincidence of leader and nation in the will (however unconscious) to lead the world. Secular-minded persons failed quite to credit Wilson's religiosity. He adored his father, a powerful Presbyterian preacher. Having always tended toward politics, the young Thomas Woodrow Wilson had learned to conflate his secular ambitions with the certainty that he represented the good and godly. He never questioned his faith, nor its expression in political good works. He knew he was right and just. "Of his sincerity, though he moved with the wind, there can be no doubt," one biographer saw him.[32]

Easily exercising the national might and overwhelming the leaders of old Europe, Wilson came to the Paris Peace Conference of January-June 1919 with a revolutionary agenda. He would dispense with the old balance of power and replace it with collective security administered by his League of Nations and guaranteeing permanent peace. For a few moments his utopianism captured the sophisticated Europeans, who secretly wanted to be saved from themselves. In February 1918, in his "Four Principles," an allocution to the United States Congress, he had said that the practice of the balance of power was forever discredited. He would replace it with "collective security," as provided in his proposal for a League of Nations. Instead of force, the agreement of partners in peace would guarantee the peace. The idea was just as crazy and impossible as the idea that Lenin, having achieved his Bolshevik Revolution in November 1917, was simultaneously trying to impose upon Russia and the world. The two great idealists dragged their more or less willing nations into a confrontation that would develop as the greatest, if not the bloodiest, of the century.

The course of the peace conference inevitably revealed, along with the impossibilities, the hypocrisies, mendacities, simple errors, and lacunae inevitable in such large collective undertakings. Its first purpose was to impose a peace treaty on Germany, now constituted as a republic, later known as the Weimar Republic and proclaimed by a Social Democratic leader on November 9, 1918. Here another lag in thinking became evident: the Allies were punishing a nonexistent imperial Germany in the reality of the weak, impoverished, and somewhat sincerely democratic republic. (Early in the war William II had been shunted from power by his own incompetence and irrelevance; from 1917 the generals Paul von Hindenburg and Erich Ludendorff exercised a semi-dictatorship; William then abdicated in the face of revolutionary actions.)

Aware of the inevitable self-interest and vengefulness of his European partners, hardly aware of America's (and his own) self-interest, Wilson had established the ideational-ideological frame for the peace in his Fourteen Points, explicated in a speech to the Congress on January 8, 1918. It was a great political stroke, for Wilson was trying to force his will upon the practiced Machiavellians Premier Georges Clemenceau of France and Prime Minister David Lloyd George of Great Britain, who had their own or opposing demands. Accepting Wilson's agenda as an undebatable imperative for the moment, they could then try to prove given details unacceptable. Some of the parts were more or less impossible: no secret diplomacy (self-evidently absurd), freedom of the seas (absurd because Great Britain would not and could not have it), tariff reduction (United States was the greatest violator and would remain so), and arms reduction "to the lowest point consistent with domestic safety" (every nation being free to determine its safety level). Some parts were self-evident and unproblematic: restoration of Belgium to itself and Alsace-Lorraine to France. Self-determination, a general aim, was reasonable in principle but devilish in detail. Thus Poland could be reconstituted as an independent country, but its border regions were problematically mixed with Germans, Ukrainians, and Belorussians. More negatively, self-determination meant the destruction of the Austrian and Turkish

Empires, and the creation of many small, questionably viable, inevitably quarrelsome nations. One of the 14 Points was blind to the more or less urgently pending future of the colonies and casually insulting to their people: "impartial adjustment of all colonial claims," claims, that is, by the imperial masters. One could nevertheless defend most of them as virtuous objectives suggesting future corrections, even hypocrisy on the colonial issue tracing a path out of colonialism. The victors, while attaining the greatest expansion for their empires, took over the German and Turkish possessions not as possessions but formally as mandates under the League of Nations (itself envisioned in the 14th Point), thus documenting a verbal-moral step, at least, toward independence. Wilson's vision had promisingly transcended the political and economic realities even as it complicated them. He was pointing accurately enough toward a future he would never see.

A month after the 14-Point speech, on February 11, Wilson introduced another objective in another speech to the Congress: peace with "no annexations, no contributions, no punitive damages."[33] The Germans would understandably feel cheated when these promises, particularly the last, would be betrayed. Wilson had later qualified that Germany should pay "compensation" for damage done to civilians, a condition to which she agreed. Clemenceau translated this as "*réparation des dommages*." At the peace conference, however, *réparation*, became an indubitably punitive indemnity, one so huge it was impossible to pay. The Germans, but also the victors and the world, choked on this last.

The conference spent little time on reparations, leaving the actual calculation to a future commission, and other economic issues, and concentrated on the obviously complex political problems. The economist John Maynard Keynes, who was the chief British Treasury representative in Paris, was appalled at this disproportion because hundreds of thousands were starving at the moment and reparations promised grave maladjustment for the future. He resigned from the Treasury and, departing his post just before the end of the conference, published his notorious and prophetic *Economic Consequences of the Peace* still in 1919. The other economic problems thrown up by the war, he direly predicted, would mean "that final civil war between the forces of Reaction and the despairing convulsions of Revolution, before which the horrors of the late German war will fade into nothing, and which will destroy, whoever is victor, the civilization and the progress of our generation."[34] One might see in his vision, combined with the Great Depression, the forces that had already produced Bolshevism and would generate fascism and Nazism, in sum World War II. Keynes stiffened his prophecy by accurately predicting the figure which the reparations commission would determine—and the economic damage.

If Wilson got much of his power from the American economy, he did not care to *think* economics and trusted that a good political settlement would help set the matter right. For him this meant the League of Nations, as written into the peace treaty. Two biographers viewed this in overlapping senses: "In comparison with this success, he doubtless regarded his concession on the matter of reparations ... as mere details." "It was a measure of Wilson's total achievements that the decision on reparations, the only issue on which he permitted his adversaries their way, was probably the worst solution reached at Paris."[35]

Wilson returned as world conqueror but the Republicans had won majorities in both House and Senate in the November 1918 elections and made difficulties. They wanted to add reservations to the terms of American participation in the League of Nations, but he refused to accept what he saw as fatally weakening it. He attempted to win the public in an exhausting, 8,000-mile speech campaign, collapsed, and on October 2, 1919 suffered a massive stroke. He was partially paralyzed and a sickroom prisoner for the rest of his life. In November the amended treaty was rejected, Wilson's followers refusing to vote for it. In March 1920 it was reconsidered, and some Democrats supported it as better than no treaty. Wilson still opposed it, half the Democrats agreeing with him; again it was voted down. By then Wilson was slipping out of history.

The nightmarish defeat or self-defeat made little difference. If Wilson's willfulness had not matched that of his enemies, the amended treaty, still a reasonable expression of Wilson's design, would have been accepted and the United States would have entered the League. And yet that would have made little difference. The scholar of law and political science had put too much weight on the formal. With United States the league would not have been much more effective. Like the United Nations today, it was not an international government able to enforce its presumably just decisions, but a useful international consultative body. Actually the League was meant to be a kind of condominium of the allied victors as world-dominant powers, thus the United States, Great Britain, and France, deciding for most other countries, which were ill-represented or unrecognized. Yet the American people, as the recalcitrance of the Republicans promised, would have found the exercise of world power too much. Without the United States it became an English-French condominium of some moderating effect—to the extent that it was effective at all. But when one considers, besides the absence of the United States, the symmetrical absence of Lenin's Bolshevized Russia and the presence of Mussolini's Italy from 1922, the stirrings in India and China, and the quiet aggressions of Japan, one can find a little to mourn. The League of Nations was not big enough for the world.

While Wilson and his associates were urging the Allies to moderate their demands on reparations, they could not persuade the American people to relax their insistence on war-debt repayment. In self-defense, even after the spirit of revenge had begun to soften, France, Great Britain, and Italy, faced with war-debt payments, defended themselves by persisting in requiring German reparation payments. Yet the United States had both the money and productive resources, while its allies struggled with huge debts and trade deficits contracted during their joint struggle. It would require time for the United States, accepting its costs, and Europe, accepting its humiliations, to agree on American world leadership. Meanwhile, in their insecure association, neither the United States nor the Allies knew what to do with Soviet Russia, while the Soviets knew what to do with the world. Too many variant, wrong-headed philosophies ruled.

Widely overshooting its intentions, deploying its economic and political resources, the United States, while overshadowing its allies, had helped eliminate Germany as a world power and found itself a much greater world power. But the American people would have none of it—or rather, just half of it. To use the neoclassical thought scheme, the world forces were out of equilibrium.

Notes

1.   James Foreman-Peck, *A History of the World Economy: International Economic Relations since 1850,* 2nd ed. (Hemel Hempstead: Harvester Wheatsheaf, 1996), 90, 94.
2.   Paul Kennedy, *The Rise and Fall of the Great Powers: Economic Change and Military Conflict from 1500 to 2000* (New York: Random House, 1987), 245.
3.   William L. Langer, *The Diplomacy of Imperialism 1890-1902,* 2 vols. (New York: Knopf, 1935), I: 67.
4.   David B. Abernethy, *The Dynamics of Global Dominance: European Overseas Empires, 1415-1980* (New Haven: Yale University Press, 2000), 81-83; Sidney Pollard, *European Integration 1815-1970* (London: Thames and Hudson, 1974), 104-7.
5.   W. N. Medlicott, *Contemporary England 1914-1964* (London: Longman, 1967), 571.
6.   Joseph A. Schumpeter, "Power and Pride" (1919) in Robin W. Winks, ed., *The Age of Imperialism* (Englewood Cliffs, NJ: Prentice-Hall, 1969), 59-60.
7.   Sigmund Freud, *Civilization and its Discontents [Das Unbehagen in der Kultur];* (New York: Norton, 1989, from Hogarth Press, 1930; tr. James Strachey). Among many relevant statements: "… contention that … what we call our civilization is largely responsible for our misery…." (38) and "… the inclination to aggression is an original, self-subsisting instinctual disposition in man and … constitutes the greatest impediment to civilization" (82).

8.　Hajo Holborn, *A History of Modern Germany 1840-1945* (Princeton: Princeton University Press, 1969), 367.

9.　Paul Bairoch, "International Industrialization Levels from 1750 to 1980," *Journal of European Economic History* 11 (Fall 1982): table, 294.

10.　Kennedy, *Rise, and Fall,* table, 200.

11.　As interpreted by Fritz Fisher, *Germany's Aims in the First World War* (New York: Norton, 1967; 1st German ed.: 1961), 307.

12.　*Ibid.*, 16. See also David Felix, *Walther Rathenau and the Weimar Republic* (Baltimore: Johns Hopkins Press, 1971), 45.

13.　Holborn, *A History of Modern Germany,* 389.

14.　Volker Rolf Berghahn, *Imperial Germany, 1871-1914: Economy, Society, Culture, and Politics* (Providence: Berghahn Books, 1994), 25-26.

15.　*Ibid.,* 228-32.

16.　Walter Phelps Hall and Robert Greenhalgh Albion, *A History of England and the British Empire* (Boston: Ginn, 1937), 748.

17.　See its per capita GDP, Angus Maddison, *The World Economy: Historical Statistics* (Paris: OECD, 2003), table, 63.

18.　Constant Southworth, *The French Colonial Venture* (London: P. S. King, 1931), 122.

19.　See Mary Evelyn Townsend, *The Rise and Fall of Germany's Colonial Empire 1884-1914* (New York: Howard Fertig, 1966; 1st ed.: 1930).

20.　*Ibid.,* 240, 264.

21.　E. Malcolm Carroll, *Germany and the Great Powers 1866-1914: A Study in Public Opinion and Foreign Policy* (New York: Prentice-Hall, 1938), 348.

22.　Chilembwe's rebellion, Robert A. Rotberg, *The Rise of Nationalism in Central Africa: The Making of Malawi and Zambia 1873-1964* (Cambridge: Harvard University Press, 1972; 1st ed.: 1965), 55-92.

23.　Quoted, Holborn, *A History of Modern Germany,* 324.

24.　Berghahn, *Germany and the Approach of War in 1914* (London: Macmillan, 1993: 2nd ed.), 38-76. He quotes an analysis of January 1, 1907 by Sir Eyre Crowe of the British Foreign Office to the effect that Germany wanted "general hegemony" or peaceful penetration, but thought the former could spill over into the latter (p. 73).

25.　Three works by American historians illustrate the sterility of the war guilt issue: Sidney B. Fay, *The Origins of the World War,* 2 vols. (New York: Macmillan, 1930; 1st ed.: 1928); Bernadotte E. Schmitt, *The Coming of the War 1914,* 2 vols. (New York: Scribner's Sons, 1930); Harry Elmer Barnes, *The Genesis of the World War: An Introduction to the Problem of War Guilt* (New York: Knopf, 1968 reprint of 2nd revised ed. of 1955; 1st ed.: 1929). All concentrated most of their attention on the leading personalities and their chessboard moves, particularly the day-to-day immediacy of 1914. Fay ascribed heavy blame to French President Henri Poincaré and made the Entente more responsible than Germany and Austria (25). Barnes said he "placed the guilt" on France and Russia, fixing on four French and three Russian leaders. He argued incredibly, inter alia, that Germany "was not as nationalistic as France, not as interested or imperialistic as Great Britain, France, or Russia, not as militaristic as Russia...." (xiii, 231). Schmitt leaned against Germany, asserting that William II and Bethmann-Hollweg "took the gambler's plunge." I: 329).

26.　Taylor, *The Struggle for Mastery,* 519.

27.　Quoted, Carroll, *Germany and the Great Powers,* 700.

28.　Quoted, Fischer, *Germany's Aims,* 103, 117.

29.　*Ibid.,* 106-8.

30.   Charles Tansill, *America Goes to War* (Boston: Little, Brown, 1932), 53, 90-115.
31.   John Keegan, *The First World War* (New York: Random House, 1998), ch. 10: "America and Armageddon."
32.   John Morton Blum, *Woodrow Wilson and the Politics of Morality* (Boston: Little, Brown, 1956), 46.
33.   The 14 Points and the American delegation's interpretation of them, quoted, Ferdinand Czernin, *Versailles 1919: The Forces, Events, and Personalities that Shaped the Treaty* (New York: Capricorn Books, 1965), 10-20; the February 11 address, quoted, Philip M. Burnett, *Reparation at the Paris Peace Conference, 2* vols. (New York: Columbia University Press, 1940), I: 359. See also Margaret MacMillan, *Paris: Six Months That Changed the World* (New York: Random House, 2002).
34.   John Maynard Keynes, *The Collected Writings of John Maynard Keynes* (London: Macmillan, 1971-89), 2: 169-70.
35.   Charles Seymour, *Woodrow Wilson and the World War* (New Haven: Yale University Press, 1921), 310; Blum, *Woodrow Wilson,* 175.

4

America at Home

During the interwar period American policy was dominated by a continuing and symmetrical failure consistent with the nation's laggard self-image to accept world leadership and to take command of its own economy. The interaction between the two was destructive. Yet the terrific success of the American economy, entirely authentic within its contemporary material limits, kept the Americans from realizing the damage they were causing themselves as well as the others. An important reason was their self-centeredness compounded by ignorance of the extended workings of their own economic policies.

America's rise to world power had been accelerated in the war, which had demanded precisely those qualities that had already made it great: its efficiency, flexibility, pragmatism, range of material resources, quality and variety of human resources, and easy-flowing democratic spirit. The other leading powers, including the loser Germany, had fought a very good—and much longer—war, and endured more protracted sacrifices, the young men dying by the millions, but the divinely favored United States, contributing modest sacrifices in life and resources, had a much larger economic base and used it appropriately.

While America's agriculture had expanded hugely to meet the new war demands, its industrial capacity has established itself on a higher level. With its steel production, ever broadening stream of automobiles, trucks and tractors, its deep pools of oil, and proliferating inventions and new or newer products, thus telephones, washing machines, vacuum cleaners, electric lights, and motion pictures, and loftier airplanes, radios, and skyscrapers, United States promised to bound even higher. In 1920 its industrial production was 40 percent to 45 percent of the world's, compared with 10.5 percent for Great Britain, 8 percent for France, and 11 percent for Germany.[1] A similar multiple appears in the comparison by the pioneering economic statistician Wladimir S. Woytinsky, who calculated the national wealth of the United States in 1919 at $255 billion, against $61.5 billion for Great Britain, $60 billion for Germany, and $45 billion for France.[2] Thus American industry was four times as great as the nearest competitor's and substantially greater than the production of all combined. If one added agriculture, the disparity was considerably greater. (In 1946, after another world war, the United States, its economy continuing to expand, would be producing 49 percent of the world's manufactured goods.)[3] However managed, the superior power of the American economy could not be gainsaid, not even by its possessor, and expressed itself variously.

In the United States, as elsewhere, industry meant progress, but agriculture fed that progress while usually being cheated of the resulting prosperity. But then American farming enjoyed its best years after the slump of the 1890s. In the next decades it shared in such industrial benefactions as electricity, milking machines, tractors, and isolation-annihilating automobiles. Then the war years raised farm incomes even higher with Russian, East Prussian, and other European croplands overrun by war. Their numbers augmented by the entrepreneurial-minded renting marginal fields, American farmers enjoyed vastly expanded demand. Prices rose dizzyingly, cotton, for example, tripling from 60¢ to $2.06 a bale, other crops faring comparably. This became part of a general inflation, the cost of living going to 105 percent above the pre-war level by 1920. Corrective action drove the economy into a year-and-a-half depression from the summer of 1920, but it lasted a generation long for agriculture. In a decade cotton fell from $1.76 to 85¢ a bale and wheat to $1.04 from $2.19 a bale; the major commodities were down to one half or even a third of the war figures.[4] Most farmers had to stand aside as others enjoyed the magical boom of the 1920s.

The war's end released hopeful but inchoate energies throughout the nation. The year 1919 was the "most strike-torn year in American history" as workers tried to preserve their wartime wages. That year 4 million of them, including 300,000 steelworkers, attempted some 3,600 strikes. The government, however, dropping wartime controls, demobilized the armed forces quickly and canceled war contracts. Entrepreneurial generosity was not encouraged and, on the whole, industry successfully frustrated coal miners (although they did win a modest wage increase) and steelworkers.[5] The poorly paid Boston police attempted a strike in September 1919, but their action released violences and Governor Calvin Coolidge won the vice-presidential nomination the next year by his reaction: "… no right to strike against the public safety."[6] Despite such actions and despite the 1920-21 depression, workers went on to enjoy the rising living standard.

Blacks also shared in the war-generated plenty. During the war hundreds of thousands escaped poverty and humiliation in the South to take jobs in northern industry. They paid the price in northern discrimination, lynching actions, and, in 1919, race riots in East St. Louis, Omaha, and, killing fifteen whites and twenty-three blacks, in Chicago.[7] They went on to form large black communities in Chicago, Detroit, and other manufacturing and urban centers.

Nearly irrelevant to this ebullition, the contemporaneous Red Scare confusedly related the threatening promise of the Soviet Union and the expostulations of two quarreling Communist parties with real action by anarchists. This was part of a last burst of action by anarchists, who had, like the Bolsheviks, hoped that the World War would give their movement a great opportunity to capture power. Lenin, who was right about the opportunity for *his* cause, then took the occasion to repress the anarchists completely in his sovietized Russia a bit later—in 1921. In United States, at the end of April 1919, members of an anarchist group vengefully, if not hopefully, mailed thirty bomb packages, nearly all of them discovered and defused, and, on June 2nd, personally delivered seven bombs. Human damage consisted of the loss of her hands by a Georgia senator's maid, and the death of two persons, one of them a watchman in New York City and the other, the bomber himself in Washington, DC. Targets of the bombs were persons who had acted against anarchists, thus government officials and judges, or such representatives of capitalism as John D. Rockefeller Sr. and J. P. Morgan Jr. Another bomb, on September 26, 1920, exploded near the offices of J. P. Morgan and Company at Wall and Broad Streets in New York City, killed thirty-three persons, and injured 200. A shaken but intact Attorney General A. Mitchell Palmer, whose home had been damaged by the self-annihilated bomber, meanwhile, then launched a series of raids, deplored by many respectable persons, which resulted in the arrests of thousands of suspected Communists and anarchists and the deportation of 600 identified as aliens.[8] The United States was becoming much less hospitable, and in this atmosphere, with unions urging it to reduce competition for jobs, Congress restricted immigration. An ineffective law of 1921, which permitted 700,000 persons to enter by 1924, led to a new law that year reducing the entry quota and basing it on a nationality mix of the 1890 census, which had few southern and eastern Europeans; the new law also forbade any Asiatic immigrants.

The Red Scare had a by-product, the only issue to arouse intellectual passion, that kept the question of radicalism alive in a time of almost moribund political discourse. It was the Sacco-Vanzetti case, which presented itself shyly in early 1920 during the Red Scare and gradually intruded into the national consciousness until it burst into world prominence in 1927. The anarchists Nicola Sacco and Bartolomeo Vanzetti were arrested on May 5, 1920 and accused of participating in two payroll holdups, one of which killed a paymaster and a guard near Boston. While sixteen eyewitnesses identified Sacco or Vanzetti in one or the other of the holdups, and the prosecution could point to such objective incriminating details as ballistics evidence and arms possession, their friends could easily argue that prejudice, in the aftermath of the anti-radical action, had dictated the verdict. (A 1991 study of the case's anarchist background, cited above, while seeing them as innocent of the holdups, concluded that both men were "involved in the [anarchist bomb] conspiracy" of 1919.)[9] The men were defended by the American Civil Liberties Union, many lawyers including the Harvard Law School professor Felix Frankfurter, and a number of such celebrated literary figures and intellectuals as John Dos Passos and Edna St. Vincent Millay, the last parading passionately for a pardon in Boston. The Soviet Union, trying to make off with an anarchist cause célèbre, inspired great demonstrations throughout the world. The American intellectuals found the case an apt metaphor for the general injustice and their own unjust plight—their impotence—in a philistine country. Sacco and Vanzetti were executed on August 23, 1927, while most Americans paid more attention to Charles Lindbergh's triumphal flying tour of the United States following his trans-Atlantic flight. In its lag effect, however, the case veered into political and economic significance. The intellectuals had been unconsciously training for their more potent roles in thinking and administering reform under Franklin Delano Roosevelt.[10]

At the same time American intellectuals joined foreigners in puzzling over a characteristic mixture of philistine and progressive aspects of American life. The decade opened up when the 18th Amendment, the prohibition amendment, went into effect on January 19, 1920—to be followed by the women's suffrage amendment, the 19th, on August 26. If the second put the nation among the leaders of social progress, the first attempted to clamp it in the rigidity of impossible virtue for a dozen years. The ideal found itself paired with efficiently organized crime, bootleggers and gangsters, obedient to economic theory, providing the supply to satisfy demand. A revived Ku Klux Klan, capable of calling a meeting of 200,000 in Indiana, put representatives into state legislatures and broadcast intimidation. In 1925, William Jennings Bryan, progressive and idealist, three times a presidential candidate and briefly a pacifist secretary of state, assisted the prosecution oratorically in a Tennessee trial convicting a high school teacher for teaching evolution. Like bootleggers' liquor it could cause internal bleeding.

Little was said on economic problems. The Socialists and Communists preached Marxian commonplaces amongst themselves. The liberal journals of opinion *The Nation* and *New Republic*, while protesting injustices and intermittently supporting black rights and feminism, failed to produce proposals for economic reform or even critiques of manifest distresses. In the decade of Babbitt, in 1928, Walter Lippmann, a former Socialist and a leading defender of Sacco and Vanzetti, wrote: "The more or less unconscious and unplanned activities of businessmen are at once more novel, more daring, and in general more revolutionary, than the theories of the progressives." After the deluge, in 1932, a group of intellectuals, including John Dos Passos, Edmund Wilson, Malcolm Cowley, Lincoln Steffens, Theodore Dreiser, Sherwood Anderson, and Sidney Hook, published a manifesto reading: "If I vote at all, it will be for the Communists."[11] (That was a temporary fever, and Dos Passos and Hook would later become outspoken anti-Communists.) Lippmann was more nearly right about the political economy than his fellow intellectuals. With new corporate efficiency businessmen were indeed revolutionizing economic life and making it miraculously better. Yet most of them were operating with little concern for the effects of their actions beyond their individual profits and losses. An accounting of the general profits and losses, with thought to economic stability, would be different.

The depression of 1920-21 had been much more of a reminder and a portent than its contemporaries realized. In hindsight we can see it as characteristic of the looser American economy, a continuation of the patterns of the depressions of the 1870s and 1890s, the Panic of 1907, and the Great Depression of the 1930s. But the United States had a short memory and minimal foresight. The 1920-21 episode was sharp and painful. In that brief period nearly 5 million persons, some 11.9 percent of the work force, found themselves unemployed. As part of the tribulations of agriculture, a half million farmers lost their farms. Business at large suffered nearly a hundred thousand bankruptcies.[12] Agriculture did not recover completely until a second world war, but only as an adjunct of an industrial economy. The latter, meanwhile, recovered exuberantly, roaring into the great golden boom of the decade.

On the rising curve of prosperity no responsible thought was given to individual security and general stability. No serious discussion was initiated on unemployment insurance, old age pensions, and other elements of a social security program, which had been initiated by Germany in the 1880s and Great Britain and France in the early 1900s. Indeed the American Federation of Labor opposed unemployment insurance as giving the government excess power over the workers.[13] At the same time, essentially a federation of craft unions, the AFL left the industrial and service workers to the winds of the marketplace and punished itself further by losing members. Americans were still betting on their risky free enterprise and seemed to be winning. The depression and excessive unemployment, 11.9 percent in 1921, soon dissipated, the latter subsiding to 7.6 percent in 1922, 3.2 percent in 1923, and except for 5.5 percent in 1924, remaining under 5 percent—as low as 1.9 percent in 1926—until 1930, when it was 8.7 percent and rising frighteningly.[14] Until 1930 almost every sector of public opinion assumed a continuation of the prosperity that had begun to blossom by the end of 1922. Even the farmers expected to share in the increased well-being. Western progressives caused minor inconveniences to the government, but President Coolidge easily resisted their demands for farm-price supports because of inevitable overproduction.

In the 1920s most Americans were sharing a real rise of some 30 percent in per capita income due to the superior productivity of their economy and the technological improvements shared by all the advanced nations. The Americans did not have to work as hard for it, their work week falling from 6 to 5 1/2 days. In 1920 the national income measured as Gross National Product (GNP) was a war- and peace-inflated $91.5 billion, but then 1921 reflected the depression at an almost shocking $69.6 billion. The year 1922 was an already recovering $74.1 billion and 1923 a well recovered $85.1 billion, the economy then booming to $93.1 billion in 1925 and beyond to $103.1 billion in 1929.[15]

Following upon the exhausting ambitions of Woodrow Wilson's leadership, the presidencies of his Republican successors soothed and, at most, modestly engaged the American electorate. Idealess and promising "normalcy," Warren G. Harding, a mediocre Ohio Senator, appointed able capacities and crooks and died, evidently of a cerebral hemorrhage, on August 2, 1923. (High-level stealing by his cronies was discovered after he died.) His vice-president, Calvin Coolidge, easily won the 1924 election on the implicit promise of minimal positive action. *His* successor, Herbert Hoover, had been secretary of commerce, a modest position he requested and used, applying his considerable ability, to prepare himself for the presidency. That ability did not, however, prepare him for the Great Depression.

The domestic administration shone with a high gloss of success and efficiency. Andrew W. Mellon, a founder of the aluminum industry and a great industrialist-banker (and, like his business associate Henry Clay Frick, a great art collector), directed the Treasury from 1921 to 1932 in the spirit of maximum laissez-faire. Given the productivity of American enterprise, he told a congressional committee: "Your government is just a business and should be run on business principles."[16] Later, reducing taxes on business, he could boast of halving government expenditures from $6.1 billion to $3 billion in seven years.[17] His rationale was the freeing of entrepreneurial funds for more productive purposes. He was making no effort to coordinate policy with the Federal Reserve System, while he defended war-debt demands and the high and (in 1930) increasing American tariffs. He rounded out his stewardship, the Great Depression causing him some embarrassment, with an honorific year as ambassador to Great Britain.

One officer of state, the ambitious Herbert Hoover, attempted to unite his engineering and business experience with economic science and undertake greater initiatives. He organized a conference on unemployment in the depression year 1921. While this was an imaginative stroke, it had little economic substance behind it and at best suggested future action. Following laissez-faire policy, President Harding would not approve any financial support for the unemployed, and the effect of the conference was nil. More in terms of his own proclivities, Hoover applied the principles of Frederick Winslow Taylor to advise industry through his new Bureau of Simplified Practice. His other efforts helped increase exports 55 percent from 1922 to 1927, a mathematically impressive performance. But the purchases of these exports were helped by American loans that began to dry up in 1927, while the high American tariffs were taking their negative effect. At the same time Hoover had been combating the monopolistic pricing by Brazil and Great Britain of such imports as rubber, coffee, potash, and nitrates. It was such sales that permitted these countries to balance off American trade advantages modestly. In essence Hoover pursued a policy of retail efficiency improvements at home and, through his economic nationalism, wholesale economic damage worldwide.[18] His presidency would be instructively painful for both the electorate and perhaps himself.

The administration failed signally to coordinate domestic policy with the economic needs of its trading partners—with its world position. One could nevertheless temper this criticism because such a practical ideal was politically impossible at this point in American history. On tariff policy the farm interest was simply too powerful, farmers naturally resisting measures that would reduce their numbers as the country became more industrialized and urbanized. On war debts the nation was also emotionally and patriotically committed to destructive, indeed self-destructive, policy. It was proceeding, in the longer run, to impoverish others and itself.

Tariff action was revived in the 1920-21 depression and carried through, even more powerfully, in the Great Depression. On May 27, 1921, after agricultural prices had collapsed the previous year, emergency tariffs were enacted on wheat, corn, meat, wool, and sugar for six months: "The representatives of the agricultural states ... had got ... carte blanche to fix as they pleased the duties on their products."[19] Colluding with them were the manufacturing interests seeking to gain unnecessary protection for their products, which were entirely competitive in world trade. The tariff changes were then incorporated in the Fordney-McCumber Tariff act of September 1922, but in their weak economic and powerful political position the farmers were able to demand still higher tariffs. In April 1929, soon after his inauguration, President Hoover, seeking to mollify them further, proposed new tariff legislation. The result was the Smoot-Hawley Tariff Act of June 1930, which increased the Fordney-McCumber rates by 20 percent—to 40-50 percent—on manufactured goods.[20] Passed the year after the Great Crash, it intensified the depressing effects abroad and at home terrifically.

All this emphasized the need for a coordinated economic policy, but the United States was far from that. Rewarded so richly in resources and personnel, the loose, free-swinging American economy resisted anything so sensible. Agriculture was one of many cases in point. The farmers, beginning to suffer the international fall in demand, were also enduring a reduction in demand for so many of them. Of course they denied it. Indeed the free play of economic forces in Adam Smith's sense had been and was still enormously productive. Thus President Andrew Jackson could kill off the second Bank of United States in 1836 and, with it, the function of central banking for nearly eighty years. The Federal Reserve System, created in 1913, had not become an effective central bank until the 1930s under the force of the Great Depression. In the 1920s, nevertheless, while trying to establish its identity, the FRS used its central financial position as best it could to attempt a measure of financial and economic coordination.

Woodrow Wilson, with his lack of interest in economic affairs, had disdained the Federal Reserve System, but the war imparted a greater usefulness to it as an agency to support the Treasury's bonds sales. Its leadership, initially mediocre, slipped further under President Harding, who made an Ohio crony head of the Federal Reserve Board ruling the system. Incompetent and lazy, the man let authority slip away from him to one Benjamin Strong, not even a number of the board. Strong held the title of governor and president of the New York Federal Reserve Bank under a supportive chairman. He managed the largest, most powerful of the twelve reserve banks of the system masterfully and had won the support of the governors of the other reserve banks. (As a young banker during the panic of 1907, he had won high regard as head of the triage committee advising J. P. Morgan which banks could be saved and which could be abandoned to bankruptcy.) During the war, organizing war bonds sales, he deployed the resources of the New York Reserve Bank of New York as the government's principal bank. After the war, operating from his bank's powerful position, he helped set FRS policy, which the board members themselves had simply failed to make under their incompetent head.[21]

Strong was able to determine financial policy in the early postwar period. He successfully urged an increase in the discount rate from 4 percent to 7 percent to break the inflationary boom and bring the economy down to a normal level. In the face of the 1920-21 depression he then urged an anti-cyclical policy to counter deflationary conditions as well. The main tool of monetary management, which he was among the first to develop, was a combination of discount rate changes and the purchase-or-sale of government securities. Slowly dying of tuberculosis, diagnosed in 1916, he spent the rest of his life gallantly trying to repair the defects of the American financial and economic order.[22]

Strong had exercised great skill in guiding the American and world economies up to the end. If he failed, he had nevertheless provided precedents for more successful action in more favorable conditions in the future. In 1927, in his last great effort, he supported an FRS move to increase the money supply and lower the discount rate by one half percent. At the moment this slightly inflationary action was favorable to the United States, which was in a very mild depression, *and* Britain and Germany, who were losing gold to the attractions of the higher United States discount rate. The immediate result relieved the Europeans but brought on a perilous rise of the New York stock market. Thus the problem grew more difficult as American and European interests diverged. With the 1926 level indexed at 100, the Wall Street market rose to 106 in January 1927, 137 in January 1928, and then, accelerating to193 in January 1929, arrived at its peak of 216 in September 1929—to collapse in October.[23] (If the figures are modest compared with the increases at the turn of the twenty-first century, conditions were very different, and the low point of 34 in June 1932 shows the extreme nature of that earlier rise and fall.) In December 1927, responding to a new weakness in the international economy, Strong sailed to England to help stabilize the Italian lira; from Europe he evidently approved an FRS decision to restrain the Wall Street boom. That month it sold $400 million of securities in open market operations and began to raise discount rates in two steps. Drawing money from Europe, a negative effect Strong wanted to avoid, this was additional evidence of the limited leverage at his disposal. In July 1928, as the market continued to rise threateningly, he tried to overcome the contradictions by vainly recommending the perhaps oversubtle operation of raising rates in the other FRS regions while keeping them unchanged in New York.[24] One simply could not guide the whole American economy by way of the stock market: Strong had given himself one more impossible task and the market had got away from him. In July, also, he tried to resign on doctor's advice. His colleagues persuaded him to stay on until the end of the year. He died on October 16, 1928.

The United States had engineered itself and the world into the greatest economic collapse in history. By February 1929 the second discount raise had left the market "nervous." The industrial production index and other indications began to drop. By August the great bull market was at its end, collapsing on Black Thursday, October 24. After a moment of apparent recovery, it fell definitively on Black Tuesday, October 29.[25] The United States and the other leading world economies, France as partial exception, soon pursued it downward.

Meanwhile, foreign customers retaliating against the Smoot-Hawley tariff, the dollar value of American exports fell from $5.24 billion in 1929 to $1.61 billion in 1932.[26] In 1929 United States sold $948.5 million in goods to Canada and bought $504.3 million worth. In three months the American tariff act called up the Canadian Emergency Tariff of September 17, 1930 listing 125 classes of American imports subject to counter-tariffs including textiles, gasoline, shoes, fertilizers, and automobiles. In 1932 exports to Canada had fallen to $241.35 million while Canada's to the United States were down to $174 million.[27] Other major trading partners acted similarly. Retaliation and the deepening depression reduced world trade down to one-third of its 1929 monetary level in 1932, although the volume held at close to two thirds.[28] The apparent disparity was the effect of falling prices, but these were another depressive influence, since buyers delayed buying in anticipation of further price decreases. The wretchedness of the situation was expressed in the 1932 unemployment figures: a quarter of the American and a third of the German work force. Everything seemed to conspire to make matters worse.

No one has shown that the succession market crash, American depression, world depression, thus the unique Great Depression, occurred as a result of the essential character of the free-enterprise system, as Marxists and Keynesians have argued or suggested. It would appear to have followed logically from fundamental and related weaknesses in the organization, leadership, and psychology of the American and international economies, which prevented the normal corrective economic action. One key factor in the linkage was the Smoot-Hawley Tariff Act. But then the new tariff was only an extension of the earlier high tariffs, which had already hollowed out the international economy. More fundamentally, the United States had too much money for its own good, hence Benjamin Strong's inevitably vain defense against the money's inflationary effects in the stock market, and the rest of the world, too little, thus Germany's desperation, Britain's deflation, and France's (and Italy's) laggard industrialization and comparatively low living standards. This imbalance created the great American bubble while impoverishing the European nations. The major economies had no defense against terrific financial and economic collapse. In the earlier great crises from the depressions of the 1870s and 1890s and the Panic of 1907 European investors had bet on the American economy and everybody had won. In 1929 the Europeans had no money to spare.

One must inquire into the validity of economic theory when its practitioners were so blind to what was coming and so helpless in dealing with it. How can the fault be allocated between theory and theorists? Why did the United States, Adam Smith's paragon in the creation of the wealth of nations, fall so far? Why did the correctives in the system of the neoclassical economists fail so badly? These questions will be addressed in the later discussion here on the basis of more data.

"No American president has come into office with a more detailed conception of what he wanted to accomplish in economic policy … than did Hoover in 1929."[29] To put it more precisely, "Hoover's election to the presidency in 1928 was a triumph of the economist-politician-technocrat."[30] Assisting his purposes as supreme political economist, Hoover had drawn upon the talents of the National Bureau of Economic Research, established, we recall, in the spirit of institutional economics, to lay out an economic program in February 1929. The program, however, showed itself to be another blind technical exercise taking no notice of the real weaknesses that caused the Great Crash later that year.

Hoover's most important constructive action was a desperate denial of his policy on war debts. Obdurately defending the idea of payment, he had arbitrarily, defensively, and rhetorically insisted that arguments against it were "false in every particular.... [E]very nation has some transferable surplus which can be made use of."[31] At best it was a meaningless statement. Effectively halting reparations and war-debt payments, international conditions finally forced the Hoover Moratorium out of him in mid-1931. But at the same time Hoover had lost control of the economy. The long interregnum from his defeat on November 8, 1932 to Franklin D. Roosevelt's accession on March 4, 1933 almost saw the total collapse of the American banking system. So began the time of unemployment, sheer hunger, shanty Hoovervilles of the Depression homeless, and breadlines. Roosevelt and the New Deal restored the banks and went on to the economy. The need was vast. The Gross National Product had gone from $103.3 million in 1929 to $56.4 million in 1933, Roosevelt's first year in office.[32] The United States had plunged into the greatest economic disaster in world history and dragged the rest of the world down with it.

At least, rethinking its economics and policies generally, it would undertake more responsible action at home and abroad.

Notes

1. League of Nations: Secretariat: Economic, Financial and Transit Department, *Industrialization and Foreign Trade* (New York: 1945), 12, diagram No. 1, "Movements of Manufacturing Production."
2. Wladimir S. Woytinsky, *Die Welt in Zahlen*, vol. 1 (Berlin: R. Mosse, 1925), table, 198.
3. Paul Bairoch, "International Industrialization Levels from 1750 to 1980," *Journal of European Economic History* 11 (Fall 1982), 301.
4. William E. Leuchtenburg, *The Perils of Prosperity 1914-32* (Chicago: University of Chicago Press, 1958), 70, 100; Frank W. Taussig, *The Tariff History of the United States* (New York: Johnson Reprint, 1931, 8th ed.; 1st ed.: G.P. Putnam's Sons, 1888), 447.
5. Robert H. Zieger, *American Workers, American Unions* (Baltimore: Johns Hopkins University Press, 1990; 1st ed.: 1986), 5-19; quotation, 6.
6. Bedford et al., *The Americans*, 474, 468; *Bartlett's Familiar Quotations* (from the Telegram to Samuel Gompers, AFL president, Sept. 14, 1919).

7.   Bedford et al., *The Americans*; Reeves, *20th-Century America*, 82.
8.   Paul Avrich, *Sacco and Vanzetti: The Anarchist Background* (Princeton: Princeton University Press, 1991), 137-62, 204-7; Leuchtenburg, *The Perils*, 71-74.
9.   Avrich, *Sacco and Vanzetti*, 159.
10. See Francis Russell, *Tragedy in Dedham* (New York: McGraw: Hill, 1962); David Felix, *Protest: Sacco-Vanzetti and the Intellectuals* (Bloomington: Indiana University Press, 1965).
11. Lippmann and the intellectuals quoted, Felix, *Protest*, 242-43.
12. Bedford et al., *The Americans*, 474.
13. John A. Garraty, *Unemployment in History: Economic Thought and Public Policy* (New York: Harper & Row, 1978), 150.
14. U. S. Department of Commerce, *Historical Statistics of the United States: Colonial Times to 1957, Series D 46-47: Unemployment 1900-1957* (Washington, 1961), 73.
15. Bureau of the Census, *Historical Statistics of the United States, Colonial Times to 1970*, part I (Washington, 1975), table, series F 1-5, 224.
16. Quoted, Philip H. Love, *Andrew W. Mellon: The Man and His Work* (Baltimore: F. Heath Coggins, 1929), 86.
17. Bureau of the Census, *Statistical Abstract of United States: 1930*, table, 172.
18. Hoover's "New Economics," William J. Barber, *From New Era to New Deal: Herbert Hoover, the Economists, and American Economic Policy, 1921-1933* (Cambridge: Cambridge University Press, 1985), 65-77; exports, 32-40.
19. Taussig, *The Tariff History of the United States*, quotation, 452-53.
20. Paul Bairoch, *Economics and World History: Myths and Paradoxes* (Chicago: University of Chicago Press, 1993), 5.
21. As shown in detail, Clay J. Anderson, *A Half-Century of Federal Reserve Policymaking, 1914-1964* (Philadelphia: FRB of Philadelphia, 1965), especially 14-30, 64-74 ("The Great Depression"). Other FRS accounts, noted here, agree with his account.
22. Lester V. Chandler, *Benjamin Strong, Central Banker* (Washington: Brookings Institution, 1958), passim. See also Sylvan A. Wueschner, *Charting Twentieth Century Monetary Policy: Herbert Hoover and Benjamin Strong, 1917-1927* (Westport, CT: Greenwood, 1999).
23. Charles P. Kindleberger, *The World in Depression 1929-1939* (Berkeley: University of California Press, 1973), table, 111.
24. Lester Chandler, *Benjamin Strong*, 454-55, 433-35.
25. John Kenneth Galbraith, *The Great Crash* (Boston: Houghton-Mifflin, 1955) 37, 93, 103-16.
26. Bureau of the Census, *Statistical Abstract of the United States*, 1940, table 552, 487.
27. Joseph M. Jones, *Tariff Retaliation: Repercussions of the Hawley-Smoot Bill* (New York: Garland, 1983; 1st ed.: University of Pennsylvania Press, 1934): on Canada, 176-210; Spain, table, 61; Switzerland, 104-38; France, 139-75; Great Britain, 211-46.
28. Lionel Robbins, *The Great Depression* (London: Macmillan, 1934), 11.
29. Barber, *From New Era*, 65.
30. Jordan A. Schwartz, *The New Dealers in the Age of Roosevelt* (New York: Knopf, 1993), 46.
31. Quoted, Barber, *From New Era*, 39.
32. U. S. Department of Commerce, Bureau of Economic Analysis, bea, *doc.gov*.

5

America Abroad

None of the leading nations had an accurate sense of its international situation after World War I. The United States proposed to leave Europe to its own impoverished resources. Of course it could not quite. Britain and France, adding to their empires, had eliminated a European threat, as they thought, and could expand their power with little concern for a reborn Russia. While Britain could attend to her imperial responsibilities, France balanced between the prospect of German reparations and a justification, as her more ambitious nationalists speculated, of using nonpayment as an excuse and capturing more of German territory on the pattern of the old revolutionary and Napoleonic conquests. Germany, thrashed but integral, agonized over defeat and present hardship more than her healthy potentials warranted. But the United States, because so much richer and more powerful, was more extravagantly wrong. It went on entangling itself in Europe even as it tried to escape it.

Looming over this Europe was a power struggle on its geographical periphery. A. J. P. Taylor concluded his *Struggle for Mastery in Europe* by saying it no longer mattered. Indeed, "All the old ambitions from Alsace and Lorraine to colonies in Africa became trivial and second-rate compared to the new struggle for control of the world." In this struggle, "Europe was dwarfed by two world powers, the Soviet Union and the United States—implacable, though often unconscious rivals … in a rivalry of idealisms."[1] Of the two United States was the least conscious of it; Lenin and Trotsky, only two months after their successful revolution, had the enemy central in their vision. Of course the idealisms were vastly different. Communist belief was integral: it demanded total command of the world for the good of the proletariat, the only class worth considering. American idealism was a patchwork of ideas of political freedom and Protestant virtues, which included temperance, good will to all (if they permitted themselves to be patronized), church-going, and staying close to home. Now, while the United States did little more than leave, Lenin, however straightened in his material position, loosed revolutionary action in Berlin from 1918 into 1919 (while benefiting from revolutionary outbursts in Hungary in 1919 and in Munich in 1918 and 1919) and elsewhere in Germany until 1923. But thereafter, with its money power United States could not help becoming a dominant foreign influence in Germany.

America had ratified the decision to reject the League of Nations with the victory of Harding in 1920. On European war debts the new president confessed, "I don't know anything about this European stuff." His cabinet, including a reluctant Secretary of State Charles Evans Hughes, was unanimous for payment. Treasury Secretary Andrew Mellon, however, wanted the Treasury to have the flexibility of negotiating with the debtor nations individually, but Congress, fearing excessive leniency, refused and instead, on February 9, 1922, passed the Debt Funding Bill setting up a debt commission to assure payment.[2] On January 19, 1923 Stanley Baldwin, Britain's chancellor of the exchequer, accepted the need to mollify obdurate American opinion and agreed to sixty-one years of payments at rates beginning with 3 percent for the first ten years and rising to 5 percent thereafter.[3] Secretary of State Hughes, who had a good sense of economics, felt he had to live with his countrymen's obduracy, however much it made his work difficult. His legal-economic legerdemain preventing disaster in the 1920s, he went on, partially at least, to solve the greatest problem of the postwar decade, the war debt-and-reparation issue.

A great lawyer of imperturbable dignity, a former presidential candidate (losing to Wilson in 1912), a past associate Supreme Court justice and future chief justice, Hughes had the necessary professional intelligence and capacity for compromise. He was between two hard rocks: the American insistence on war-debt payment and the Allied demand for reparations, if not as compensation for war damage but at least as a help in paying onerous debts left behind by the war. Indeed Hughes agreed with the Europeans. In an interview with the London *Times* of March 2, 1922 he warned that the United States would not relent on war debts but hinted he would like to do so. A *Times* editorial explained his sense: "Europe is invisible from the Mississippi Valley." Granted that, the old Allies would have been crazy to give up on reparations. Additionally, France in the person of the intensely nationalistic Raymond Poincaré, former president (1913-20) and premier from January 1922 to March 1924 (and for four other times), hoped for an excuse to inhibit German resurgence by occupying the Rhineland.[4] Although, alleging German failure to pay reparations, he did occupy the Ruhr mining area on January 11, 1923, he was forced to accept the financial settlement that Hughes was securing. American subtlety defeated European overreach. Meanwhile, however, the Germans reacted to the incursion into the Ruhr with strikes and mass action. In the disorder and violence, the German mark went to 4.2 *trillion* to the dollar on November 20, 1923. This was the height—or depth—of the German hyperinflation, the sheer irrationality and nausea of which demanded a sensible solution.

Hughes had to soften the reparations demand in a way the Allies, especially the French, would accept, while leaving the war debts inviolate. His ultimate strength—his solution—was American money power, which would defeat American obtuseness. He got the idea, which he half-seriously attributed to God, while discussing the issue at a meeting of the American Historical Association in New Haven on December 29, 1922. The core of it was, as he put it, to remove the problem from politics and devolve it on non-political experts.[5] Of course this was a perfect lawyer's falsification, since the experts would have to obey the government leaders, who were obeying unfriendly public opinion. But there was a crack in this pitiless logic through which American money power would flow. The need was so great that everyone entered into the lie. The point was that the American government was not contributing any of its money, but that its sponsorship of the action would attract and reassure private investors. These individuals and companies would provide finance under a nonexistent governmental guarantee.

The mechanism of mendacity was a committee chaired by Charles G. Dawes, a Chicago banker and future United States vice president (under Calvin Coolidge) and including British experts (but not the uncooperative John Maynard Keynes, who thought the war debts were too absurd). When Harding died, on August 2, 1923, Calvin Coolidge rather subtly conveyed his government's fundamental irresponsibility by telling Dawes, "I have said that you…represented not the government, but the American mind."[6] The Dawes Committee plan, going into effect on September 1, 1924, began with the Allied powers actually granting Germany a loan of $200 million and a year's moratorium. Of course these concessions satirized the sense of demanding reparations in the first place, but the responsible leaders all cooperated in a charade of international good will. The theory was that Germany would be able to pay after the two-year respite. In a sense she was, that is, by way of more loans. She would then begin paying at an annual rate of $250 million for the first year, the installments rising to $625 million in the fifth year. No decision was made beyond that; no one could show how she could pay on her own. Nevertheless, signaling a great change in the economic air, the $200-million loan was an enormous success. Everyone wanted to lend the money. Americans, offered a *tranche* of $110 million, oversubscribed it by a multiple of eleven. French, British, and other purchasers were equally enthusiastic. One powerful reason, now that the Allied governments had seemingly guaranteed the Dawes Plan, was the fact the Germans, in their desperate financial situation, had to pay 8 percent to 9 percent interest, double the normal commercial rate. At this price Germany was reintegrated into the economy and polity of Europe and the world.[7]

Germany never had the money to pay reparations. She was not permitted to build up the great trade surpluses which would have provided it, since the old Allies were her major trading partners and refused to accept trade deficits for themselves. But under the Dawes Plan from 1924 to 1929 she did pay $2 billion (plus $4 billion exacted earlier). She got it, private loans then following, from optimistic foreign investors. The operation worked on the principle of a classic Ponzi swindle, which attracts new investors with disproportionate returns. The funds of these new investors, and not the profits, finance large payments to the original investors and attract more. Eventually a doubt arises, the investors begin to flee, and the scheme collapses. This would happen to Germany as involuntary swindler during the Great Depression.

In this way the United States, the Soviet Union eliminated as a powerful factor in Germany by 1923, became a master of the German political economy. American policy was getting what it wanted: a stable and profit-creating economic partner. But the short-range solution disguised, and helped build, the long-range structure of disaster. The falsity of reparations was a core part of the falsity of the European situation.

The Dawes Plan was followed by the Young Plan, another admission of the madness of reparations. Beginning on September 1, 1930, it was meant to be a permanent settlement, but also failed to provide the income to pay reparations. It reduced annual payments to $400 million, which then would rise to $600 million, more mathematical than actual relief, while prescribing their continuance until *1988*. In mid-1931 the Depression overwhelmed the new plan after Germany had paid an additional $700 million financed chiefly by foreign loans. Before then, however, the plan had even worse political than economic effects.

Hughes cannot be blamed if his strategy had avoided a great disaster at the cost of building up to a greater one. He had given the major nations a half dozen years to repair matters on the thesis that one must get through today before attending to tomorrow. His country, the leading of the leading nations, would fail him. This partial success of American policy had been preceded by a completely empty action. Again Hughes had been responsible; again it was excusable. In fact all the other American foreign-policy initiatives were simply false and empty.

The first major example was the Washington Conference on the Limitation of Armaments from November 12, 1921 to February 6, 1922. Behind it was the slightly chastened American public opinion and the theory that armaments caused war. If the United States had avoided the responsibilities of membership in the League of Nations, it might find a way to general peace by reducing military arms, hence the Washington conference. Hughes made the best of it, most particularly since the country was resisting paying more taxes for Army and Navy during a period of promised peace. He proposed a radical reduction of the battleship fleets, the United States in the lead, by destroying thirty capital ships out of sixty-six. This spectacular idea outran any rational sense in the logic of peace. But it had great effect at the time. The United States wanted to limit Japanese expansion and proposed a 5:5:3 ratio for the American, British, and Japanese battleships. This was accepted, but the Japanese secured the promise of the United States to freeze the fortification of its Pacific island possessions (the British following suit), an agreement causing subsequent pain after the Pearl Harbor attack. The Japanese also evaded the American intent of keeping her out of China. Since only capital ships were designated, other nations, thus France and Italy, built more cruisers and lighter vessels.[8] The agreements were worse than empty, they were negative in effect, a false path to peace and another example of the American effort to outwit reality.

When Calvin Coolidge began his full term in 1925 he was content to let Hughes go for a more pliant Frank B. Kellogg, the ambassador to Great Britain. The mediocre Kellogg was better adapted to the intensified falsity of American policy. Resolutely colonial, Coolidge distrusted Europeans. In a note to a publisher he wrote: "Of course I do not want to implicate ourselves in Europe.... We have interests there which I want to look after for our own sake, but we cannot attempt to shield them [the Europeans] from the results of their own actions." Correctly, he accused them of wanting to use reparations as a defense against war debts; of course he was right. But penury, which Coolidge did not address, dictated this intent: Europe did not have the money. More personally, he told the British ambassador's wife that he would never visit Europe "because he could learn everything he needed to know by remaining in America."[9]

Coolidge's major effort in foreign policy was a revival of the American anti-armament campaign. In February 1927 he called upon the major powers to meet in Geneva to resolve their naval rivalry. While Great Britain and Japan accepted, France and Italy declined. Their argument was that this cut across to the disarmament efforts of the League of Nations, a reminder of the failure of the United States to join it in the first place. The conference opened in the late spring in Geneva but Calvin Coolidge stayed home as usual and the participants were second-rank diplomats. Coolidge wanted to extend the Washington treaty to the lesser vessels, while the British and Japanese demanded concessions that hollowed out the sense of a possible agreement. After six weeks the conference ended in August without any.

A final effort was forced upon the United States by France's Aristide Briand, frequently prime minister and/or foreign minister in the 1920s. In 1925, as foreign minister, he scored a great success by concluding the half-pacific Locarno Treaty with Gustav Stresemann, foreign minister of Germany, both winning Nobel Peace prizes. Seeking to mollify the United States after the French refusal to attend the Geneva conference, Briand seized upon an idea proposed by a Chicago lawyer, the outlawry of war. It was intensely advocated by the influential Columbia University president Nicholas Murray Butler and the Columbia University professor James T. Shotwell. Briand proposed renouncing war between France and the United States, a fine, benign project. Coolidge and Kellogg were cool to it because it suggested a kind of negative military alliance between France and the United States, but it had too much support to be ignored. They resolved the problem by inviting the participation of other allegedly pacific nations. The eventual agreement became the vague expression of irresponsible goodwill. Sixty-two nations joined, the first fifteen, led by Kellogg, signing it in Paris on August 27, 1927. Rather honestly, Briand granted: "Peace is proclaimed ... but it still remains to organize it." Herbert Hoover, the new president, declared the treaty in force in the White House on July 24, 1929.[10] A British study remarked on the "escapist quality of every aspect of United States diplomacy."[11] The United States, meanwhile, was expanding its naval program in view of the construction increases by the other naval powers.

Hoover's secretary of state, Henry L. Stimson, a fine civil servant, attempted to reverse the practical isolation practiced by Coolidge and tighten relations with the other major powers. He had modest success in moderating naval rivalry but could not move Hoover on war debts, which he recognized as a major disturbing factor. But then he had to contend with the effects of the Wall Street Crash, the beginning of the Great Depression, and the collapse of world trade. The 1930s were beginning with disaster and getting worse.

We have been planing above Europe and seeing only the outer shapes of its nations, not their interior existence and peoples. To make sense of what American policy did to Europe, not omitting what it did to itself, we should selectively examine it—its people, its agonies, and, necessarily, its lies.

The onset of the Great Depression, the war losses, and war-debt and reparations issues should not distract us from an awareness of the increases in material well-being during the 1920s. These resulted from the inevitable improvements in economic productivity, assisted by war-driven efficiencies. Compared with the United States, which had a per capita gross domestic product (1990 international dollars) of $5,500 in 1920 and $6,900 in 1929, France went from $3,230 to $4,770, Germany from $3,000 to $4,050, and Great Britain from $4,550 to $5,500 in those bookend years.[12] The figures, however, would have been somewhat higher if the United States had pursued a more generous trade and tariff policy. This does not dispose of the war-debt and reparations problem. In order to pay the American war debts and the Allied reparations, the payers (thus Allies and Germans) had to build up trade surpluses, but the United States and its tariffs blocked both possibilities, hence their neuralgic-economic importance. It all goes back to the terrific blankness of the nation about its international position.

France did have serious complaints, thus the terrific pressure of debts left behind by the war, with ten of its departments devastated by the fighting and the memory of its 1,400,000 military dead. Protesting war-debt payments, she hoped to use reparations as a defense, if only a partial one. The 1921 French budget foresaw revenues of 23.1 billion francs and expenditures of 43.8 billion francs for a deficit equivalent to $1.6 billion. The deficit was carried in its budget under the heading, "Recoverable Expenditures," with the explanation that they were "mainly covered by loans in anticipation of reparation payments."[13] Few of these latter appeared. If this looked dismal for France, she suffered less financially than the other major European combatants. We have seen that even as she demanded reparations, she was using their absence to expand her occupation of western Germany. Furthermore, driven by need, she managed her finances more artfully than Great Britain. While Britain paid half of her war costs by taxes, France paid but 14 percent. The effect of the resultant deficits naturally was inflation, reducing the franc to one fifth of its prewar value (as measured by the dollar, which lost *half* of its value). Trusting that German reparations would make up the losses (while Germany had planned to do the same to the Allies), France did not try to strengthen the franc. Instead she effectively swindled her bondholders who had helped finance the war by letting the bonds fall with the franc. Giving herself a great advantage in foreign trade, she went on to leave her currency undervalued into the 1930s. As a result of such financial irresponsibility, France never experienced the unemployment suffered by the United States, Britain, or Germany. In her worst year, 1936, she had 5.4 percent unemployed (of her insured working force). In 1932 she counted 274,000 unemployed while Britain and Germany reached their maximums of 2.8 million and 5.6 million jobless, respectively.[14] Addressing these experiences, John Maynard Keynes translated their lesson into the depression cure of his General Theory—governmentally managed inflation.

On the economic side we can see Great Britain, under the force of the Great Depression, providing a symmetrical lesson on the evils of financial virtue. Alone among the European combatants, she had formally remained on the gold standard during the war (although she had to cheat mathematically to do so). She slipped off visibly in early 1919 when American aid stopped. Actually, clinging to gold was an archaic skill like winning at whist, and probably harmed the country by reducing the demand for her high-priced exports and producing a passive trade balance by the spring of 1915, an imbalance to be mindlessly replicated in the 1920s. Consistent with that policy, Britain at first attacked the postwar inflation by increasing the bank lending rate in 1920. John Maynard Keynes, still mostly orthodox, had argued for staying on gold in 1914 and he now urged a drastic bank-rate increase from 6 percent to 10 percent as a counter-inflationary action. The government found 1 percent sufficient. Indeed the one point drove unemployment from 2.8 percent in 1921 to 14.8 percent in 1922, the level remaining above 10 percent for the rest of the decade—to rise to 22.5 percent early in the Depression.[15] While nearly all professional economists held grimly on their old rigors, Keynes turned into an inflationist by the fall of 1921 and demanded a bank-rate reduction.[16] But he was out of step with his country. With Keynes protesting vainly, and Labor and Liberal parties agreeing with the Conservatives, Britain moved inexorably back to gold and gold standard in 1925.

Here is where Benjamin Strong, the New York Reserve Bank governor, acted in place of the American presidency, the Department of State, and the Treasury Department. He gave the Federal Reserve System, thus the nation, a financial foreign policy. According to that policy he proposed stabilization plans for France, Poland, Romania, and Italy. But all of Strong's efforts and the influence of the FRS could not counterbalance the negative effects of American tariff and war-debt policy. Another negative factor was the laggard economic thinking at the time, Strong supporting Great Britain's return to the gold standard in 1925. In Britain it was expected that the return would "reestablish the former domination of the London monetary market and be to the general benefit of the country's economy."[17] Agreeing, Benjamin Strong offered to lend Great Britain substantial funds to help.[18] His generosity, incidentally, enlisted Britain to defend the value of the gold hoard the United States was amassing. But the pound was not worth $4.86, the old "parity" to which she returned, and hence confirmed British labor and goods as too expensive in foreign trade. Her laggard evaluation of her situation and her financial and economic probity punished her with a dreary period of unemployment and labor strife, as employers tried and failed to reduce wages. In fact economic primacy had gone to the United States; Wall Street, aided by the Dawes Plan, had supplanted London's Threadneedle Street as the world's financial center. Britain had to undergo the general strike of May 3-12, 1926 set off by the particularly intransigent coal miners with the wavering support of the Trades Union Congress, the central labor organization. While the other unions dropped away, the miners stayed out for seven months before giving up. The Conservative government, breaking the strike with the help of middle-class volunteers, provided a fine subject for left-wing propaganda.

If France and England suffered considerably, Germany got the worst of American economic and political destructiveness.[19] At first the United States had little to do with her, while Lenin's achievement, both his ideology and his command of Russia, became an immediate presence there. On October 7, 1918 a left-wing Social Democrat proclaimed revolution in Bavaria, the first in a series of uprisings. At the end of the month a naval mutiny, surely suggested by the Bavarian and the Bolshevik examples, prevented the mad intention of German fleet commanders to sally out to sabotage the peace negotiations. On November 9, after energetic demonstrations in Berlin, the Social Democratic Party took over the nation's leadership in a sequence from the emperor's ministers to a liberal prince. Left-wing Social Democrats, calling themselves Spartacists and accurately seeing the party as nonrevolutionary, proposed to follow Lenin's example. Their leaders were Karl Liebknecht, son of a live-in Marx protégé, and

Rosa Luxembourg, an incisive personality and a virtuosa of dialectics. On December 19 or 20, 1918 they were joined by Karl Radek, the Communist International—Comintern—representative and a personal emissary of Lenin himself. On December 30, 1918 to January 1, 1919 the Spartacists organized themselves as the German Communist Party.

From January 4, in Berlin's revolutionary unrest, Liebknecht and Luxembourg led an urban revolution, but the Social Democrats called in the Frei Corps, volunteer military units—many nationalistic and superpatriotic—to save the provisional government. On the night of January 15-16 the Spartacist leaders were captured and killed.[20] The Social Democrats carried through a peaceable election giving them 40 percent of the vote; they headed the government in cooperation with the Catholic Center (20 percent of the vote) and the Democrats (19 percent). This was the Weimar Republic, so-called because it first met in Goethe's Weimar for safety. The three parties formed the Weimar Coalition governing the republic most of the 1920s, sometimes with the addition of the more conservative German People's Party. More risings took place until 1923, when in October and November Communists briefly and vainly got control of the provincial governments of Saxony and Thuringia, in the southeast and center-east. The republic could maintain itself against all Communist efforts, only succumbing to the American-determined economics and Nazi brown- and blackshirts by January 1933.

The war and Marxian socialism created a third force, fascism-Nazism. The feasance and nonfeasance of American policy did not affect Italy as directly as Germany, although more generous economic measures might have reduced the attractions of fascism for Italy. Its leader, Benito Mussolini, began as a radical Socialist whom the war taught to join nationalist to socialist promises. While the Italian Socialist Party sincerely threatened revolution, ultrarevolutionary Socialists organized themselves as the Italian Communist Party on September 1920. With both Socialists and Communists leading violent strikes and factory takeovers, Mussolini could promise middle-class Italians he would protect their property and lives. On October 1922 fascists carried out their March on Rome and took power. The election of April 1924 confirmed Mussolini as national leader and by July 31, 1926 he was legally dictator, *Il Duce*.[21]

This was a model for Adolph Hitler, a homeless Austrian and veteran of the German army. Beginning as a patriotic spy for the military in Munich, he found the Bavarian area a rich site for his ambitions. The left-wing Social Democratic leader in Munich was assassinated by a right-wing fanatic, and with a Communist regime in Hungary from March to

August 1919 a Bavarian Communist group took over the city on April 7. The Weimar government sent in military units who retook it on May 1-2 and shot odd suspects. Presently a reactionary government, friendly to Hitler's aims, took control. In September 1920 Hitler, assigned to investigate a tiny group of cranks and oddly charismatic, made a speech, captured the support of the group, and impressed a larger audience at its first public meeting on October 16. By November Hitler's National Socialist German Workers Party, broadcasting a virulent anti-Semitism and nationalism, had become a political force in Bavaria. Hitler organized his brown-shirted SA in 1921 and the more elite black-shirted SS in 1925. He attracted his first important crowds to protest Allied reparation demands in 1921. In January 1923, with Germany failing to pay reparations and the French entering the Ruhr, the political-economic chaos generated the year's inflationary burst and encouraged Hitler to attempt his Beer Hall Putsch of November 8-9. With its failure Hitler was arrested, tried, and sentenced to eight months of comfortable captivity, during which he wrote his *Mein Kampf*.[22]

Assisted by the Dawes Plan, the heart-wrenching period of hyperinflation behind them, the Germans could enjoy the temporary, false-bottomed prosperity of the later 1920s. In the study *The Diplomacy of the Dollar*, an American adviser on economic affairs noted: "American buyers of German securities financed the recovery of her republican Germany, the repair of the German monetary and banking system, and the payment of German reparations during the twenties."[23] With a secure currency supported by American funds, Germany also endured increased unemployment, since employers could no longer pass on wage increases to more resistant consumers. The prosperity temporarily eased the unemployment problem, but the Wall Street collapse would make it much worse.

In July 1929 Germans could feel the indignation over the Young Plan, which they had not felt strongly enough to feel over the Dawes Plan. This gave Hitler valuable assistance to emerge from his post-Putsch slump. Leaders of the right-wing Nationalists, Pan-German League, and Stahlhelm (a veterans' organization) joined the Nazis in organizing a national committee to demand a plebiscite on the plan. This meant an enormous accession of respectability for the head of a fringe party with handful of deputies in the Reichstag. The legislature was certain to ratify Germany's acceptance and the anti-Young Plan campaign got only 13.8 percent of the vote in December. But Hitler, exercising his oratory, again represented the popular negative sentiment on reparations and positioned himself and the party effectively to move toward power.

By 1929 international conditions lifted German unemployment to 13.1 percent, and steady deterioration then set in: 15.3 percent in 1930, 23.3 percent in 1931, and a maximum of 30.1 percent in 1932. Germany had a higher proportion of unemployment than any other major nation, United States second to it with 24.9 percent, its maximum, also in 1932.[24] The Social Democratic chancellor found the situation unbearable by early 1930, and led his party out of the cabinet. The new government, taking office on March 30, 1930, was profoundly different, more than indicated by the leadership of a Centrist chancellor and the absence of the Social Democrats. Heinrich Brüning, an ascetic economic expert out of the Catholic labor movement but respectful of laissez-faire, proposed a strategy that might lead Germany out of the reparation trap. A few weeks before he took office he told the Reichstag his aim was to win a reparations moratorium. In order to do so Germany had to prove its good faith by practicing the most rigorous economies.[25] The hope for a moratorium was not as absurd as one might think; Germany actually got it a year and a season after Brüning took office. The relief, however, could not save his government.

Brüning's economic intent had required a new politics. He had planned to relegate the Reichstag to the situation of a Greek chorus, accepting the fact of its self-imposed impotence, free to deplore but not to act. He would govern by decree, with the support of the elderly President Paul von Hindenburg, under powers granted by the Weimar Constitution. It would be a dual dictatorship although subject to recall, a violation but not quite a betrayal of its democratic character. New elections on September 14, 1930, however, showed that his government was a thinning shell and greater powers were in the streets. Hitler paraded his strength with his brownshirt formations, who fought Social Democratic and Communist groups, while the Nazis went threateningly and powerfully from 12 to 107 Reichstag seats (out of 577). The Communists themselves, enemies of the Nazis but also of the Weimar Republic, increased their representation in the Reichstag from 54 to 77. The majority of the Reichstag deputies were actually enemies of its representative character. For a fragile moment, however, the Reichstag (and Hindenburg) permitted Brüning to govern. Here is where and how American economic policy crashed into the shaky German economy.

It was American funds, lured by the Dawes Plan, that had created the German prosperity. Now the funds flowed out. At first the problem had been the American boom, investors preferring American stocks by 1928. In that year Germany received almost $1 billion in capital imports, nearly all of it from the United States, the figures falling to $482 million in 1929, $129 million in 1930, then into a *deficit* of $540 million in 1931.[26] The reversal was deadly. Meanwhile, in May 1931, Austria's Creditanstalt, the largest bank in central Europe, went bankrupt, dragging down with it the great German bank, the Danat, the next month. All this savagely undercut Brüning's positive measures. His program, meanwhile, imposed three terrific wage and price reductions accompanied by import reductions. For world trade his policy represented one blade of the scissors, the American Hawley-Smoot Tariff Act of 1930 representing the other. From 1929 to 1932 Brüning reduced imports from $3.37 billion (13.4 billion Reichsmarks) to $1.18 billion. With other nations retaliating, German exports fell from $3.5 billion to $1.43 billion.[27] John Maynard Keynes, who spoke to the chancellor in Berlin on January 11, 1932, wrote, "Germany today is in the grip of the most terrible deflation that any nation has experienced. We need to have an imaginative apprehension of all this." Few had it. Less than a decade earlier Germany had experienced a comparably terrible hyper-inflation. No fool, Brüning told Keynes he saw no alternative.[28] Keynes could not gainsay him. The Allied nations, who had put Brüning in that position, offered no help.

On June 20, 1931, almost a year earlier, President Herbert Hoover, at last admitting the destructiveness of reparations and war debts, and implicitly conceding the connection between the two, had called for a year's moratorium on both. But after a year, persuaded by intrigues and the dismal economy, President von Hindenburg dismissed his "hunger chancellor" on May 30, 1932. It had taken the leading nations that much time, bitter French resistance to delaying it, until the Lausanne Conference of June-July 1932 recognized the impossibility of reparations (and war debts) and effectively ended them. It was, thus, after Brüning's fall, but the conference decision could not have saved him. The forces of disintegration had been too strong, German politics ratifying American economics and Soviet sabotage. The German Communist Party had suicidally helped Hitler and his Nazis destroy the Brüning regime. After seven months and two ephemeral chancellors, on January 31, 1933, Hitler took power as legal chancellor. Actually set by a dissident Dutch Communist, the fire which gutted the Reichstag building on February 27 gave him an easy excuse to clamp his dictatorship upon the nation and move it toward war. Americans had a heavy responsibility for his rise to office.

The other major powers had played minor roles in the struggle of titans. More subordinate to the United States than they could admit to themselves, the British and French, trying self-defeatingly to extend their old power, failed to fit Germany into a contemporary European structure maintaining peace. The French, furthermore, had lusted for unattainable German treasure and impotence. Mussolini was happy to play a game of aggression and, eventually, to join Germany in conquest. The only way all their efforts could work cooperatively was in the common act of making war.

Neither the United States nor Soviet Russia had been able to do with Germany what it wanted. Operating on the cheap, the United States wanted to integrate a peaceful and profitable Germany in a peaceful European community. The Soviets, led serially by Lenin and Stalin, wanted to enlist it in world revolution, but lacked the national and ideological power. The joint American-Soviet failure helped fashion Hitler's terrific instrument of aggression, a direct threat to the existence of the Soviet Union while making great but enlivening demands on the American political (and military) economy. After the defeat of Germany and the disappearance of Hitler would come the direct confrontation for world mastery, the United States at last recognizing its global power and the Soviet Union pursuing its Marxian objectives.

The United States had been the subtlest Machiavellian of them all, however innocent it was of the thought. It had created a situation encouraging a medium-sized Germany to have another try at world power. This evoked the effort of the more eligible Soviet Russia, a much larger national entity, to seek it. The sum ultimately would give the advantage to the still larger and overwhelmingly efficient American economy in achieving world power, thus the Cold War and its denouement.

Notes

1.   A. J. P. Taylor, *The Struggle for Mastery in Europe*, 568.
2.   Robert K. Murray, *The Harding Era* (Minneapolis: University of Minnesota Press, 1969), 360-67; quotation, 360.
3.   Medlicott, *Contemporary England,* 171-73.
4.   Poincaré quoted, "It would pain me if Germany were to pay....We are driving toward the occupation of the left bank of the Rhine," Max Sering, *Germany under the Dawes Plan* (London: P. S. King, 1919), 44.
5.   Betty Glad, *Charles Evans Hughes and the Illusions of Innocence* (Urbana, IL: University of Illinois Press, 1966), 221; Hughes's actions, 218-31.
6.   Quoted, Robert H. Ferrell, *The Presidency of Calvin Coolidge* (Lawrence: University Press of Kansas, 1998), 148.
7.   The Dawes Plan and reparations, Charles P. Kindleberger, *A Financial History of Western Europe* (London: George Allen & Unwin, 1984), 302-4; Harold G.

Moulton and Leo Pasvolsky, *War Debts and World Prosperity* (Washington: Brookings Institution, 1932), 161-62; Medlicott, *Contemporary England*, 198; Stephen A. Schuker, *The End of French Predominance in Europe: The Financial Crisis of 1924 and the Adoption of the Dawes Plan* (Chapel Hill: University of North Carolina Press, 1976).

8.   Margot Louria, *Triumph and Downfall: America's Pursuit of Peace and Prosperity 1921-1933* (Westport, CT: Greenwood, 2001), 37-63; Selig Adler, *The Uncertain Giant 1921-1941: American Foreign Policy Between the Wars* (New York: Macmillan, 1965), 62-67.

9.   Quoted, Ferrell, *The Presidency of Calvin Coolidge*, 145.

10.   Briand quoted, Ferrell, *Peace in Their Time: The Origins of the Kellogg-Briand Peace Pact* (New Haven: Yale University Press, 1952), 218; see also Adler, *The Uncertain Giant*, 84-89; Louria, *Triumph and Downfall*, 125-38.

11.   Medlicott, *Contemporary England*, 217.

12.   Maddison, *The World Economy: Historical Statistics* (Paris: Organization for Economic Cooperation and *Development*, 2003), hereafter *The World Economy*, tables, 62, 88.

13.   League of Nations, *Memoranda on Public Finance 1921-22* (Geneva: League of Nations, 1923), 45-46.

14.   Albert Sauvy, *Histoire économique de la France entre les deux guerres* (Paris: Fayard, 1965), table, 2: 554.

15.   Mitchell, *European Historical Statistics*, tables, 65, 69.

16.   Keynes article, "The Depression in Trade," Sunday *Times*, *Collected Writings*, vol. 17, 259-65.

17.   Medlicott, *Contemporary England*, 220.

18.   Chandler, *Benjamin Strong*, 316-31.

19.   On the Germany of this period, besides Holborn, *The History of Modern Germany*, see also (the Democrat) Erich Eyck, *A History of the Weimar Republic*, 2 vols. (Cambridge, MA: Harvard University Press, 1962-63); and the socialist-minded Arthur Rosenberg, *A History of the German Republic* (London: Methuen, 1936).

20.   On Rosa Luxembourg and *her* revolution see Peter Nettl, *Rosa Luxembourg: Abridged Edition* (London: Oxford University Press, 1967; 1st ed.: 1966).

21.   Most of the background, Denis Mack Smith, *Modern Italy: A Political History* (Ann Arbor: University of Michigan Press, 1950).

22.   On Hitler, Joachim C. Fest, *Hitler*, Trs., Richard and Clare Winston (New York: Vintage, 1975); Alan Bullock, *A Study in Tyranny* (London: Oldhams, 1952); on the right-wing military units, Robert G. L. Waite, *Vanguard of Nazism: The Free Corps Movement in Postwar Germany 1918-23* (Cambridge, MA: Harvard University Press, 1952).

23.   Herbert Feis, *The Diplomacy of the Dollar* (Baltimore: John Hopkins Press, 1950), 39.

24.   Mitchell, *European Historical Statistics*, tables, 66, 68; U. S. Department of Commerce, *Historical Statistics of the United States: Colonial Times to 1951*, 73.

25.   Brüning's speech, February 11, 1930, Wolfgang J. Helbich, *Die Reparationen in der Ära Brüning* (Berlin: Colloquium, 1962), 30.

26.   Aldcroft, *From Versailles to Wall Street*, table, 264.

27.   Walther G. Hoffmann, *Das Wachstum der Deutschen Wirtschaft seit der Mitte des 19. Jahrhundert* (Berlin: Springer, 1965), table, 520-21.

28.   Keynes, "An End to Reparations?" *New Statesman*, 16 January 1932; Keynes, *Collected Writings*, vol. 18: *Activities 1922-1932: The End of Reparations* (London, 1978), 366-67.

6

New Deal at Home and Abroad

Franklin Delano Roosevelt (January 30, 1882-April 12, 1945) led the United States out of the Great Depression through his New Deal, a political promise became a dynamic policy. If that first characterization of his leadership is true enough, it must be accompanied by a second thought: an internationalist, he led the nation masterfully into World War II, victoriously in that war, and large-heartedly toward the organization of the peace in the form of the United Nations. This could be called a New Deal in foreign affairs, as it brought the United States out of the psychic vestiges of colonial status and isolationism. Roosevelt's second aim was second only chronologically. His policy was integral: he saw himself presiding over a healthy nation in global comity.

Roosevelt arrived in presidential office as Wilsonian and naval interventionist, the latter tending to be forgotten because it was seemingly inconsistent with his character as an outspoken reformer and progressive. Elected a New York State senator in 1910, the young Roosevelt became a leader of a group of reformers opposing Manhattan's Tammany Hall machine. After being reelected in 1912 he had the standing to be appointed assistant navy secretary the next year. His politician chief giving him wide latitude, young Roosevelt became an aggressive and able administrator during his seven years in that office. A skillful negotiator with the Congress, he strove to develop the submarine, expand the Navy, and create the Naval Reserve. He resigned to run vainly as Democratic vice-presidential candidate at the beginning of a decade of Republican ascendancy. Earlier, he told the Democratic National Committee that the party should define itself as unambiguously progressive, clearly opposed to Republicans as conservatives. He came to his high office with acute sense of the nation's defense needs but as an internationalist. He also came as a cripple, having been struck with paralysis from the waist down in August 1921. He fought his way back to politics on heavy metal braces.

In his Inaugural Address President Roosevelt affirmed: "Our international trade relations, though vastly important, are in point of time and necessity secondary to the establishment of a sound national economy." He reiterated: "[T]he emergency at home cannot wait on that accomplishment."[1] He immediately demonstrated his ability to make a ruthless choice between national and international when addressing the appearance of the World Economic Conference in the early days of his administration. The intent of the conference had been entirely reasonable and virtuously international: stabilize the world's currencies, then gyrating wildly under the effects of the depression and Britain's departure from the Gold Standard in September 1931. Roosevelt had dispatched Raymond Moley, his chief policy adviser, to represent him in preliminary discussions. The new president was caught between his desire for international cooperation and his aim to counter the general deflation. Moley tried to compromise with the British by agreeing to an "innocuous" statement about the American intent to reestablish gold in due time. But Roosevelt was pondering the devaluation of the dollar and Moley's report precipitated this message on July 2: it was wrong for the conference "to be diverted by … a purely artificial and temporary experiment affecting the monetary exchange of a few nations only." The idea of stabilization submitted unthinkingly to the "fetishes of so-called international bankers."[2] With that Roosevelt repudiated his representative and, rejecting international cooperation at that moment, effectively annihilated the conference.

Although it upset his own purposes as policymaker and theorist, John Maynard Keynes, who was proposing an international bank and had been conferring cooperatively with Moley, immediately saw the sense of Roosevelt's action. His response was expressed the next day in the headline to an article written for *The Daily Mail*: "PRESIDENT ROOSEVELT IS MAGNIFICENTLY RIGHT." Keynes specified, "It is a long time since a statesman has cut through the cobwebs as boldly as the president of the United States."[3] While Keynes had hoped for Britain's advantage and the discussion of his own international-bank idea, the decisiveness and superior potentials of Roosevelt's stroke captured his enthusiastic assent. In the long run Britain and the world would benefit if the greatest economic power would rebuild its economy behind the defenses erected by the necessary national egoism.

The American experience of the Great Depression confronting Roosevelt precisely illustrated the values and limits of neoclassical, institutional, and Keynesian economic theory—and the values and limits of the economists and political leaders dealing with it. Supply and demand expressing the fundamental economic laws without fail, no one has been able convincingly to argue attaint to the perfection of neoclassical economics. The depression, however, showed what the great founders of neoclassical theory knew but what their followers tended to forget, that noneconomic factors could disrupt the economic verities to terrific effect. Institutional economics claimed to make corrective adjustments to the fairness and efficiency of the economic order by such means as law and administration. The economists of this persuasion, however, could not deny that the economic laws tended to resist such improvement. Thus minimum wage laws, for example, discouraged the employment of marginal workers as too expensive, harming perhaps more than helping labor. In another approach, the economics of John Maynard Keynes, expressing itself in his *General Theory of Employment, Interest and Money* (February 1936), ignored institutional economics and claimed to correct the deficiencies and injustices of neoclassical economics. But *The General Theory* could not free itself from the established theory while claiming to improve on it radically.

A masterful deployer of talent, Roosevelt had to contend, like Hoover, with the problematics of the available economic advice. The most vulnerable point was the sheer helplessness as taught by the then dominant school of neoclassical economics, which accepted the axiom that efforts to improve upon the natural self-corrective powers of the economy would only make matters worse. This kind of thinking, however, was purely abstract and limited to the economic laws. As narrated above, the Great Depression can be explained simply but much less abstractly by the fateful interaction of politics and economics in the given circumstances. Trained not to darken their minds with such distracting counsel, the neoclassical economists could only hope that prices—and wages—would fall far enough to encourage purchases and lead to recovery. The resultant hardship, expressed in the terrific unemployment and business bankruptcies, further reduced demand and so provided a practical rebuttal to such an abstract solution. All this opened the way to the institutional economists, who proposed to organize economic reality, not submit to it, the candidate Roosevelt drawing upon them for advisers. Indeed the situation in the 1930s permitted them to revive their powers, lost a generation earlier in combat with neoclassical wisdom. Roosevelt, a personality demanding to *act*, had sought precisely such a rationale of economic action.

Attempting to solve the greatest economic problem in the nation's history, Roosevelt, artful politician but no pretender to great intellect, had to draw upon what was inevitably an ambiguity of professional advice. He possessed, however, a quality that had placed him in office, a profound, widely attentive and responsive political instinct that comprehended reality; he could *feel* what was right where more intellectual persons were deaf and blind. Unlike Hoover, with his pretentious knowledge of business economics at least, Roosevelt never tripped up himself by thinking competitively with the experts. His style was to support the most plausible experts within the context of the political realities—and drop them when that support could not help them out of obvious failure.

Governor of New York State when the Great Depression struck, Roosevelt had been thinking and moving toward responsible, solid, and comprehensive presidential leadership for many years. He could use his position to experiment with practical policies that would presently be adapted to the federal government. As a realistic politician, he had refused to take clear positions on a number of difficult issues. Indeed, in February 1932 Eleanor Roosevelt was so furious with her husband that she would not talk with him for days. As an old supporter of the League of Nations, he had now opposed America's entry. His reason was simple: he was trying not to offend William Randolph Hearst, the powerful anti-League publisher. He had to get elected to do what had to be done.[4]

One important element of Roosevelt's style, both in campaigning for office and in the exercise of that office, was his use of the Brain Trust. The core of it was three Columbia University professors, the political scientist Raymond Moley, and the institutional economists Rexford G. Tugwell and Adolph A. Berle., Jr. Understandably, given their theoretical block, no neoclassical economists got close to Roosevelt. Neither Tugwell nor Berle were economic theorists; indeed most professional economists would not recognize them as economists. After his New Deal experience Tugwell would function and teach as a political scientist, and Berle was a professor of corporate law. In 1932, with Gardiner C. Means as a research assistant, Berle published that classic of institutional economics, *Modern Corporation and Private Property*. The dominant neoclassicals having failed to do it, allied experts in political science and institutional economics like Berle gave Roosevelt the ideational tools to operate on the economy.

In April 1932, so earning their distinction as Brain Trust, Moley, Tugwell, and Berle assigned themselves the planning and coordination of the economic sectors, thus dominating the vagaries of the failing market economy. This was the genesis of Roosevelt's New Deal, an aptly political name Moley had thought up for the reform and recovery program they were creating.[5] In this way Roosevelt was moving in the direction of correcting the fragmented policies that had too much characterized the American economy.

Roosevelt knew just what he proposed to do as president. Of course that did not include the specifics; in fact, as a great politician, he knew he would have to deal with the unexpected. But he knew where to locate the nodal points of the political economy. The Brain Trust, assisted by other experts, gave him the armament he needed to win the election overwhelmingly and take up his terrific responsibilities. It did not matter that Roosevelt had advocated balancing the budget *and* increased spending to succor the unemployed, among other contradictory policies. The overriding theme of his campaign had been "bold and persistent experimentation."[6] The American people had agreed with him and gave him 23,815,539 votes against Hoover's 15,359,930 votes, while the Democrats won tremendous majorities in the Senate and House: 60 to 35 and 310 to 117. He had a mandate to do whatever he proposed to do.

"New Deal" meant reform, a better social order for the disadvantaged, a sincere objective of Roosevelt and a passionate one of his wife. In the circumstances this required recovery, the reformers seeing the two joined in the sense that reform meant improving the incomes and the lives of those disadvantaged. The sum would provide a greater national income. Conservatives, as they continue to do today, heatedly questioned that logic. They wanted recovery without, as they saw it, an inevitably counter-productive reform program.

Roosevelt's early period in office, known to history as the (rounded off) "Hundred Days," set a record of presidential activism. The biographer Kenneth Davis saw him: "On constant display were his zestfulness, his incredible good-humored patience, his tenacity, his persistence, his driving forcefulness, and throughout and overall, a radiant energy, extravagantly spent from some seemingly inexhaustible resource."[7] First he had to halt the collapse of the nation's banking system. A number of states provided the precedent, having closed their banks already, and he immediately declared a national bank holiday. The banks could reopen on March 13 but not all, by any means, were sound. Out of 24,504 commercial banks with $49 billion in deposits at the end of 1932, 11,878 with deposits of $23 billion were functioning on March 15, 1933.[8] It had been a disaster but he had contained it. In the longer run he would make use of Hoover's Reconstruction Finance Corporation to support the banking system.

Roosevelt launched into a number of actions, some of them contradictory. He stopped gold transactions, preparing for departing from the gold standard on April 19 by way of an embargo on the export of gold. These were all urgent emergency measures, intermixed with others of less positive value. He called a special session of the Congress on March 9 to support his actions and on March 12, Sunday, gave the first of his reassuring "Fireside Chats" over the newly generalized radio. His aristocrat's confidence and commanding charm seduced the public and tamed the Congress. He asked the latter for economy and cut federal employees' pay and veterans' pensions by 15 percent,[9] an action that was psychologically reassuring if economically dampening, indeed negative in economic effect. The New Deal would proceed with similar contradictions. One could not ascribe pondered economic theory to such ad hoc measures, but they fit comfortably into the frame of institutional economics as prefigured in the Brain Trust's conceptualizing and would lead to more explicit implementation of its ideas. Moley soon departed after his repudiated assignment at the World Economic Conference. The two others never held important positions. Rexford Tugwell, the most explicit apostle of planning in the pure spirit of institutional economics, applied his ideas to some modest effect in the Agriculture Department as assistant secretary, later undersecretary, to the secretary, the populist Republican Henry Wallace. Berle was also not easily integrated into the New Deal, later becoming an inconspicuous assistant secretary of state for Latin America from 1938 to 1944. Their lackluster careers reflected the experience of their institutional economics in New Deal practice.

Effectively economic dictator, Roosevelt had extraordinary freedom to act. Due to the frightening nature of the economic situation and the huge majorities he enjoyed in the Congress, he had more power of decision than any president, including himself, before or after the Hundred Days. The American situation was oddly comparable to that of Germany precisely at the moment. On January 30, 1933 Adolf Hitler had become chancellor of the formally democratic government. Establishing himself as unqualified dictator, he set off on his military purposes and so created a foreign affairs problem, which Roosevelt knew he must address. From the beginning both met with little opposition, most of it verbal and chastened.

The early thrust of the New Deal was to establish greater governmental control over the economy in the sense of the Brain Trust technocrats. With its conscious planning this was carried out by the National Recovery Administration, chief among the alphabetically designated agencies, under the National Industrial Recovery Act of June 16. This was the summit of the Hundred Days. Also created by then were the Agricultural Adjustment Act, the Farm Credit Act, and the Civilian Conservation Corps, while $500 million was given to the states for relief, in eloquent contrast to Hoover's refusal to provide them with federal funds. The early New Deal, however, rose and fell with the NRA.

Roosevelt pursued institutional economics further. His new point man was an unlikely retired general, the hard-drinking Hugh S. Johnson, who became administrator of the NRA. Johnson's qualifications were not irrelevant; a West Pointer, trained, however, as a lawyer, he had organized the draft in World War I, when he worked with the financier Bernard Baruch, head of the War Industries Board of that war. Johnson's function, an exercise in institutional economics, was to write and administer the basic codes, eventually numbering 557, setting a floor to prices and limits on production. As the president was devaluing the dollar to 59 percent of its value, this was meant to assist in a counter-deflationary price increase.[10] The supply-and-demand logic of the market frustrated Johnson's purposes.

Another New Deal experiment had failed. Johnson simply could not overrule the economic laws, however much political power supported him. Increased prices discouraged consumption and regulations enraged business. Opposition to his efforts to manage the economy began to embarrass the administration, and Roosevelt gently dismissed him in September 1934. Not much later, on May 27, 1935, the Supreme Court declared the NRA unconstitutional as an improper delegation of legislative power. Most of the Agricultural Adjustment Administration, trying similarly to manage prices and production on the farms, was declared unconstitutional in early 1936. Like Moley and Johnson, Rexford Tugwell presently departed from the government. The New Deal survived in less institutionalist character.

The evaluation of all such experiments is decisively ambivalent. Most economists agree with Peter Temin, an economist of a later generation, who said that the NRA was a failure: "What it gained by improving expectations it took away by raising nominal and real wages."[11] This indicates the problem with the institutionalist theory as earlier expounded by the work of the pioneer Wesley Mitchell, founder of the National Bureau of Economic Research (ch. 2) and, perhaps more pertinently, by Adolf Berle. Like Mitchell, Berle can be accused of "measurement without theory." In a classic of institutional literature, Berle argued that big monopolies determined prices, but his vast compendium of data provided no evidence for it. With the facts going in one direction and the theory nowhere, the book has been widely and respectfully mentioned, but rarely read and never applied.[12]

The results of this cerebration and policymaking were not, however, as sterile as the individual ideas themselves. Stripped down, pragmatic elements continued to function. Planning and coordination remained as rational and necessary. Among the bureaucratic survivals, some programs of the AAA increased farmers' purchasing power somewhat while restricting production. (Of course this meant higher prices for consumers, the poverty-stricken among them; such were the painful contradictions of the economic situation.) The AAA tried to manage seven commodities—wheat, cotton, rice, hogs, corn, tobacco, and dairy products, eight more being added by 1935. This should be set in the context of the century, when American farmers were being reduced from 60 percent to 1.8 percent of the national population. The farmers, operating with characteristic American efficiency, were their own worst enemy and not the banker of populist image. A farm worker in 1990 could produce 15 times as much as his 1910 predecessor and the number of farms had fallen from 6.4 million to 2.1 million, while the size of the farms tripled.[13] The AAA slowed and softened the descent, while many farms were becoming more or less industrialized parts of the economy, thus agribusinesses, which were more and more integrated into the urbanized American society. Both NRA and AAA served usefully by improving morale in a desperate moment. Roosevelt's experimentation, some of it more hard-headed, could then move on to recovery on the basis of better economics, as provided by John Maynard Keynes.

Intensely concerned with the great economic problems and anxious to apply his developing theory to them, Keynes proffered his advice to the president. Felix Frankfurter, then a well-connected Harvard Law professor, plotted the connection by arranging to publish an open letter of Keynes to Roosevelt in the New York *Times* of December 13, 1933. Keynes established: "You have made yourself a trustee for those in every country who seek to amend the evils of our condition by reasoned experiment within the framework of the existing social system." He was firmly affirmative and negative, thus "I put in the forefront…a large volume of loan expenditure," but warned less tactfully that Roosevelt was getting "crack-brained queer advice" from some of his advisers.[14] Clearly Keynes was standing on their heads the New Deal policy emphases. He distrusted the NRA, AAA, and similar manipulative operations of institutional economics, while encouraging the president to accept the deficits the New Deal programs were inevitably accruing. This would be the implicit sense of his *General Theory of Employment, Interest, and Money*, then in process. Roosevelt, who had campaigned on the promise to balance the budget, was embarrassed to see his deficits burgeoning well beyond the point he had condemned in Hoover's record. This was in accord with general opinion, which believed in paying the bills. Only Keynes knew the secret: deficits bringing modest inflation could be therapeutic in a time of intense deflation. In any case, Keynes argued that raising taxes to pay government expenses, including the necessary relief for the unemployed and impoverished, meant taking away with one hand what was being given inadequately with the other. A personal meeting of statesman and theorist in the White House on May 28, 1934 did not help. Keynes found Roosevelt disappointingly like a businessman, and Roosevelt was baffled by Keynes's "whole rigmarole of figures."[15] But, both pragmatists, neither gave up on the other.

Further substantiating Keynes's ideas, although not meant to do so, were Roosevelt's early actions in office. Truly sympathetic himself and further impelled by a social-minded wife, he had early set up the Civil Works Administration as successor to the Federal Emergency Relief Administration to employ as many as 4.3 million persons by early 1934. Appalled, however, at the amount of funds pouring out, the president ended its life. After briefly returning to the first agency, he then created the Works Progress Administration under Harry Hopkins in 1935, and now more resolutely endured the rising costs.[16] However much he resisted, the president had to see the federal deficit rise from $2.6 billion in 1933 to $4.4 billion in 1936; he had been more Keynesian than he realized.[17] The WPA became a great employer of the unemployed, some of them in make-work and others paid to act, play music, or produce regional guides. Conservatives jeered at these "boondoggles," but they nourished the culture, saved lives, and, perhaps, the economy.

The deficit had countered the destructive deflation, which expressed the essence of the Great Depression. This was Keynes's cure along with his advice, which Roosevelt was instinctively following, that the government should control the economic system more purposefully—thus balance off, but not inhibit, the economic freedom that made the American political economy so great in the first place.

Another great New Deal reform was the Social Security Act of August 1935, which Roosevelt had aggressively sponsored from mid-1934. Accurately sensing its importance for the economy and society, he wanted "the greater security of the individual." To the old-age pensions of the original bill he added unemployment insurance as an additional element of security.[18] In this the United States was only following the example of social programs beginning in Germany in the 1880s and England

and France early in the century. It had taken the United States too long to recognize the hard sense—social, political, and economic—of these programs. The original act provided only modest payments financed to a great extent by the beneficiaries themselves in their payroll taxes, which were, furthermore, regressive. The lower-paid paid more proportionately, since everyone began paying up to a certain point, with the better-paid receiving the rest of their incomes (payroll) tax-free. Yet the sum was insurance for the economy as a whole: everyone gained.

The National Labor Relations Act, also in 1935, tried to right the balance, as labor and progressives saw it, between labor and capital. The bill provided for voting procedures protecting labor against intimidation and greatly encouraged labor action, although the workers had not waited for it. In the 1930s union membership rose from less than 3 million to almost 9 million as labor asserted itself. In 1934, before the law was passed, 1.5 million workers went out on 1,800 strikes. On April 9, 1935 the Congress of Industrial Organizations was organized out of unions departing the American Federation of Labor and its principle of organization by crafts. The CIO's great industrial unions, accepting everybody, succeeded grandly in unionizing the United States Steel Corporation (making good the defeat of the steelworkers' craft union by Henry Clay Frick in 1892), and also, as recounted in Chapter 1, the great automobile companies.[19] This righting of the capital-labor social balance made economic sense: the economy functioned better with a more sophisticated workforce that could respect itself.

The New Deal had shifted the economic, social, and political power away from the white Anglo-Saxon Protestant business leadership, incorporated in Henry Ford and Andrew Mellon, toward a more meritocratic coalition of intellectuals, writers, journalists, academics, social workers, union leaders, government administrators, and other representatives of, or sympathizers with, the middling and working classes. "Ordinary" workers and struggling clerks and storekeepers benefited to the extent that they had jobs and little businesses, surely better than unemployment and bankruptcy. More important for the general well-being, power was no longer monopolized by a self-regarding elite, its vision limited by its interests. It went to a range of elites responsive to a greater heterogeneity of interests, needs, or demands. The nation was becoming more democratic mentally, socially, economically, politically, and, as a result, more productive. Racial inequality remained a problem, indeed *the* major injustice, although more blacks were moving into industrial jobs and unions. Farmers benefited chiefly, perhaps, by escaping their farms or, at least, in a spillover from the expanding industrial and service economy, thus enjoying roads, automobiles, and rural electrification.

The sum of the changes was economic coordination that could prevent disasters of the magnitude of the Great Depression. This meant a revolution in administering the economy. The impelling need had been to reduce the old fragmentation of functions and, for the first time in American history, make the president an economic leader. Grover Cleveland, helped by J. P. Morgan, had contended with financial panic, Theodore Roosevelt had manfully faced up to monopoly, and Woodrow Wilson had reduced tariffs and abstractedly accepted the creation of the Federal Reserve System. The fragmentation endured. The Hundred Days, however, saw Roosevelt as more than an economic leader; he was an economic dictator, all major strands of governance in his hands. Never again would tariff policy go off in one direction, and financial and foreign policy in still other directions. Congress, however, presently began to defend its prerogatives of decision; Roosevelt had enough tact to yield to its codeterminations except for a failed effort, in 1937, to make the Supreme Court more tractable. It had been a terrific struggle pitilessly revealing his deviousness: he wanted to add as many as six new justices to overbalance the court's aged and indeed reactionary majority. But it threatened the division of powers inherent in the Constitution.[20] This was a case of a strong leader being misled by his strength, and learning better. The economy, properly, remained established under executive leadership with legislative approval.

All the government's programs to succor the needy and unemployed gave it more power. If the relief agencies vanished with good times, the Social Security operations became more important. The federal government was doing more. One explicit indication was the proportions and magnitudes of federal, state, and local spending. In Coolidge's time, in 1927, the federal government spent 3.7 percent of the GNP against the states at 2.2 percent and local governments at 5.9 percent; in Roosevelt's 1936, federal spending was 11.1 percent against 4.7 percent for the states and 4.5 percent for the localities. Total government spending then was 20.3 percent, of which the federal government accounted for half, a tripling of its 1927 figure. Toward the end of the last century total government spending would continue to increase—to some 40 percent of the GNP, more than three fifths of it federal at 25 percent.[21] The sense of the word "federal" was fading to "national" in the process.

One quiet administrative act of financial coordination had major economic effects, the restructuring of the Federal Reserve System. This completed its establishment as a central bank. No longer would the New York Reserve Bank, as it did under Benjamin Strong, become a functionally irresponsible leader-by-default of the whole system, although it would remain a major force as agent of open market operations. The Banking Acts of 1933 and 1935 gave the FRS chairman and board of governors the power to name the twelve presidents of the Federal Reserve Banks. The acts also gave the Federal Reserve Board sitting in Washington the power to make the buy-and-sell decisions of its Open Market Committee and change the reserve and discount requirements. The 1935 law was largely drafted by Marriner Eccles, a Utah banker who had arrived, independently of Keynes, at the idea of deficit-financing as a counter to deflation. Eccles became a strong chairman, giving the example for decisive leadership of the system. Through the FRS, able better to manage the economy, the government now controlled banking and credit.[22] All the financial sectors were now integrated in the economy under clear and responsible leadership.

By the mid-1930s, as a historian quoted here earlier noted, the American recovery was "very impressive" in terms of gross national product, having improved by a third, but "anemic" by the more human index of unemployment.[23] The GNP rose from its 1933 nadir to $66 billion in 1934, $73.3 billion in 1935, $83.7 billion in 1936, and $91.9 billion in 1937—when it fell to $86.1 billion in 1938 and recovered just barely to $92 billion in 1939.[24] Unemployment, meanwhile, rose from 1.6 million (3.2 percent) in 1929; 4.3 million (8.7 percent), 1930; 8 million (15.9 percent), 1931; 12 million (23.6 percent), 1932; and 12.8 million (24.9 percent), 1933—when it began, agonizingly, to fall. It then eased down to 11.3 million (21.7 percent) in 1934; 10.6 million (20.1 percent), 1935; 9 million (16.9 percent), 1936, and 7.7 million (14.3 percent), 1937. It then shot up to 10.4 million (19 percent) in 1938 before falling off rather weakly to 9.5 million (17.2 percent) in 1939.[25] The New Deal had stumbled.

John Maynard Keynes had a simple explanation: the president had not followed his advice. Instead of manipulating the nation's institutional structures with WPA and other acronymal agencies so much, even granting they provided succor and confidence, the administration should have concentrated on increasing inflation by refusing to cover all expenses and taxes. From 1933 to 1936 that is just what happened when the budget deficit had doubled. But under terrific pressure from the mostly conservative press, disbelieving in Keynes and what appeared to be magic, the president was led to change his policy. Promising fiscal virtue, he increased taxes in 1937. Doubling that effect, fearful of inflation, the Federal Reserve System misused its new powers to increase the reserve and margin requirements of its banks in three moves between August 1936 and May 1937.[26] Among the reasons were the conservative advice of Treasury Secretary Henry J. Morgenthau, supported by such bankers as George L. Harrison of the Federal Reserve Bank of New York (Benjamin Strong's old bank), and informed financial opinion generally.[27] A wise administrative measure, coordination of the monetary sector of the economy, took perverse effect because of the bad economic thinking directing it. The Recession of 1937-38 promptly followed.

By the spring of 1938 the administration recognized Keynes's wisdom. Accepting his instruction and the sense of the Recession, other presidential advisers, Harry Hopkins and the economist Leon Henderson among them, persuaded Roosevelt to reverse direction. On April 14, 1938, he demanded from the Congress $3 billion for relief, public works, housing, and aid to state and local governments: "For the first time the administration committed itself to a calculated strategy of fiscal stimulation," explicit deficit-financing.[28] Neoclassical economics had shown itself helpless before noneconomic factors causing the Great Depression; institutional economics, lacking any coherent theory, had failed. Keynesian theory, patching up the first, replaced it and shouldered aside the second.

This initiated the Keynesian conquest of American economic policy, much of the world following, and led to the United States Employment Act of 1946. The act committed the American government "to promote maximum employment, production, and purchasing power," creating the Council of Economic Advisers to advise the president to that end.[29] It was a promise, at least, of more economic coordination. (Keynes had anticipated this measure in a memorandum fired at Prime Minister J. Ramsay MacDonald in the December 1929 calling for a kind of economic general staff to guide the government guiding the economy. This led to the Economic Section of the Cabinet Office institutionalizing the British government's economic advice.) And so, pursuing Keynes's ideas and its own slower inclinations, the United States achieved a broad integration of the economy under democratic management and with expert advice.

The Keynesian victory occurred despite (and to an extent also *because*) of the fact that few persons, indeed few economists, have ever read the painfully difficult *General Theory*. The *policy* of deficit-financing was the *conclusion* of the hermetic theory. Keynes had *theorized* that modern economy, while generating more wealth, perversely tended toward stagnation: "Moreover the richer the community, the wider will be the gap between its actual and its potential production; and therefore the more obvious and outrageous the defects of economic system."[30] With its egalitarian and populist suggestions, this seemed brilliantly to describe the Great Depression, particularly as experienced in the huge unemployment in the United States (and Germany and The Netherlands). But Keynes was describing the effects of the exceptional situation of the Great Depression, an explanation failing to accord with earlier and later economic history. His theory cannot account for the great economic expansion up to 1929, which resumed all the more forcefully in the latter half of the twentieth century. This discussion has shown the destabilizing results of World War I, American tariffs and war debt (and reparations) policy, the perverse interaction between the American and the other major economies, the decline of American agriculture, and the deflationary bias of most, and the most important, governments. The narrative, thus, does not require any conceptualizing beyond the neoclassical theory.[31] Yet pragmatically Keynes had been right and neoclassical economists wrong. He had blindfolded and confused his readers (himself also perhaps) to arrive at his contention, a variant of one broadcast by monetary cranks for years. Eager to persuade, Keynes the theorist and policymaker, had produced a paralogical construction that would, he correctly saw, rationalize sensible policy. This was, I argue, the essence of his genius. He had concocted a mad theory that would have positive results, a merely correct theory would fail to achieve by alienating with its austerity.[32] The subsequent career of Keynesianism, operating in the inflationary 1960s and 1970s, will suggest additional glosses.

Assisted by deficit financing, United States emerged from its recession in 1939 to find its economy carried upward on the inevitable inflation of wartime. War is a great depression therapy: the Great Depression dis- solved. While the nation did not enter the war until the end of 1941, it was producing more and more to meet Allied, and after the fall of France, British needs. In current dollars the GNP rose from $92 billion in 1939, $101.3 billion, 1940; $126.7 billion, 1941; $161.8 billion, 1942; $198.4 billion, 1943; $219.2 billion, 1944; and $223 billion, 1945.[33] Wartime inflation exaggerated these proportions by 20 percent. In 1939 9.5 million were unemployed, 17.2 percent of the labor force, which provided a valuable reserve army for the expansion of industry, a great positive factor when the nation entered the war. In 1940 unemployment fell somewhat--to 8.2 million, 14.6% of the labor force, but then it dropped to 5.6 million in 1941 (9.9 percent), 1 million (1.9 percent) in 1943, 670,000 in 1944 (1.2 percent) and, with the war ending in the West in May and in the East in September, slightly more than 1 million (1.9 percent) in 1945.[34]

This intensive engagement with the domestic problems of the nation during the Great Depression did not abate Roosevelt's concerns about its international position. Even as he was expanding his administrative powers over the American political economy, he was feeling his way to a wider leadership early and late. With a natural leader's instinct for power, spilling over, as we have seen, into the excess of his designs on the Supreme Court, he was thrusting toward more influence globally. Behind the "façade of indifference [he] remained vitally concerned with international affairs," a close student of his foreign policy cited here put it.[35] This was all conditioned, however, by the dead weight of isolationism, which had rejected the Wilsonian prescriptions and now, contemplating the aggressions of Hitler and Mussolini, clung to old fears and limits. Determinedly, Roosevelt worked around this central impediment as he had labored with the paralysis that struck him back in 1921.

Roosevelt began modestly in Latin America, a foreign-policy area that threatened little resistance. Yet he made it meaningful. He proposed the Good Neighbor policy, an innocuous undertaking that nevertheless suggested wider concerns and expressed a new style. With it he repudiated the unilateral use of the nation's massive power in the hemisphere. America's military units were withdrawn from Haiti, and new treaties with Cuba and Panama formally, if not quite actually, ended their status as United States protectorates. In December 1932 he signed the Montevideo Convention on the Rights and Duties of States, renouncing unilateral intervention in Latin American countries.

In this spirit and quietly contradicting his nationalistic annihilation of the World Economic Conference, Roosevelt had installed the Tennessee senator Cordell Hull, an enemy of tariffs, as a long-enduring (eleven years) secretary of state. With Roosevelt's support in principle, despite presidential tergiversations on occasion, Hull reversed the old tariff momentum and got the Reciprocal Trade Agreements Act through Congress on March 2, 1934. This permitted the president to lower rates as much as 50 percent, actually producing modest improvements in the early years but leading to the broad free (or freer) trade policy of the post-World War II era, thus the eventual development of the General Agreement on Tariffs and Trade of 1947, becoming the World Trade Organization in 1995. And so, in Roosevelt's long-term sense, the United States turned away from one of its most destructive economic policies and initiated the world's vast trade expansion of the later twentieth century.[36]

From 1935, as more and more aggressions occurred, Roosevelt directed his attention to Europe in an exercise of a new and revised Wilsonianism. With Mussolini threatening to invade Ethiopia, which he did on October 30, and with the appearance of a hitherto forbidden German air force, the president commented feelingly and historiographically to his ambassador in Rome: "These are without doubt the most hair-trigger times the world has gone through in your lifetime or mine. I do not even exclude June and July 1914." He had to employ his subtlest gifts to defeat the stolid negatives of isolationism. If not his greatest, it was his finest battle. In 1933 he had challenged the naysayers successfully by establishing diplomatic relations with Soviet Russia in the person of its able Foreign Commissar Maxim Litvinov. This was grand Realpolitik but it had to be slowly applied or it would be crushed.

Roosevelt began in 1935 by losing a last Wilsonian skirmish. In a perhaps stale spirit, internationalizing Americans proposed that the United States enter the World Court, the ineffective judicial body of the League of Nations. On June 29, 1935, with opposition by William Randolph Hearst and the influential and demagogic radio priest, Father Charles Coughlin, the Senate failed to provide the necessary two-third majority approval. The issue was trivially symbolic, one more redundant denial of America's international character. Early that year, sensitive to the increasing dangers, Roosevelt nevertheless successfully requested more than a billion dollars for the defense budget. This, however, provoked a wide range of resistance including the reactions of a minority of fascist-Nazi well-wishers like Charles Lindbergh, who admired Nazi efficiency. On another flank Oswald Garrison Villard, the respectable editor of the mildly left-wing *Nation*, was appalled at the thought of a "Christian nation ... planning to spend $1.125 billion [upon the] military ... when more than 20 million Americans are in the breadline."[37] In greater bulk, on April 6, 1935, 50,000 veterans paraded for peace in Washington and 175,000 college students carried out a one-hour strike for it. If the resistance was confused, it was substantial. Such sentiments produced the Neutrality Law of August 31, 1935 forbidding trade indiscriminatingly with combatant nations. The law, as well as another, in 1937, frustrated Roosevelt's desire, at least, to be able to define aggressors as unsuitable recipients. More, such obstacles were an agony for a leader demanding to lead and seeing disaster in a paralysis of policy. Drawing upon his rich political experience Roosevelt's temperament roused his virtuosity to overleap the resistance.

Helplessly at first but accurately, Roosevelt was reacting to a series of aggressions beginning with the destruction of the Versailles system: German withdrawal from the League of Nations, March 1933; Mussolini's invasion of Ethiopia, October 1935; German militarization of the Rhineland in defiance of the Versailles Treaty, March 1936; the Spanish Civil War and the destruction of the Spanish Republic, July 1936-March 1939; the *Anschluss*: the German seizure of Austria, March 1938; the Munich humiliation of British Prime Minister Neville Chamberlain and French Premier Édouard Daladier, who agreed to the award of the Sudeten area of Czechoslovakia to Germany, September 29-30, 1938; German occupation of the rest of Czechoslovakia, March 15, 1939; Nazi-Soviet Pact, August 23, 1939; German invasion of Poland, and British and French war declarations against Germany, September 1 and 3, 1939; German invasion of Denmark, Norway, the Netherlands, Belgium, and France, April to June 1940, a defeated France signing an armistice on June 22; the hard-fought air "Battle of Britain," late summer, 1940; German invasion of Soviet Russia, June 22, 1941.

With his consummate political tact Roosevelt was always a few steps ahead of his nation, careful not to go too far or fast. He responded only with a Fireside Chat when World War II broke out: "[T]his nation will remain a neutral nation." He added: "I cannot ask that every American remain neutral in thought." At that time public opinion surveys reported that more help to the allies would "produce an outpouring of opposition." He was nonetheless building the foundations of substantive action. With the fall of France in June 1940 Roosevelt could act to the extent of securing the passage of a selective service act in September. He also named the internationalist Republican Henry Stimson, who had been secretary of war under Taft and Hoover's secretary of state, as war secretary again; and Frank Knox, another Republican, as navy secretary. The naming of Republicans was a call for national unity as well. Stimson expeditiously began the drafting and training of 14 million men and women. Before the end of 1940, in September, the president began to send aid to Britain in the form of fifty overage destroyers in return for the use of British bases in the Western Hemisphere, another way of aiding the embattled country. On March 11, 1941 he also achieved the passage of the Lend-Lease Act to help the British, later others, eventually with $50 billion of military supplies through leasing or lending, repayment not required (unlike the situation in World War I). Isolationists correctly and vainly protested the aid as a warlike intervention and the violation of the neutrality laws. Lend-Lease, certainly in his style, may have been Roosevelt's idea. On Friday, June 5, 1941, more overtly, he ordered the Marines to occupy Iceland. On August 9-11, 1941, just after the German invasion of Soviet Russia, he met Prime Minister Winston Churchill in the Atlantic to sign the Atlantic Charter agreeing to virtuous international arrangements and implying a moral alliance with a combatant nation. Churchill thought: "There seems little question that Roosevelt now wished to take the United States into the war."[38] His actions were clear enough. In 1936 he had famously announced: "I hate war!" He put it pathetically: "I have seen blood running from the wounded.... I have seen the dead in the mud."[39] But he was accepting war for the peace he could see beyond.

Japanese overt aggression interlocked with Roosevelt's passive aggression. He was provided with a great threat and an opportunity. Moving their forces from China, from December 1940 to May 1941, the Japanese swept through Southeast Asia—Indonesia, Thailand, Burma, and Indonesia—to the Indian border. Refusing to fuel this aggression, Roosevelt cut off 95 percent of Japan's oil supply. Requiring retreat if enforced, this was a direct challenge to Japanese ambitions. Of course Roosevelt knew what he was doing. At a "war council" meeting on November 25 Navy Secretary Stimson's diary noted the chance of a surprise attack in two days and "the question was what we should do." The conferees considered "how we should maneuver them into a position of firing the first shot without allowing too much danger to ourselves."[40] Even if the decision was not so clear, Roosevelt and the American leadership saw no chance to avoid war except by self-betrayal or dishonor. Unfortunately the Army and Navy commanders in Hawaii did not react appropriately to a Washington warning. On December 7 surprise air attacks on Pearl Harbor struck in two waves from 7:55 AM, Hawaii time, killed 2,403 persons, and destroyed or put out of commission the bulk of the fleet, including seven battleships and most of the aircraft. On December 11 Hitler, joining the Japanese, declared war on the United States, preventing a split in American war operations. Roosevelt and now his people were facing up to the responsibility of war. Later, at a press conference in December 1943, Roosevelt told a reporter that "Dr. New Deal" had now called in "Dr. Win-the-War" to complete the assignment.[41] This was part of a New Deal for the United States and the world that would extend his vision beyond the war. Whatever mistakes the United States had made or would make, it was entering into its global responsibilities. Roosevelt's leadership projected itself powerfully beyond his lifetime.

If the American economy had shown its worst side in generating the Great Depression, it showed much of its best in World War II: its tremendously efficient industrial plant, flexibility, administrative imagination, sheer inventiveness, management of personnel, financial deftness, and democratic responsiveness to need. "The Great Depression was ...

the most important event of the 20th century," one economic historian put it. "The mobilization of the American economy in World War II is close second."[42] Once again the United States validated Adam Smith's appreciation of the American economy's potentials. The nation now exerted the qualities that had made it a world leader before 1900 and an efficient ally in World War I. Labor and capital cooperated fluently in the transition to war and its prosecution. The War Production Board (on the model of the War Industries Board of World War I) oversaw the manufacture of 300,000 aircraft, 5,425 merchant ships, 72,000 naval vessels, 87,000 tanks, and 2.5 million trucks. Women's employment increased from 14 to 19 million. Discrimination against blacks by employers and, especially unions, was reduced by executive order, although race riots in northern cities in 1943 suggested the order's limits.[43] The American military fought as efficient a war. Supported by devastating air power, it landed a tremendous force on the European continent in the face of experienced German resistance and presently moved on into the German heartland. It had meanwhile taken limited island bases against the Japanese in an equally successful land, air, and sea offensive that was remarkably economical of American lives.

The American economic performance during the war confirmed the great accomplishment of Roosevelt and his New Deal. Theodore Roosevelt had wrestled athletically with the great railroads and other industrial concerns. Similarly, the younger Roosevelt lustily attacked the "economic royalists," but never seriously threatened their functional leadership. Neither Roosevelt questioned the verities of Adam Smith's invisible hand of self-interest and the enlivening value of competition. Franklin Roosevelt's heritage was a nation so well-ordered that it was capable of winning the peace as triumphantly as the war.

During the war federal spending rose to nearly half of the GNP; in 1939 and 1940 it was at an annual rate of 2 percent; in 1941 it reached 11.2 percent; in 1942, 31.6 percent; in 1943, 43.1 percent; 1944, 45 percent, in 1945 dropping to 39 percent. The deficit increased from $6.2 billion in 1941 to level off at about $57 billion in 1943. Much of the costs were paid by tax increases, the federal income tax rising from $2.2 billion in 1939 to $35.1 billion in 1945.[44] War bonds, efficiently marketed, helped substantially and also reduced the inflationary pressures while rationing controlled prices effectively although inconveniently. If shortages inevitably occurred, the nation, emerging from the Great Depression, nevertheless lived much better than before, the great GNP increases more than adequately providing for both military necessity and civilian comfort. Except for the victims and their families (322,000 Americans killed,[45] little more than half of the fatalities in the Civil War), it was a "good" war for America.

Approaching the end of the war, economists, the unrepentant neoclassicals and other theorists joining the Keynesians, worried gratuitously about the expected consumption collapse and depression. It was one more example of their failure to pay sufficient attention to history and interactions beyond economy. Keynesians (Keynes himself would die on Easter Sunday 1946) believed in the economy's endemically weak consumption and excessive interest rates, and both Keynesians and neoclassicals neglected the great differences between the old and the new postwar periods. If new problems doubtless threatened, many of the old ones had vanished. The United States, instructed by history, would not demand huge payments from those it had helped, while it was energetically driving toward radically reduced tariffs and much freer trade. Economists had simply assumed the replica of the previous reduced spending and consumption collapse. Nothing of the sort happened. One new factor was the coming of the Cold War, with its promotion of new military expenses. Another major one, for which Keynes and his followers deserve the credit, was the implementation of his policies, thus the American Employment Act of 1946 and earlier, in 1944, the adoption of a similar employment policy, along with a vast expansion of social welfare, in Britain. Other nations, except the Soviet Union and its bloc, followed.

The vast wealth United States had poured into its prosecution of the war was easily converted into serving the civilian economy. Young adults found that unlike their parents, they could quickly own their own homes with the assistance of federal loans, another novelty. Automobiles, radios, and, very soon, television sets poured off the assembly lines. *We remind ourselves that real American per-capita income was multiplying by seven in the century.* A greater proportion of Americans were enjoying good living. The problem of depression was solved for the century. Of course the political economy contained other difficulties, the natural products of the new American wealth in a relatively poor world. The country was accepting the burden of much greater international responsibility and expense, compounded with proliferating risks. The U.S.S.R. posed a great practical and theoretical threat. World War II had flowed into the Cold War, John Maynard Keynes and Karl Marx dividing most of the world between them.

Notes

1. Quoted, Robert Dallek, Franklin D. Roosevelt, *American Foreign Policy, 1932-1945* (New York: Oxford University Press, 1995;1st ed.: 1979), 23.
2. Quoted, Kenneth S. Davis, *FDR: The New Deal Years 1933-1937: A History* (New York: Random House, 1986; 1st ed.: 1979), 192-93.
3. Keynes, *Collected Writings*, vol. 21: 273.
4 Kenneth S. Davis, *FDR: The New York Years 1928-1933* (New York: Random House, 1985; 1st ed.: 1979), 242, 259-60.
5. See "The Genesis of the 'New Deal,'" *ibid.*, 291-337.
6. Roosevelt quoted, William J. Barber, *Designs within Disorder: Franklin D. Roosevelt, the Economists, and the Shaping of American Economic Policy, 1933-1945* (Cambridge: Cambridge University Press, 1996), 19.
7. Davis, *The New Deal Years*, 523.
8. Eugene N. White, "Banking and Finance in the 20th Century," in Stanley L. Engerman and Robert E. Gallman, eds., *The Cambridge Economic History of the United States* (hereafter *CEHUS*), 3; *The Twentieth Century* (Cambridge: Cambridge University Press, 2000), 761.
9. Barber, *Designs within Disorder*, 26; William E. Leuchtenburg, *Franklin D. Roosevelt and the New Deal 1933-1940* (New York: Harper & Row, 1963), 37-61.
10. Barber, *Designs within Disorder*, 40; Leuchtenburg, *Franklin D. Roosevelt and the New Deal, 53-79.*
11. Peter Temin, "The Great Depression," in *CEHUS*, 323.
12. Adolf A. Berle and Gardiner C. Means, *The Modern Corporation and Private Property* (New York: Harcourt Brace & World, 1932; revised ed., 1967).
13. Alan L. Olmstead and Paul W. Rhode, "The Transformation of Northern Agriculture," in *CEHUS*, 729-35, 693, 697.
14. Keynes, *Collected Writings*, vol. 21: *Activities 1931-1939: World Crises and Politics in Britain and America* (London: Macmillan, 1982), 289, 296, 290.
15. Account of meeting, Frances Perkins, *The Roosevelt I Knew* (New York: Viking, 1946), 225. Labor Secretary Perkins had arranged the meeting with Felix Frankfurter.
16. Leuchtenburg, *Franklin D. Roosevelt and the New Deal 1932*-1940, 120-39.
17. W. Elliot Brownlee, "The Public Sector," *CEHUS*, 1039-40.
18. Barber, *Designs within Disorder*, 95-98.
19. Robert H. Zieger, *American Workers, American Unions* (Baltimore: Johns Hopkins University Press, 1994; 1st ed.: 1986), 26-61.
20. The "court-packing" issue, Davis, *FDR: Into the Storm 1937-1940: A History* (New York: Random House, 1993), 47-68.
21. Table, Brownlee, "The Public Sector," *CEHUS*, 1,014.
22. White, "Banking and Finance," in *ibid.*, 764-73; Barber, *Designs within Disorder*, 86-94; Leuchtenburg, *Franklin D. Roosevelt and the New Deal*, 158; Davis, *FDR: The New Deal Years*, 537-41.
23. Temin, "The Great Depression,"*CEHUS*, 325.
24. Commerce, U. S. Department of: Bureau of Economic Analysis, GDP, bea, *doc. gov.* Recent records report GDP instead of GNP, but the two are close enough for our purposes.
25. Labor, U. S. Department of: Bureau of Labor Statistics:, Composition of the Civilian Labor Force . . . 1929-2001, *bls.gov.*
26. White, "Banking and Finance," *CEHUS*, 770.
27. Elliott A. Rosen, *Roosevelt, the Great Depression, and the Economics of Recovery* (Charlottesville: University of Virginia Press, 2005), 179-91.

28.   Barber, *Designs within Disorder*, 114.

29.   Employment Act quoted, Robert Lekachman, *The Age of Keynes* (New York: Random House, 1966), 171.

30.   John Maynard Keynes, T*he General Theory of Employment, Interest, and Money* (London: Macmillan, 1936), 31. *The General Theory* is vol. 7 of *The Collected Writings of John Maynard Keynes*, 30 vols. (London: Macmillan, 1971-89).

31.   Besides those already mentioned here, studies of the Great Depression consulted include: John A. Garraty, *The Great Depression* (New York: Harcourt Brace Jovanovich, 1986); Lionel Robbins, *The Great Depression* (London: Macmillan, 1934); Peter Temin, *Lessons from the Great Depression* (Cambridge: MIT Press, 1989); Mark Wheeler, ed., *The Economics of the Great Depression* (Kalamazoo, MI: Upjohn Institute, 1998); Thomas E. Hall and J. David Ferguson, *The Great Depression: An International Disaster of Perverse Economic Policies* (Ann Arbor: University of Michigan Press, 1998); H. Clark Johnson, *Gold, France, and the Great Depression* (New Haven: Yale University Press, 1997); John Kenneth Galbraith, *The Great Crash, 1929* (Boston: Houghton-Mifflin, 1955); Ben S. Bernanke, ed., *Essays on the Great Depression* (Princeton: Princeton University Press, 2000); Patricia Clavin, ed, *The Great Depression in Europe, 1929-1939* (New York: St. Martin's Press, 2000); Charles P. Kindleberger, *The World in Depression 1929-1939* (Berkeley: University of California Press, 1973); Derek H. Aldcroft, *From Versailles to Wall Street 1919-1929* (Berkeley: University California Press, 1981); and Milton Friedman and Anna Schwartz, *A Monetary History of the United States, 1867-1960* (Princeton: Princeton University Press, 1963).

     No writer directly and completely addressed the interaction element, thus interaction between the American and other economies, and between economics and politics. Economic theorists dealt with economics as an unbounded abstraction or concentrated on the economy of the given nation without sufficient regard to international effects. Centering on theory, the economists paid scant attention to the historical context.

32.   This is based on my critique of the General Theory, developed in my *Biography of an Idea: John Maynard Keynes and The General Theory* (New Brunswick: Transaction Publishers, 1995) and summarized in the chapter, "A Life in Theory," 225-55, in *Keynes: A Critical Life* (Westport, CT: Greenwood Press, 1999). I argue that Keynes based the General Theory on two subtheories, that the provider of the funds to the market alone determined the cost price—interest rate for short—and the producer-borrower had to accept that price; and that consumption failed to absorb all the produced values. The first contention is simply incredible. About the second, Keynes granted that he had no evidence to prove it and it denies the evidence of economic sociology and economics that demand is, in general, insatiable.

33.   GNP (or GDP, i.e. "domestic" as opposed to "national"), U. S. Department of Commerce: Bureau of Economic Analysis, bea, *doc.gov*.

34.   U. S. Department of Labor: Bureau of Labor Statistics, Compensation of the Civilian Labor Force, 1929-2001, *bls.gov*.

35.   Robert Dallek, *Franklin D .Roosevelt and American Foreign Policy*, 20.

36.   See Peter H. Lindert, "U.S. Foreign Trade and Tariff Policy," *CEHUS*, 454-58.

37.   Both quoted, Dallek, *Franklin D. Roosevelt and American Foreign Policy*, 101, 111.

38.   Quoted, ibid., 197, 201, 285.

39.   Quoted, Davis, FDR: *The New Deal Years,* 640.

40.   Quoted, Basil Rauch, *Roosevelt from Munich to Pearl Harbor: A Study in the Creation of a Foreign Policy* (New York: Barnes and Noble, 1967; 1st ed.: 1950), 472.

41. Quoted, Dallek, *Franklin D. Roosevelt and American Foreign Policy*, 443.
42. Hugh Rockoff, "The United States: From Ploughshares to Swords," in Mark Harrison, ed., *The Economics of World War II: Six Great Powers in International Comparison* (Cambridge: Cambridge University Press, 1998), 81.
43. Reeves, *Twentieth Century America*, 127-28.
44. Mark Harrison, "The Economics of World War II: An Overview," in Harrison, ed., *The Economics of World War II*, table, 83; Brownlee, "The Public Sector," CEIIUS, 1, 446-49.
45. Reeves, *Twentieth Century America*, 137.

7

USSR: Another Political Economy

In 1835 Alexis de Tocqueville saw America and Russia "marked out by the will of Heaven to sway the destinies of half the globe."[1] Each would also sway the other. If the Soviet Russian influence on the United States would be ideologically louder, the American effect on the land of Lenin, Stalin, and successors would be quietly and powerfully important to its development as well as its fate.

Earlier influences on Russia, after the Byzantine imprint and the Russian Orthodox Church, had been German culture and French Enlightenment, the Enlightenment exploding into the French Revolution. Russia was self-admittedly "backward" and its peasants, comprising 90 percent of the population, had been long mired in serfdom. It had experienced nearly three centuries of national submission to the Tartars followed by the modernizing savagery of Ivan the Terrible (1533-82) and Peter the Great (1682-1725). Russia's victory over Napoleonic France and the resultant contact with Western Europe had sensitized its officers and educated persons to the greater freedom and dignity of these other peoples.

One effect of it all was the rising on December 26, 1825 by 3,000 officers of the elite guards demanding the throne for the liberal older brother of the designated czar and liberal guarantees, thus "Constantine and Constitution!" The leading conspirator, however, had planned to execute the imperial family and create a Robespierran dictatorship while freeing the serfs, hardly a completely liberal objective. A stab of Russian violence, too characteristic of the past, accompanied the demonstration, one enthusiast assassinating the governor-general who was trying to damp it down. Assuring his reign, Czar Nicholas brought up a cannon and cleared the square with volleys of grape shot. Among the guards, of the 189 defendants known to history as Decembrists, five, including their leader, were hanged, thirty-one imprisoned, and the rest exiled to Siberia, these latter providing living martyrs with their long punishment.[2]

Inspired by the action and its evocation of a free society, the demand for reform continued to seethe during the rest of the regime of Nicholas (1825-55). If the new movement was mostly talk, the proximity to action was close. Reform faced with reaction, in effect, meant revolution. From the time of Nicholas revolutionaries fought a shooting and bombing war against the government and social order.

An intellectual form of resistance to the regime, calling itself vaguely Populism, was articulated by Alexander Herzen (1812-70). A superb writer, wealthy scion of a great lord, Herzen was able to publish his ideas in a newspaper safely situated in the West and smuggled into Russia.[3] The young people he inspired presently were mocking him as timorous and backward. Admiring them and deploring their manners, he did not repudiate them. We can best appreciate the Populists[4] through Fyodor Dostoevsky, who joined the reform-minded Petrashevsky group in St. Petersburg in the late 1840s. With a few others he found himself accused of revolutionary plotting in 1849. Whether or not they were consciously guilty, they meant revolution. After a mock execution, one of the accused going mad, he spent four years in prison labor and six years as a private soldier. Using his experience to write *Devils* (1871-72), one of his five great novels, Dostoevsky is our guide. In some translations the title has been transposed to *The Possessed*, which is more meaningful in English. Addicted to roulette as well as fanaticism, the redundantly possessed novelist belongs in the novel as much as his characters. Refusing to remain a vaguely social-minded Populist, he later developed into a reactionary chauvinist with particular disregard for Poles and Jews while, however, retaining his sympathy for the peasants.[5] He used *Devils* to inform on himself and his erstwhile comrades. In 1873 he sent a copy to the future Czar Alexander III, writing: "It's almost an historical study, in which I've sought to account for the possibility of such monstrous phenomena.... It's this kinship of ideas ... that I've tried to show in my work."[6] Thus Dostoevsky—supremely great novelist, revolutionary, and betrayer of the revolution.

Dostoevsky's novel will bring us to Lenin, Stalin, Gorbachev, and Putin. It was crystallized in his mind by the story of Sergei Nechaev, who collaborated with the great, mad Mikhail Bakunin on his *Catechism of a Revolutionary* (1866), which preached murder for the cause. Nechaev then returned to Russia, where, in 1869, he persuaded a revolutionary group to kill a member who was questioning his leadership. Nechaev could escape to Switzerland, while sixty-seven less agile group members were arrested and tried. Extradited back to Russia, Nechaev was convicted and, and after charming his visitors, died in the Peter-Paul Fortress in St. Petersburg in 1882. Czar Alexander II was assassinated the next year.

Dostoevsky doubled his Nechaev into two protagonists, the intriguer Peter Verkhovensky and the straight-arrow officer Nicolai Stavrogin. Verkhovensky organizes a conspiracy among reform-minded friends of his liberal father and inspires the murder of a group member in the Nechaev manner. Other small-town events include a charity festival during which the unruly guests ignore the liberal speaker, a workers' strike, suicides, a series of fires, a childbirth, and several gratuitous murders. Verkhovensky announces his purpose: "We'll stir up such trouble that everything will be shaken loose from its foundations." The murder conspiracy is discovered and police arrest the other plotters, but Peter Verkhovensky himself, it is suggested, slips away to continue pursuing his revolutionary aims.[7]

If Mark Twain's Huckleberry Finn lit out for ultimate freedom in the Territory, another member of the group, the comrade "with long ears" explained his system: "Beginning with the idea of unlimited freedom I end with unlimited despotism."[8] This was not quite a prediction by Dostoevsky, although it suggested the ambiguity of idealism.

The new generation combined idealist action with rebellion. The "Go to the People" movement of 1873-74, when young people invaded the countryside to enlighten the peasants, was also meant to radicalize the exploited. It radicalized the idealists more than the peasants, who often denounced their saviors to the authorities. But the movement was a rich matrix for revolutionary action.

Populists were presently assassinating hated officials and stirring up peasant revolts. On March 13, 1881, mounting an operation in military style, a group of thoroughly professional revolutionaries closed in on the emancipator Czar Alexander II and assassinated him. The authorities annihilated their group; others more and more ideologically sophisticated followed. On May 20, 1887 Alexander Ilyich Ulyanov, a university biology student, was executed for participating in a failed Populist plot to assassinate Alexander III. The young man was the older brother of the seventeen-year-old Vladimir Ilyich Ulyanov, who would call himself Lenin. Two years later Vladimir Ilyich discovered Marx's *Capital*; reading it was a revelation, a fine proof of Marx's revolutionary genius. Lenin would always retain a core of Populism, with its tendency toward terror, the Marxist ideals providing a sophisticated rationale for it. Nor would Marx object. Indeed, the old revolutionary had celebrated the assassination of Alexander II in a long letter of family gossip to his daughter

Jenny. The Russians were "brave people with no melodramatic poses, straightforward, realistic, and heroic." The deed was "historically unanswerable…there is as little point in moralizing argument for or against as there is in the case of the earthquake at Chios."[9] For the first time in his life Marx, who had looked on imperial Russia as a bastion of reaction, had responded to something Russian with unqualified approval.

Lenin found like-minded persons and entered the life of a labor activist and revolutionary while functioning formally as a lawyer. In December 1895, arrested with fifty-six others, he was in prison as a revolutionary agitator and after fifteen months was sent to Siberian exile for three years. He thereupon exiled himself to freedom in the West to make his revolution. From his early twenties his life had become a concentrate of revolutionary-socialist action and thought, in that order.

Lenin became a member of the All-Russian Social Democratic Workers' Party, founded in 1898, and in 1903, at its second congress, established himself as a dominating, but not dominant, leader in it. At the congress, meeting in Brussels and continuing in London, he split the party to gain his ends, hence the Bolsheviks (members of the majority) and Mensheviks (members of the minority). The names themselves were a valuable public relations victory for Lenin; they were nicknames for the winners and losers in one crucial vote at the congress although the Mensheviks were far more numerous as a faction or party. His flourishing of a name implying majority suggests Lenin's skill in making the verbal best of recalcitrant reality.

We are tracking Lenin in detail because he was so paradigmatic as Marxian revolutionary, because, thus, he uncannily fixed the pattern for the creation and shaping of Soviet Russia—and its threat of world revolution. Perhaps only Alexander the Great placed so personal a stamp on history and geography.

In March 1902, Lenin had published the pamphlet *What Is to Be Done?* expounding the principle of revolutionary action leading to the Bolshevik-Menshevik split. He wanted a party dictatorship barely disguised under the oxymoron "democratic centralism." The party was fighting a revolutionary war and, as he put it at the triumphant eighth party congress in 1919, "Outright military discipline is indispensable."[10] Lenin made it clear: a party of professional revolutionaries and not the workers would lead the revolution. This was in the sense of Marx, who in the *Communist Manifesto* had given his Communist League "the advantage … over the great mass of the proletariat of clearly understanding the line of march."[11] Of course Lenin would command the party as the party commanded the proletariat. Such presumption was justified only if the thirty-three-year-old Lenin was one of the greatest leaders of world history, and indeed he was.

While this is an intensely Russian story, it plunges into the world outside—extending to America. In a sense greater than Lenin or his comrades realized, and without giving up any of his Russian essence, he half-Americanized himself as revolutionary. He became an admirer of Frederick Winslow Taylor (1856-1915), the great American engineer-ideologue of scientific management. In what a study of Taylor's influence calls "The Great Diffusion," his ideas, despite the earlier opposition by American organized labor, spread widely under impetus of production needs during World War I. Paul Valéry, a philosopher as well as great poet, wrote: "The world, which calls by the name of 'progress' its tendency toward a fatal precision, moves on from Taylorization to Taylorization." The conception was really so simple that it could be overlooked. With time and motion studies, thus the core of "scientific management," Taylor could eliminate workers' waste motion in the production process. During the war the American army applied his ideas to ordnance and, besides Henry Ford, they even found acceptance by American unions and the Marxian philosopher Antonio Gramsci.[12] This is all part of the broad sense of Alfred Chandler's study of American management practices that had shown how far advanced they were (ch.1). It is a sign of Lenin's genius that he was open to ideas so antipathetic to his Marxian view of capitalist exploitation and capitalism's eventual self-destruction. One sign was his early creation of Soviet Russia's Supreme Economic Council. Stalin's Five-Year Plans were fitted precisely into this Leninist-Taylorite conception.

In prison and exile Lenin had turned himself into an earnest scholar of the Russian economy, researching and writing his *Development of Capitalism in Russia* (1899), an impeccable example of a dissertation meriting a doctorate. Yet he used his earnest scholarship to subvert economic science in the interest of his politics. The book was a political action attacking Populism and peasantry. (In 1901 the Populists had established themselves formally as the Socialist Revolutionary Party.) Lenin agreed with Marx that industry and proletariat and not agriculture and peasantry meant progress. This led him, falsely claiming "the complete disintegration of the peasantry," to deny the magnitude and vigor of the peasant economy.[13] Yet his appreciation of economic progress led him to an intense interest in technology, which he studied in books sent to him in his exile, as a factor in building a post-revolutionary Russia.

Lenin's socialist way was competing with those agents of exploitation, Sergei Witte (1849-1915) and Pyotr Stolypin (1862-1911), who had been driving Russia forward in bourgeois terms.[14] A railway administrator and finance minister, Count Witte had built thousands of versts of railways, restructured the Russian State Bank to finance industry, and put Russia on the gold standard. Fatally self-defeating, the czar, however, never forgave him for helping save the government as prime minister after the Revolution of 1905 and dismissed him the next year. Stolypin, succeeding Witte, permitted the peasants to buy their way out of the rural communes, a primitive and inefficient form of communism. He was assassinated in 1911 by an anarchist. Right and left were making life easier for Lenin and his revolution.

The Revolution of 1905, guided by the St. Petersburg Soviet (existing from October 27 to December 16, 1905), was another help to Lenin and his Bolsheviks. The Soviet (the word "soviet" means "council" or "assembly") began as a coordinating center of a series of strikes protesting the czarist government and its losing war with Japan. It led to the creation of a legislature, the Duma, permitting democratic and radical parties to operate eloquently, if impotently, at the center of Russian politics.[15] Lenin, back in Russia, made good propaganda use of it. By 1907, however, the czar and his court were resisting change, and Lenin found it prudent to return to exile.

We can leave the study of Lenin's capture of power to the historians of Soviet Russia, but we pick out the details that show the reasons for his success, thus, the *sense* of the Soviet Union and its conflict with the United States. Looking back at the Soviet Russian collapse, how can we explain its creation and existence until 1991? We pursue Lenin's politics—and economics.

On April 16, 1917 Lenin arrived back in Petrograd at its Finland Station virtually running, brushing past the welcoming committee to mount an armored car and make his first speech, a demand for immediate revolution. The February Revolution of 1917 had begun when hungry women attacked the bakeries and food shops. On the precedent of 1905 strikes erupted and broadened into a general strike. The czar abdicating, the Provisional Government, formed of members of the Duma, found itself contending with the Petrograd Soviet, created on the model of the 1905 soviet. While the Provisional Government was chiefly composed of bourgeois Constitutional Democrats, the Soviet, with an unwieldy 3,000 delegates from various more or less radical organizations, was dominated by Mensheviks, with a minority of Socialist Revolutionaries and a handful of Bolsheviks. It is indicative of Lenin's political genius that he won power in these circumstances a half-year later.

Lenin's "April Theses" in *Pravda*, the Bolshevik newspaper, called for a generalized civil war between proletariat and bourgeoisie, and Soviet control of the land, banks, and capitalist enterprises. He denounced all compromise with Provisional Government, Mensheviks, and Socialist Revolutionaries—all non-Bolsheviks.[16] He was telling the Petrograd workers what they wanted to hear. In his slogans, indeed, in all his actions, Lenin was also laying down the major outlines of his tactical and strategic success.

While the Mensheviks were losing supporters, the Bolsheviks were winning more and more popular support in the continual elections, increasing their membership in the Petrograd and Moscow Soviets, and the other soviets. By September, with their allies, the Left Socialist Revolutionaries, the Bolsheviks had won majorities in Petrograd and Moscow. With its military-style, decisive, unified leadership, unique among all parties, their party was gaining the adherence of major military units in the Petrograd area, including the sailors of Kronstadt, the naval base nearby. It was also organizing the Red Guards, worker detachments more or less drafted from the factories. By June Lenin thought he might be ready.

Mounting great demonstrations, the Bolsheviks lunged toward power three times, but twice, on June 22-23 and July 16-17, sheered off. Despite great mass support, Lenin's instinct made him indecisive. He was positively decisive on November 6-7.

The July effort had been particularly dangerous for the Bolsheviks. Against such an obvious threat, the Provisional Government ordered Lenin's arrest and seized other party leaders. Accused of being a German spy and, more credibly, receiving German funds, Lenin slipped away, eventually to hide in Finland. He was still the Bolshevik leader, sending commands to the operative leadership, which for the moment meant Joseph Stalin, who kept the party in active being. At that moment also, abandoning the socialist ideal of ownership in common, Lenin capitulated to the peasants' desire for individual land holdings to gain some support among them. His first formal act on taking power was to issue a decree providing for individual ownership.

On the night of November 6-7 the Bolshevik insurrectionary machine had easily overwhelmed scattered resistance, and taken over the communications centers, military headquarters, government buildings, and then the Winter Palace, seat of the broken Provisional Government: Thus the Bolshevik Revolution. Validating all of Lenin's decisions, it had been the right moment. Within the grand penumbra of Lenin's presumptions, again and again he showed his tactical genius. Getting to work immediately to organize his communist state, he swept away one egregious expression of revolutionary democracy, the Constituent Assembly, in the process of election before the Bolshevik coup, which met on January 18-19, 1918. It was a momentary embarrassment for the Bolsheviks, who had gotten 175 of the 707 seats, compared with a majority of 416 going to the peasant-sympathetic Socialist Revolutionaries. (The Mensheviks, lacking a political strategy, got only 16 seats.) Bolshevik force forbade a second meeting.

With his absolute power Lenin was earnestly trying to make his Russia function according to Marx's *Communist Manifesto* and *Capital*. As argued here (ch. 2), Marx had been a great thinker and economist without, however, possessing any real affinity for economic theory. Lenin followed him in his own flawed economic conceptions, thus believing that eliminating capitalists and capitalism would mean eliminating all exploitation and permit the proletariat to enjoy the fruits of its labor. This would lead to the wrenching violence of early Communism and the institutionalized cruelty of the Communist regime, but also, given Lenin's subjacent realism, the retreat into compromise.

One early expression of revolutionary purity was the creation, on December 7, of the Vecheka, known for short as the Cheka, the All-Russian Extraordinary Commission for Combating Counter-Revolution, Sabotage, and Speculation, thus the secret police. The Cheka had direct powers of executive action, including the imposition of the death penalty. Giving it maximum powers Lenin specified: "The paragraph on terror must be formulated in as wide terms as possible." He saluted his first creation: "Our excellent Cheka," "our brave Chekists."[17]

Following Marx, Lenin proposed to replace self-interest with altruism in his Communist society. All members would become proletarians freely giving their work contributions to society and receiving their just rewards. This massive effort to be good rather than greedy might require aid from the brave Chekists, but this was just a transitional phrase. Lenin was attempting a revolution in economic motivation profounder than his political revolution.

If the Bolsheviks had given it acuter point, economic policy under the Provisional Government and Petrograd Soviet had been toxic to rational economic operations. Except for the Constitutional Democrats, soon rudely driven beyond the political fringe, all the leading parties from March 1917, the Mensheviks and Socialist Revolutionaries, as well as the Bolsheviks, gave no thought to encouraging production and supplying consumption. They had assumed the economic sectors were naturally operative and that the aim was to share the fruits therefrom equally. In power, the Bolsheviks, on principle, encouraged the workers to take over the factories and, as a political tactic, the peasants to continue to seize the landlords' land. The factories were producing less and less, the workers, in the circumstances, more concerned about rights and food than work, and the Bolshevik administrators learning on the job. In the country, the Bolshevik government undercut its support of the peasants by attacking private trade, again on principle, inevitably preventing them from getting sufficient returns for their crops. The sum, disorder imposed upon disorder, was War Communism, an effort to manage the governmental whirlwind.

Under Lenin's Supreme Economic Council, founded on December 15, 1917, the major banks and firms, Lenin terming them the "commanding heights" of the economy, were taken over. But the new masters' many fallacies in thought and policy had immediate, destructive effect. Production plunged, consumption hungered, famine was next. Workers deserted cities to get closer to food in the villages, Petrograd losing two-thirds of its population. In 1917 the city had 2.6 million inhabitants; in 1920, 1.2 million: "The proletarian dictatorship had triumphed but the proletariat had nearly vanished."[18] In March and April 1918 Lenin recurred to Frederick Winslow Taylor. He made notes: "Raise productivity ... learn socialism from the big organizers of capitalism ... Tailor's [sic] system, Motion study [in English] ... the Soviet government plus Prussian railroad efficiency, plus American technology ... etc., plus, plus equals socialism."[19] But chaos dominated. To get anything economic done required orders; a ramification of orders replaced Adam Smith's pervasive and invisible hand of individual self-interest. As any training sergeant would attest, sadistic bullying is a useful part of social discipline. The system worked, but cruelly, in the same manner military discipline drove infantrymen to climb a hill in the face of enemy fire. Stalin, who enjoyed discovering and punishing enemies, would brutally and variously incorporate its essence.

The period of War Communism coincided with the Civil War between the new regime and the range of enemies it quickly created. Internally, these were the resistant parties identified loosely as Whites and more or less supported by some Russian military units and externally these were variously engaged foreign powers, some helping the Whites. At one point eighteen competitive governments under varied patronage were set up in

Russia's breadth. This is another argument for Lenin's practical wisdom. Beyond his monolithic Bolshevik force Russia has splintered itself into anarchic fragments. All the errors of the Bolsheviks could not produce nearly so much disintegration as the various contradictory forces who were as hostile to each other as to Lenin's party. Lenin also had to make an accommodation with the Germans. This led to the Treaty of Brest-Litovsk of March 3, 1918, Russia losing 34 percent of its population, 42 percent of its agricultural land, 54 percent of its industry, and 89 percent of its coal mines.[20] Lenin accepted the treaty over the protests of leading Bolsheviks as necessary in the face of German power. The dénouement on the Western Front proved him right.

Trotsky had been commissar of foreign affairs and after refusing to make the agreement with the Germans that Lenin had accepted, became a more successful war commissar. Deploying an astonishing talent for war and management, he won the Civil War for Lenin. Violences of a more specific nature were also occurring. On July 16, 1918 the czar, his family, and retainers were shot with Lenin's approval—to prevent the imperial family from becoming a rallying center for the Whites. Ten days earlier Socialist Revolutionaries, indignant about Lenin's capitulation at Brest-Litovsk, assassinated the German ambassador. Then, on the morning of August 30, a young man shot and killed the Petrograd Cheka chief; in the afternoon a madwoman, an old terrorist, shot Lenin twice in the neck as betrayer of the revolution. Evidently not badly hurt, Lenin was back at his desk in three weeks, but with his encouragement the first Red Terror responded. The victims of reprisals were persons who happened to be prisoners at the time or were denounced by informers, relatives of officers, noblemen, and middle-class persons arrested on suspicion. In an expression of the terror Lenin had proposed eager Communist Party units throughout the country took the initiative to kill. Thousands died.[21]

While fighting for its life, on March 4, 1919, Lenin's government founded the Third International, the Comintern, and took the offensive superbly as the incorporation of the world revolution. Of course this cut across the lines of proper diplomatic intercourse. Lenin gave the orders, transmitted through Gregory Zinoviev, established as chairman of the Comintern's executive committee. The duty of the foreign Communists, represented by nineteen questionable delegations, some of them Bolsheviks of non-Russian origins, was to serve the world revolution's fatherland. Implementing Soviet foreign policy, the Comintern was meant to transform the foreign parties into "a single world Communist Party," as Zinoviev explained at its second congress in July-August 1920.[22] Thus global communism and the early challenge to American power.

Comintern policy, that is to say, Lenin's policy, was much more effective, indeed, genial in addressing the colonial peoples. For the wrong reasons Lenin had theorized that the colonies were the most vulnerable flank of the great powers. Their existence had explained an apparent weakness in Marxian theory, the failure of increasing poverty to appear in modern capitalism, as *Capital* had predicted. Colonial exploitation had simply slowed the process, Lenin theorized. But, as we have seen (Ch. 3), colonies seldom paid, capitalism stubbornly producing more wealth on its own. The great-power weakness lay elsewhere, in the fact that the best spirits in the colonies felt humiliated by their imperial masters and receptive to the Soviet Union's support. Of course Lenin proposed for the colonies the same role he gave to the Russian peasantry, appendage to the Soviet proletariat, that is, his Communist Party. This policy, as Lenin's peasant policy had done, would serve the Soviet Union in future great-power competition.

If Lenin's policies were indeed successful, indeed epochal, they had nevertheless provoked dangerous opposition. The sailors of the nearby naval base Kronstadt now turned against the regime they had helped empower. On March 2, 1921 they rebelled and demanded a truly democratic socialism, the election of new soviets, and the secret ballot. Lenin resisted the spirit of 1917. On March 7-18 War Commissar Trotsky, aided by one of his best officers, the future Marshall (and Stalin victim) Michail Tukhachevsky, sent troops across the ice of the Bay of Finland to retake the base. Hundreds, "if not thousands," of sailors were shot. Later in 1921, such were the cascading Bolshevik effects, Tukhachevsky had to subdue starving Volga peasants.[23]

Defeating Lenin and his Bolsheviks, resistance by suffering peasants to grain requisitions provided the fundamental, *economic* argument on policy. On February 24, before the Kronstadt sailors made their message clear, Lenin granted that the forcible requisitions policy should be replaced by a tax in kind. The party purists resisted, but the sailors gave Lenin his ultimate argument, as their rebellion was being crushed. The new tax brought with it the other changes, which constituted the New Economic Policy (NEP). Once again Lenin made the correct tactical decision. Since the peasants could not travel hundreds of versts to trade their crops, the state had to permit private traders to buy and sell. This was the end of War Communism and the restoration of private commercial operations—American-style capitalism!—throughout the Soviet economy. Of course the party, always enduring pangs of conscience for its betrayal of Marxian purity, kept control of Lenin's commanding heights of the economy. The Supreme Council of the Economy, in an early example of privatization, leased some 10,000 private enterprises by early 1922. If most were small, a few employed as many as 1,000 workers by 1925. The hyperinflated currency was replaced by a newly stabilized ruble. Revived capitalism saved the economy and the Communist state. This solution to the problem of survival would be the first great dilemma of the Soviet Union.

A remarkable renewal of trade and economic vigor ensued, but not so fast that it prevented disaster: "Uncounted millions died" as a result of famine and typhus. Statistics, however questionable, traced a pattern of relative recovery. Total industrial production in 1913, as measured in the inflated 1926-27 rubles, was worth 10.25 billion rubles in 1913, 2 billion in 1921, and 11 billion in 1926. For those years electricity was at 195 million, 520 million, and 3,508 million kilowatt hours and the grain harvest produced was 80.1 million, 37.6 million, and 76 million tons.[24] Of course the living standard remained abysmally low by Western European, not to mention American standards. But Lenin had saved his revolution. He could die, as he did on January 21, 1924, secure about that, although unhappy about too many of its epiphenomena.

From May 26, 1922 Lenin had suffered a series of strokes that left him half-paralyzed and unable to speak. Selflessly, desperately, he tried to save his revolution from internal as well as foreign enemies. He was particularly unhappy about Joseph Stalin, who used his position as party secretary to make the party Secretariat the administrative master of the Soviet state. Testing out his power, Stalin had insulted Lenin's wife. Lenin, however, suppressed his unhappiness and humiliation because he had effectively created this indispensable monster, the other equally unhappy party leaders accepting this final judgment. With his Supreme Economic Council and other instrumentalities of Communist governance, Lenin had laid down the main elements of his system: a compound of knout-driven Russian socialism and Taylorist-American efficiency. Only Stalin could manage Lenin's organizational and killing machine.

Stalin's first task was to resolve the dilemma of the Soviet Union's socialist order coexisting with NEP capitalism. It is a measure of his deadly genius that he succeeded.

Stalin had to find the right moment to return to Communist purity. He was contending with the obvious value of the NEP, which showed in the figures for grain production. In the years 1922-25 it had been an average of 57.7 million tons annually while rising to 73.5 million tons in 1926-29. More precisely, however, the figure for the year 1925-26 was

76.6 million tons, but it slipped to 73.1 million tons in 1926-27, held at
73.3 million tons in 1927-28, but again slipped to 71.7 million tons in
1928-29.[25] Clearly no more improvements could be expected: agriculture
and the economy were in stasis. A return to pure communism, given the
insistent and hopeful nature of the Communist ideology, could promise
economic recovery as well. To this one might add the alien assistance,
rendered virtuous and vigorously approved by Lenin, of Frederick W.
Taylor's scientific management as directed by the Supreme Economic
Counsel, that is to say Stalin.

By the time Lenin died Stalin had consolidated all power in his hands.
This gave him the authority to impose his judgment on circumstances,
to decide that a given year was too soon or too late—and, most advan-
tageously, to define the judgment of his rivals as wrong and suspect.
Another factor enhanced his strength. By 1921 all other revolutionary
parties, thus Mensheviks, Socialist Revolutionaries, and anarchists,
were legally forbidden. Bolshevik rivalries became internalized and as
deadly. In the Leninist-Bolshevik manner Stalin could denounce incorrect thinking by Communists as counter-revolutionary, deserving of the
fate of the other heretics.

Historians of the Soviet Russia of the 1920s recount in detail the various moves in its politics, but the major factor was the economy or, more
broadly, the political economy. More nearly right then his rivals, Stalin
could fluently annihilate them in the Bolshevist manner. In the tortuous
maneuvering, given the opportunity by Trotsky's actions, Stalin first
operated as a moderate, and as such, a proponent of the NEP. In 1923
Trotsky had spectacularly attacked the party for capitulating to NEP
capitalism at home and failing to pursue revolution abroad.[26] None of the
other leaders could agree to such a quixotic view. The result was support
for Stalin by Zinoviev, now Leningrad (as Petrograd had been renamed)
party boss, and Lev Kamenev, Communist leader in Moscow. But then
he could turn against them for qualifying their NEP position. By 1927
Stalin could expel both Zinoviev and also Trotsky from the Communist
Central Committee. In 1929 Trotsky was driven from Russia to Turkey;
he was assassinated by a Stalin agent in Mexico in 1940.

The mild theorist and editor of *Pravda* Nikolai Bukharin, meanwhile,
had supported Stalin against a too precipitate radicalization of the economy.[27] In 1929, however, he realized that Stalin meant pure power and
forced industrialization, and began to resist.. With his absolute power
Stalin could easily dispose of him.[28]As absolute master of Soviet politics,
Stalin launched himself against the economy.[29]

"The events of 1929-34 constitute one of the great dramas of history," in the words of Alec Nove, the economic historian of the Soviet Union.[30] The events meant another Russian revolution. In the next four years Stalin broke the peasant resistance to change and began to transform Soviet Russia from an agricultural to an industrial country. The industrial side of his revolution consisted of the Five-Year Plans, which consigned the NEP, in Trotsky's words, "to the dustbin of history,"[31] and modernized industry with the support of agriculture. In 1928 Soviet Russia was 70 percent peasant and agricultural. In 1967, on its fiftieth anniversary, it was almost 60 percent industrialized and the world's second greatest industrial power.[32] Stalin had Taylorized, thus Americanized, the Soviet economy (but not, we should note, the society).

In October 1927 the Central Committee had already determined on the first Five-Year Plan, the agency of the new economic revolution. Formalized by December of that year, the policy began to be implemented in 1929. Stalin was denouncing the kulaks, who were 3 percent to 5 percent of the peasantry, and claiming to support the majority "middle" and marginal poor peasants against them, but he proposed to exploit all of them. This was just what Bukharin had feared. In 1924-25 the country had still been too poor. In 1928-29 Stalin's USSR would find sufficient agricultural capital to finance his aims for industry, however cruelly. To be a viable state in the twentieth century the Soviet Union needed a great industrial expansion. The lie about the kulaks deceptively hid the truth.

Betraying Lenin's policy of granting the land to the peasants, Stalin simply annihilated private agricultural ownership in a few years. In four months, by March 1930, he had driven 55 percent into collectives, the kolkhozes. That pace was too much even for him; he retreated in a *Pravda* article of March 2, 1930: the party cadres had got "dizzy with success" and gone too far. Blaming his subordinates, he could save the regime and his own power. The peasants were able to win back more than half of their holdings in the next three months. But he lunged forward again in 1931 to regain almost all of the ground lost. In 1932 collectives reached a figure of 61.5 percent, going to 71.4 percent in 1934, and 89.5 percent in 1936.[33] If Stalin brushed aside the human costs, the agricultural losses were enormous.

The peasants were damned if they would let Stalin steal their land and livestock. In the first months they slaughtered and ate 15 million cows and oxen (more than half of the nation's cattle stock), 40 million goats and sheep, 7 million pigs, and 4 million horses.

One historian reported: "An epidemic of orgiastic gluttony spread from village to village….Men, women, and children gorged themselves, vomited, and went back to the fleshpots…and the drinking was…hard and deep."[34] Stalin punished the recalcitrants, labeled as kulaks, by three waves of deportations into regions unprepared to support life, in 1929-30, 1931, and the end of 1930, a total of 1.3 to 1.5 million households, thus 6-7 million "souls," as the Russians say. Those peasants who remained on their holdings were not much better off. He rationalized his starvation policy as a defense against the peasants' starving out Soviet power. Famine spread over huge areas, most particularly in the Ukraine in 1933, the authorities cordoning them off and keeping out food and observers. By way of famine and hardship from 1932 to 1939, with the "normal" population increase flattened, "somewhere along the way well over 10 million people had 'demographically' disappeared."[35] This figure includes perhaps 4 million peasants who died in 1933.[36] For Stalin the point was to modernize the Soviet Union as a defense against its enemies and, clinging to Lenin's ultimate objective, leading the world toward universal communism. If Lenin's ruthless statesmanship had created the Russian communist revolution, Stalin's sadistic statesmanship had consolidated it.

Could this have been accomplished less cruelly, less murderously? Moshe Lewin, the author of the splendid study of Soviet agriculture quoted here, has resisted the sense of his own facts. "On the basis of the material here presented, some of my readers have reached the conclusion (which I do not share) that the solution envisaged and adopted by Stalin was, in fact, the only solution possible."[37] Sympathetic broadly to socialism, Lewin could not accept that it demanded such sacrifices. By way of the Stalinist horrors, the peasant proportion of the Soviet Union's population fell from 66.7 percent to 14.9 percent between 1913 and 1979.[38] We might recall that the United States had eliminated most of its farmers by then, but in a less deadly manner. Within the limits of ideology and economic efficiency Stalin had to exploit the inefficient peasantry to finance industrial efficiency, thus Taylorization. In the same movement he had to eliminate individual farming, since ideology could not permit the continued existence of private operations in two thirds of the economy. Furthermore the Soviet Union had the mission of converting the heretical world to socialism. With privately managed agriculture the regime would have lost its moral legitimacy. Like Lenin, Trotsky, and Bukharin, Stalin had to lie and kill.

Four elements were necessary to approach the Marxist-Leninist-Stalinist consummation: industrialization by way of the Five-Year Plans (including mechanization of agriculture through industrial spillover, thus tractor stations), sophisticated personnel, slave labor, and the Great Terror. All this is part of the promise of Dostoevsky's long-eared comrade and the logic of Lenin's policy.

Simultaneously with the collectivization horrors, Stalin's Five-Year Plans began to drive industry forward. Earlier, he had told industrial managers: "To slow down the tempo means to lag behind…. The history of old Russia shows … that because her backwardness she was constantly being defeated" (while expanding over one sixth of the earth, he did not say). He launched into numerical exorbitance: "We are behind the leading countries by 50 or 100 years. We must make up the distance in 10 years." The latter figure, however, was only too accurate, if we count the time to the German invasion. Along with realism, however, Stalin was, in the opinion of Adam Ulam, "inebriated with a vision of a mighty and industrialized Russia 'overtaking and leaving behind' Britain, Germany, and even America."[39] Of course this was more modest than Lenin's vision of a communist world.

Driven by Stalin's insatiable will, the first Five-Year Plan began to take administrative effect in late 1928, Stalin continually forcing changes upward in tempo and figures. He changed the terminal date from September 30, 1933 to December 31, 1932, actually making it a four-year plan. Coal was projected to go from 35 million tons in 1927-28 to 75 million tons in 1932-33, but that was amended to 95-105 million tons; the actual figure recorded was 64 million tons. This assumes, to the doubt of expert observers, that the "actual" figure is correct. We should beware of "statistical inflation," the economic expert Alec Nove cautions, a warning that should be attached to every Soviet Russian statistical claim. The impulsion to match reality to extremes of the ideological imagination, combined with a lack of correctives available only in a free society, was an endemic element in the Soviet political economy and society. The other key figures of the plan were similarly recorded as planned, amended upwards, and "actual," thus oil, from 11.7 million tons, to an optimal 21.7, to an amended 40-55, to the "actual" 21.4 million tons. Ulam noted that electricity began with 500 million kilowatt hours, to go to 22 billion, achieving 13 billion kilowatt hours (if that). The target for automobiles and trucks set in 1932 for 1937 was 300,000 to 400,000, then raised to one million; the figure of 100,000 was later reported for1936.[40] It should be conceded that the achievement of real production increases was nevertheless substantial: no other country progressed so fast. No other country suffered so much.

Based on a flawed view of society, driven toward an impossible secular heaven, covered with a drumbeat of propaganda, the Soviet modernization, in industry as in agriculture, was shot through with lies. The regime controlled all expressions of opinion, from newspapers, periodicals, and books to schools and governmental and dependent organizations. Cheating had to make up for impossible fulfillment. Caricaturing Taylorism in effect, one example of many was the case of the coal miner Alexei Stakhanov, who was set up in 1935 to dig 102 tons of coal in a single shift as an example. This was seven times the normal amount, but the other miners were doing all the auxiliary work which Stakhanov would normally do. The action was attended by loud publicity as a method of propagandizing greater work norms. Resentful workers were reported to have lynched imitators attracted by such rewards as better housing, and the operation was dropped by 1940.[41]

"[A]midst the turmoil of economic transformation and terror...a new kind of society was taking shape," as the study of Soviet society put it, cited above (n.38). "At its core were the new technical graduates." Beginning in the 1930s, Stalin provided the necessary educational opportunities to create the skilled personnel managing his industrialized economy. By 1939 graduates of higher education were a modest 1.3 percent of the working population, but still a substantial improvement over previous years, while secondary education had already arrived at a figure of 11 percent. Twenty years later, despite the war, the proportions were 3.3 percent and 40 percent; twenty years after *that*, they were 10 percent and 70.5 percent. The technical graduates included Leonid Brezhnev and Alexei Kosygin, who became leaders of the Soviet state in 1964, and also Andrei Sakharov, undertaking his education as physicist, who would famously oppose their policies. In the 1980s, the historian could write, "The Soviet Union is now a highly educated society."[42] Stalin deserves much of the credit.

If Lenin remained a gentleman and Stalin showed himself to be of a criminal nature, Lenin was nevertheless the originator of every major impulse and consummation, constructive or deadly, of the Stalinist state. If he had been behind industrialization and education, he had also organized labor camps and originated the policy of terror. In a letter to a provincial soviet on August 9, 1918, besides the "the mass terror against kulaks, priests, and White Guardists," he went on to propose that "unreliable elements should be locked up in a concentration camp...."

(Note the word "elements," dehumanizing the victims of the action.) In Lenin's time, by 1922, the Soviet state had created 190 camps with 85,000 inmates. In 1930 the Gosplan, the State Planning Committee, was instructed to incorporate the work performed by those deprived of liberty into the planned economy of the country. A special department of the Commissariat of Internal Affairs, abbreviated as GULag, the Chief Administration of Camps, was set up to operate them.[43] Stalin's labor camps were direct descendents of Lenin's concentration camps. Firing up the first Five-Year Plan with human briquettes, Stalin generalized the model vastly.

The Five-Year plans required more intensive exploitation of the Soviet Union's rich human and natural resources, much of the latter in mortally distant and dangerous locations. Gold was in the Kolyma area, in far northeastern Siberia, and timber and coal in much of the Siberian region. Of course transportation facilities over the Soviet Union's great surface had to be comparably expanded. To satisfy Stalin's killing urgency, humans were hurled into areas most promising of industrial values. In his masterpiece, *The Gulag Archipelago*, Alexander Solzhenitsyn has listed the major slave labor projects: the Baltic-White Sea Canal (1932, also called the Belomar Canal), the Moscow-Volga Canal (1936), and the Volga-Don Canal (1962); construction of a dozen railroads, two highways, three hydroelectric stations, and several complexes for the production of steel, copper, paper, and chemicals; construction of eight cities and, additionally, a number of centers of modern industry; mining of radium, coal, gold, apatite, fluorite, and rare metals; and timber in the European north of Siberia, logging camps constituting half of the archipelago.[44] The many hundreds of camps were a core sector of the Five-Year-Plan economy. What was the investment in human beings?

The most secure estimates, according to a study by Anne Applebaum published in 2003, have some 18 million persons passing through the camps between 1929 and 1953, besides another 4 million war prisoners sent there while another 6 million Russians were dispatched to remote exile. Forced labor could thus be summed to 28 million souls. The camp population ranged from 179,000 in 1930 to 2,525,351 in 1950. Camp life was deadly. Excluding the fates of special exiles, deaths have been calculated at 4.2 percent of the camp population in 1930, rising sharply to 15.3 percent in the final years of the collectivization drive, then falling to 4.2 percent in 1934, but then rising to 24.9 percent in the starving war year of 1942, falling slowly to 22.4 percent in the almost equally bad year 1943 and more swiftly to 9.2 percent in 1944.[45] The normal ration combined with exhausting general work broke down and killed all who could not escape it as Solzhenitsyn did by achieving extra rations as a mathematician. But then no one could escape the outdoor prison Soviet Russia, including Stalin and his minions.

While the camps had done so only incidentally to their purpose of extracting labor, the Great Terror expressed the essence of the Soviet state even more purely by eliminating life. What was its practical sense? One would think that by 1934 Stalin had established total control over party and state apparatus, that his Five-Year Plans plus collectivization had effectively socialized the economy. The reason is suggested by Adam Ulam, who saw it being acted out in the proceedings of the Communist Party's 17th Congress, the "Congress of the Victors," meeting from January 26 to February 10, 1934. Waves of adulation washed upon Stalin. Suggestively, a party history of 1962, in the time of Nikita Khrushchev, remarked that it was a "scene of the most excessive praise" of Stalin. The "excessive praise" was an element, Ulam interpreted, of a "plot by adulation." The lesser party leaders wanted to limit Stalin's destructiveness, surely threatening them, by rendering him impotent. They would raise him to a higher level of superiority by relieving him of the sweaty tasks of administering everything; he would lose control of his party and administrative machine. A party history written during the Khrushchev period, according to Ulam, speaks of the intent "to transfer Stalin from the office of general secretary to some other post."[46] They would do to him what Hercules had done to the giant Antaeus, who was invincible as long as he kept his feet on the ground, in contact with his mother Terra. But then Stalin knew very well how he had treated the helpless Lenin. We can appreciate this if we refer to Mao Zedong's experience in China's 1960s. Mao had actually been removed from the levers of power, but fought his way back, declaring war on the party in the Cultural Revolution, a multiplicity of civil wars in which millions died. He had to raise up a force outside the party, thus the anarchic youth, particularly students. Having broken the party, he used the army, initially intimidated into neutrality, to restore order, smother the student movement, and reassert his control over the party and country. Stalin was too practiced in revolution to let matters go that far. He assured his continuance in power by internal blood-letting.

The plot revolved around the assassination of Sergei Kirov on December 1, 1934. Head of the Leningrad fief as successor to Zinoviev, he was, by definition, a future rival of Stalin's. A half-mad young man, with the connivance of Stalin's secret police almost certainly, was the unquestioned perpetrator. Whether Stalin was complicit or not, he found the assassination a splendid excuse to secure the command of party and military forces. Stalin's means was a set of three show trials of the old Bolsheviks (and a few associates) in August 1936, January 1937, and March 1938. Nearly all, including Bukharin, Zinoviev, and Kamenev, were immediately shot after the inexorable guilty verdicts. Stalin, commanding absolute power of persuasion in the Soviet Union and much persuasion in the minds of Western intellectuals, had established sufficient rationale for his Great Terror.

As prepared by the three great trials, the holocaust of the Communist Party endured from the end of 1936 to the end of 1938. Of the 1961 delegates to the 17th Party Congress of January 1934, 1,108 were arrested and most of them shot. Of the Central Committee of 1934, 98 of its 139 members and candidate members were arrested and most of them shot. Of the party, some 850,000 or 36 percent of its members, were purged. Perhaps a total of two thirds of a million were shot.[47]

Meanwhile a concentrated attack was launched more swiftly on the armed forces in mid-1938. Eight leading military men, beginning with Deputy War Commissar Marshal Michael Tukhachevsky (conqueror of the Kronstadt sailors in 1921) and Army Commander Yona Yakir, were tortured or beaten to provide confessions of treason, tried on June 11, 1937, and forthwith shot. The wives of such military defendants were either shot or sent to camp. The executions proliferated throughout the military, including navy and air force. In sum the executed included 3 of the 5 marshals, 13 of 15 army commanders, 8 of 9 fleet or leading admirals, 50 of 57 corps commanders, 154 of 186 lower ranks fared better proportionately. Among those of field rank or the equivalent, only about one half of the officers from the company level upward were tried, nearly all to be found guilty and shot. The army was crippled, as its early defeats showed, but not so badly that it could not recover. [48]

One must ask the technical question of how Stalin did it and the political question of why. As for the first, if the operation was difficult, Stalin, an efficient executioner and genius at conspiring and killing, knew how to divide and isolate his victims. The military had been kept out of politics and remained content to enjoy its privileges. All society was permeated with spies beholden to Stalin, who, furthermore, had another armed force securely in his hands, that of the NKVD, the People's Commissariat of Internal Affairs. In July 1934 the NKVD had absorbed the OGPU, the old secret police. Thus Stalin commanded a unified army of his secret police; the NKVD usefully checkmated the army, arrested its commanders, and shot them. Against such power the civilian party and even the armed forces were helpless.

But then why did Stalin do it? The military had never resisted and the resistant old Bolsheviks had been eliminated effectively by 1930 and formally at the three great trials. Why go beyond that? But Stalin had been right to interpret the adulation of the 17th Party Congress suspiciously. He realized his command was becoming unbearable to the party. Beyond that, terrific repression was needed to maintain control over society; any relaxation would have weakened his power. The only way to maintain his position was to keep his political opponents off balance. With his lust and instinct for power, Stalin knew a man would betray him before the man knew it himself. Continually generating new victims, the repressive system condemned Stalin to condemn his subjects to the end. But then he enjoyed it.

Stalin's great state machine was in good working order when World War II began. Whatever its defects, the military character of the Bolshevik party carried through in the Soviet state; whatever utopian dreams Lenin and his comrades nurtured, Soviet Communism was better able to wage war than provide the promised good and just life for its people. Despite colossal failures for which Stalin was responsible, it was in a position to defend itself successfully, if just barely. Building upon Lenin's achievement and Frederick W. Taylor's technical advice, Stalin had collapsed time and expeditiously constructed a modern political economy, but with the fundamental difference that its individual components were inefficient slaves. The Soviet Union fought a harrowing war, twenty million or more of its people dying, about nine million of them military personnel and the rest civilians. In Leningrad, virtually cut off for most of the war, perhaps a million, 40 percent of its population, died of malnutrition or hardship.[49] The highly militarized economy had been expending some 20 percent of its GDP on defense before the war. Now as one historian saw it, the nation had a "superior capacity for integration and coordination." Thus it "could commit a very high proportion of national resources to war effort."[50] In 1942, it was spending 55% of GDP on defense, perhaps the highest proportion anywhere.and this with a terribly impoverished population.[51] The State Committee of Defense took over from the Council of People's Commissars (the peacetime "cabinet") and directed the totally militarized economy, but then this was in Lenin's sense as an extension of revolutionary war. The highly centralized war direction meant that mistakes at the top were particularly harmful, and Stalin had made almost fatal ones, beginning with his earlier destruction of most of the higher officers and continuing with his refusal to believe intelligence reports of the coming German attack. The immediate results had been the annihilation of much of the air force on the ground, the loss of vast stretches of territory and great numbers of his troops, and the threat to Leningrad and Moscow. By November 1941, besides many factories, the Soviet Union had lost more than 50 percent of its coal, steel, pig iron, and aluminum. In that November industrial production was barely half what it had been a year earlier. Hitler's mistakes saved Russia.

Stabilizing the front in the winter of 1941-42, the Soviet war command shifted some 10 million of its people eastward as it built up its industry in the Urals. By 1945 half of its metallurgical output came from the new plants, compared with 20 percent before the war. Soviet statistics on wartime production are particularly doubtful, but the country was able to manufacture great numbers of aircraft, tanks, and other war materiel, while American Lend-Lease provided substantial additions.[52] At war's end, face-to-face with the American army, Soviet forces were in Berlin and deep in central Europe. From its advanced positions, armed with a powerful ideology, the Soviet state could resume Lenin's revolutionary war against international capitalism as led by its erstwhile war ally, the United States. All this was consistent with Lenin's original conception of making revolution in the military manner. The Soviet Union proved itself as a military machine but, departing from the raison d'être of governance, not as a human habitat. That would become its greatest problem in the postwar future.

Notes

1. Tocqueville, *Democracy in America*, 141.
2. See G. R. V. Barratt, *Voices in Exile: The Decembrist Memoirs* (Montreal: McGill-Queens University Press, 1974).
3. See his *My Past and Thoughts*, abridged, ed., Dwight Mac Donald (Berkeley: University of California, 1982; 1st ed.: 1973); Martin Malia, *Alexander Herzen and the Birth of Russian Socialism* (Cambridge: Harvard University Press, 1971).
4. On the Populists see the classic Franco Venturi, *Roots of Revolution: A History of the Populist and Socialist Movements in 19th-Century Russia* (New York: Grossett & Dunlop, Universal Library, 1966, 1st [Italian] ed.: 1952), and the superbly workmanlike Adam B. Ulam, *In the Name of the People: Prophets and Conspirators in Prerevolutionary Russia* (New York: Viking, 1977).
5. See Joseph Frank, *Dostoevsky: The Seeds of Revolt, 1821-1849* and *Dostoevsky: The Years of Ordeal, 1850-1859* (Princeton: Princeton University Press, 1976, 1983).
6. Quoted, translator's introduction, Fyodor Dostoevsky, *Devils*, tr. Michael B. Katz (Oxford: Oxford University Press, 1992; 1st ed.: 1871), ix.
7. *Ibid.*, 441, 523-86, 704-5.
8. Quoted, *ibid.*, 235, 426.
9. April 11, 1881, Marx, *Werke* ([East] Berlin: Dietz, 1973), vol. 35: 179.

10. On *What Is to Be Done?*, Adam B. Ulam, *Lenin and the Bolsheviks* (London: Fortuna-Collins, 1973: 1st ed.: 1965 as *The Bolsheviks*), 228-51; "military discipline," quoted, Robert Conquest, *V. I. Lenin* (New York: Viking, 1972), 39.
11. Marx, *Collected Works*, (New York: International, 1976), vol. 6: 497.
12. Robert Kanigel, *The One Best Way: Frederick Winslow Taylor and the Enigma of Efficiency* (New York: Viking, 1997), "The Great Diffusion" (486-570); quotation, 486.
13. V. I. Lenin, *Development of Capitalism in Russia: The Process of the Formation of a Home Market of Large-Scale Industry* (Moscow: Foreign Language Publishing House, 1956; 1st ed.: [Russian] 1899); "disintegration," 66.
14. See Theodore von Laue, *Sergei Witte and the Industrialization of Russia* (New York: Columbia University Press, 1963); Abraham Ascher, *P. A. Stolypin: The Search for Stability in Late Imperial Russia* (Stanford: Stanford University Press, 2001).
15. See Abraham Ascher, *The Revolution of 1905*, 2 vols. (Stanford: Stanford University Press, 1988, 1992).
16. David Shub, *Lenin* (New York: Doubleday, 1945), 221-22. On the 1917 events see also Marcel Liebman, *The Russian Revolution* (New York: Vintage, 1970).
17. Leonard Schapiro, *The Communist Party of the Soviet Union* (New York: Vintage, 1971; 1st ed.: 1960), 267-70; "paragraph on terror," quoted, 269; "excellent Cheka," quoted Ulam, *Lenin and the Bolsheviks*, 548.
18. Isaac Deutscher, *The Prophet Unarmed: Trotsky 1921-1934* (London: Oxford University Press, 1959), 7.
19. Quoted, Louis Fischer, *The Life of Lenin* (New York: Harper & Row, 1964), 258.
20. John Wheeler-Bennett, *Brest-Litovsk: The Forgotten Peace, March 1918* (New York: Norton, 1971; 1st ed.: 1938), 269.
21. Ulam, *Lenin and the Bolsheviks*, 563, 564. See Shub, *Lenin*, "Terror and Civil War," 344-76.
22. On the Comintern, Schapiro, *The Communist Party of the Soviet Union*, 196-210 (quotations, 199) and Ulam, *Lenin and the Bolsheviks*, 646-76.
23. Schapiro, *The Communist Party of the Soviet Union*, 205-8 ("if not thousands," 267); Ulam, *Lenin and the Bolsheviks*, 618-20; Deutscher, *The Prophet Armed, Trotsky: 1879-1921* (New York: Vintage, 1965; 1st ed.: 1954), 510-14.
24. Alec Nove, *The Economic History of the U.S.S.R* (New York: Penguin, 1984; 1st ed.: 1969), 86, 94; on the NEP, 83-135.
25. Moshe Lewin, *Russian Peasants and Soviet Power: A Study of Collectivization* (New York: Norton, 1975; 1st [French] ed.: 1966), 172-73.
26. Schapiro, *The Communist Party of the Soviet Union*, 282-83.
27. Stephen F. Cohen, *Bukharin and the Bolshevik Revolution* (New York: Vintage, 1975), "The Duumvirate: Bukharin as Co-Leader," 213-42.
28. Robert Conquest, *The Great Terror: A Reassessment* (Oxford: Oxford University Press, 1990), 7-36.
29. On these complex actions, Shapiro, *The Communist Party of the Soviet Union, 271-312; 365-68; on* Trotsky, Deutscher, *The Prophet Unarmed* I, 201-471; on Bukharin, Cohen, *Bukharin and the Bolshevik Revolution,* 270-336.
30. Nove, *An Economic History of the USSR*, 160. Much of the following depends on *ibid.*, 160-87. See also the valuable Lewin, *Russian Peasants and Soviet Power*, passim; and David Mitrany, *Marx against the Peasant: A Study in Social Dogmatics* (New York: Collier, 1961; 1st ed.: 1951).
31. Hurled at the Mensheviks leaving the Congress of Soviets on the occasion of the

Bolshevist seizure of power in November 1917, quoted, Deutscher, *The Prophet Armed: Trotsky, 1879-1921* (New York: Vintage, l965), 31; Schapiro, *The Communist Party of the Soviet Union, 282.*

32.   E. H. Carr, "A Historical Turning Point: Marx, Lenin, Stalin," in Richard Pipes, ed., *Revolutionary Russia: A Symposium* (Cambridge: Harvard University Press, 1968), 362.

33.   Nove, An *Economic History of the USSR,* 174.

34.   Isaac Deutscher, *The Prophet Outcast: Trotsky, 1929-1940* (Oxford: Oxford University Press, 1963), 118 ("epidemic or orgiastic gluttony"); Nove, *An Economic History of the USSR,* 174; Lewin, *Russian Peasants and Soviet Power,* 515.

35.   Nove, *An Economic History of the USSR,* 180.

36.   Ulam, *Stalin,* 346.

37.   Lewin, *Russian Peasants and Soviet Power,* 12.

38.   Geoffrey Hosking, *The First Sociaist Society: A History of the Soviet Union from Within* (Cambridge, MA: Harvard University Press, 1985), statistical table, 481.

39.   Ulam, *Stalin,* 340, 341.

40.   *Ibid., 322-23.*

41.   Hosking, *The First Socialist Society,* 158.

42.   Ibid., 403-5; quotations, 206-26, 403-5; quotations, 206,403.

43.   *Ibid.,* 71-74; quotations, 71.

44.   Alexandr I. Solzhenitsyn, *The Gulag Archipelago* (New York: Harper & Row, 1975), 2: 591-94.

45.   Anne Applebaum, *Gulag: A History* (New York: Doubleday, 2003), 580-83.

46.   Quoted, Ulam, *Stalin,* 372.

47.   Schapiro, *A History of the Communist Party of the Soviet Union,* 420-27, 440; in his *Bukharin and the Bolshevik Revolution* Stephen F. Cohen gives the figure of the executed, but his source is unclear, 341.

48.   Robert Conquest, *The Great Terror: A Reassessment* (New York: Oxford University Press, 1990), 182-213; Ulam, *Stalin,* 446-59.

49.   Nove, *An Economic History of the USSR,* 286. A later Soviet estimate is 26-27 million, Mark Harrison, "The Soviet Union: The Defeated Victor," in Harrison, ed., *The Economics of World War II: Six Great Powers in International Comparison* (Cambridge: Cambridge University Press, 1998), 291.

50.   Quotation, Harrison, "The Soviet Union ," 271; see Nove, An Economic History of the USSR, 275-77.

51.   Quoted, Nove, *An Economic History of the USSR,* 274.

52. · *Ibid.,* 271-77.

8

Hitler's Germany as Facilitator

We have seen how the United States created itself as a political-economic superpower and how Lenin's and Stalin's Soviet Union recreated Russia, rising upon its Communist ideology, to become a countervailing threat and more, a promise to become a unique global power. If this last presumption was more mad than real, the Soviet Union, with a population a third greater than that of the United States, thus 196 million as against 133 million in 1940, its vast geography, and its effort at industrial modernization, was a sufficiently real great power to be taken seriously. But how did Germany compare with these huge countries? Her population then was at 70 million, barely more than half of the American and only somewhat more than a third of the Russian. Now factor in their respective gross domestic products in 1940: the backward Soviet Russia at $420 million (1990 international dollars); Germany, with triple the Soviet *per capita* income, at $377 million, and the United States with its huge GDP of $930 million.[1] Have we been viewing Germany through the magnifying glass of her fantasy?

Considering these proportions, a conspiracy theorist might begin with the American-Soviet Russian relation. He might see manipulation here, if not by the United States, then as self-manipulation by the Soviet leadership in imitating the American-style industrial modernization exemplified in Frederick Winslow Taylor's efficiencies. More visibly, United States joined in impoverishing and frustrating a defeated Germany to the point where it selected an irrational leader to thrust it into an impossible quest of world power. Thus, as contended here, the United States, while innocent of the thought, can accurately be accused of this Machiavellian policy, if not conception. It required only the perverse statesmanship of Hitler acting as facilitator, while innocent of the thought like the American leadership, to carry out his part of the logic. Germany's likely defeat would set up a confrontation that the United States was likely to win.

139

We should recognize that Hitler was a genius, however perverse. He could not have accomplished all that he did without extraordinary powers. Of course he lied and cheated, but then so did Machiavelli's Cesare Borgia, Frederick the Great, and Napoleon Bonaparte. If he lacked their distinction, his gutter-level being was better fitted for his unhappy era, during the backwash of great military defeat and the petty wretchedness and humiliation endured by the Weimar Republic. Many Germans lusted for petty revenge. All of Hitler's qualities were appropriate: the autodidact's simple solutions, the marginal man's envy of the more fortunate, the Viennese self-indulgence in anti-Semitism, the war nostalgia. A defeated person from the beginning, he could speak for a defeated nation in denial.

Hitler was notoriously cold, with an attenuated relation to other human beings. He gave evidence of no sense that the others could have feelings independently of him. His own were a solipsistic orbit around himself when not simply hateful toward designated enemies. He could kill millions without hesitation, the statesmanship his situation and taste required.

All the women in Hitler's life suffered. The young Hitler easily separated from his widowed mother to lead an aimless life in Vienna. He appears to have been affected by her death, but only after he had remained away while she had sickened and died. The two other women in his life, both passive and pallid, suffered so much from his coldness that the first, his niece and possible mistress, committed suicide, and the second, his official mistress Eva Braun, tried to commit suicide on her own earlier and then obediently joined in his state suicide.[2] Magda Goebbels, wife of Joseph Goebbels, his propaganda chief, had close contact with him and determined: "In a sense Hitler is simply not human—insensible and untouchable." Yet Hitler had shown great anguish when his mother died and made a cult of mourning his niece. That much feeling, rising perhaps from deep unrecognized need, gave him the capacity for public hysteria as expressed in the ravings of his speeches. Engaging the nation in hysterical nationalism, it was immensely useful for a demagogue. In any case, his administrative genius, possibly inherited from his customs-official father, combined with an affinity for low emotions, gave him his instinct for taking advantage of others' individual and national weaknesses. He was a world-historical manipulator. One marvels at his ability to win out in many crucial situations.

A major crisis, a little over a year after he came to power, took the murderous form of the Night of Long Knives. Ernst Röhm, head of the brownshirted SA and representing radical bully-boy egalitarianism, was proposing to oppose Hitler's accommodation with the army and conservatives. Accompanied by faithful supporters, Hitler resolved matters by personally descending on Röhm, striding into his bedroom, and ordering his arrest on April 30, 1934. Without a trial or other pause Röhm was presently shot, along with some 200 other SA leaders. Hitler also took the opportunity to eradicate such selected enemies as a Bavarian leader who had refused to cooperate with him during his Beer Hall Putsch and General Kurt von Schleicher, who had preceded him as chancellor. The action consolidated Hitler's command of Germany. Stalin, a kindred nature, understood him well and commented to a colleague, "What a great fellow. How well he pulled it off."[3]

At all the key points of his political life Hitler triumphed until he plunged beyond the improbable into the impossible. As we have seen, he could take advantage of a long string of political errors and worse: the destructive peace terms of 1919, the various failures of the political parties of the left and right, America's dramatic entrance into, and deceptive semi-departure from, European affairs, the friendly example of Mussolini's fascism, and the Soviet Union's convoluted promise, threat, and vulnerability.

In 1936, emboldened by Germany's political and economic successes, and by the easily perceived weaknesses of his political enemies and victims, Hitler began his overt actions to destroy the Versailles system and go over to the attack. Feinting and threatening, he marched his troops into the Rhineland on March 7 to wipe out its demilitarized status. Correctly, he had predicted that France and Great Britain would not resist. This was the first break in the cordon around Germany established by the Versailles Treaty. With impunity, cooperating with Mussolini, he supported Francisco Franco's forces after they began the Spanish Civil War in July of that year, Franco's successes and his victory by March 1939 further weakening the position of the democracies. Meanwhile, on March 11, 1938, Hitler bullied and threatened Austria to succumb to the *Anschluss,* its absorption by the Reich. He immediately intensified the pressure on Czechoslovakia in the name of the three million Sudeten Germans. On September 29, 1938, effectively forcing the capitulation of France and Great Britain in the persons of their leaders, who came to him in Munich, he sent troops into the Sudetenland, rendering the surviving lump of Czechoslovakia defenseless. On March 15, 1939, as the Spanish Civil War was ending, Hitler swallowed the rest of the country: another Franco-British capitulation. He now threatened Poland, clearing the way by the terrific reversal of the Non-Aggression Pact with the Soviet Union on August 23, 1939. Invading Poland on September 1 and annihilating its forces of 3 million in 36 days, he was rather surprised to find himself at war with Great Britain and France, but went on to more victories.

Hitler ceded Poland's eastern areas to Soviet Russia, a reasonable price for Stalin's complicity, and beginning on April 1, 1940, after using the lull of the "phony" war to prepare more surprises, attacked Norway, Denmark, the Netherlands, and France. By June 22 he had knocked France out of the war. But Great Britain was obdurate and just well enough defended by the English Channel and a few fighter aircraft. So, after more intoxicating successes, he went to Russia. A half year later, on December 7, 1941, Japan attacked Pearl Harbor, the various aggressors joining forces around the world. Once again Germany found herself fighting on two fronts in defiance of fairly recent instruction, but then his genius had already overrun many old limits.

Hitler erected his brilliant military triumphs upon a remarkably sensible, successful economic base. This remains a reflection on the leadership of his enemies from the United States to the USSR. When he came to power Germany was facing "formidable" economic problems, perhaps the greatest, certainly the most poignant, being unemployment. The country had the largest proportion of unemployed of any major nation, a third of the workforce at more than 6 million officially recorded, compared with United States at one quarter out of work. But to this could be added one or two million for those Germans only partially employed or the unemployed who had dropped from the registered list.[4] Undertaking vigorous action, Hitler cut the six-million figure by one-third in a year. In four years, by the end of 1936, he had effectively eliminated unemployment. By 1938 his government was conscripting workers to reduce the labor shortage.

Hitler's achievement was effective politics and economics conjoined. Silently dropping all of his earlier extravagant promises while keeping much of their psychological aura, he pursued his reemployment policy without vitiating its substance by frightening the business leaders. In his first two years he spent 5 billion Reichsmarks on employment measures, 4 percent of the gross national product.[5] Compared with that, the United States, as we have seen, had actually spent less than 1 percent when it increased its deficit from $2.6 billion to $4.4 billion from 1933 to 1936. The American deficit reflected modestly increased spending and decreased unemployment, thus the modesty of the result. Shaming the Americans, the German achievement—the Nazis', Hitler's—was as solid as it was ambitious.

The German economic program began with its great success in reducing unemployment. It extended to construction operations, thus work on roads, including the excessively famous Autobahnen, but also on unspectacular road and bridge repair. Ending the unemployment among building workers, substantial funds went to subsidies for housing. The post office and railroads employed an additional 250,000 workers in their own work schemes. Hitler's administration assigned oversight over many of these projects to officials whose "primary interest was in reemployment and the refurbishment of public services," thus those with relevant experience and incentive.[6]

Such excellences were contemporaneous with other operations closer to the essence of Nazism. Winning admiration with these authentic achievements, Hitler immediately launched a wave of terror. Then the shocking Reichstag fire of February 27 permitted him the use of an emergency decree to destroy independent political parties and eliminate all liberty. This was implemented violently by his SA and SS private armies. From midsummer, concentration camps sprang up to contain the victims of their arbitrary arrests, 100,000 by the end of 1933.[7] The camps continued to proliferate, particularly after the war began. Jews who could not escape the country were harassed, murdered, or flung into the concentration camps preparatory to the Holocaust. Hitler could actuate the economic levers more easily.

Employment and reemployment were powerful arguments with labor, which had to see unions wiped out by May 1933. Workmen found themselves in the replacement organization of the Arbeitsfront, which "developed a certain sense of power" by claiming, at least, to improve working conditions. Of course strikes were forbidden, while the Arbeitsfront bestowed such sops as cheap vacations in the affiliated organization seductively entitled "Strength through Joy."[8] It might be unjust to suggest any resemblance to the Soviet model, since Hitler also cosseted the business community.

After the first two years the economy swung over into military preparedness, which was Hitler's fundamental and ultimate unemployment cure, but no one could accuse him of betraying his promises. From the start he had promised war. On February 8, 1933, hardly settled into office, Chancellor Hitler laid down the proportions of his program to a meeting of his cabinet. If his party's 1920 program, which was never altered, "read like a letter to Santa Claus," the cabinet heard "the future of Germany depends exclusively and alone on rebuilding the armed forces."[9] But Hitler was leading the National Socialist German Workers Party and meant every word of it although he made no promise that he would keep the workers alive to enjoy the party's socialistic benefits. As politician he knew he had to depend on their good will. All this was nicely resolved in those first two years and he could swing over into rearmament even before the second year was over.

Hitler had moved slowly into war preparations because of his ideology and because he liked technical modernization for its own sake. The welfare of the workers themselves, furthermore, suggested the extent and limits to his "socialism." Hitler told a meeting of party leaders in July 1933: "We have the power to throw out every general director, but ... can bread be provided for workers like this?"[10] He had effectively, if not formally, abandoned the strictures of his socialist-sounding 1920 program about "interest-slavery" and was willing to provide hospitable conditions for profit-making. Yet he limited free enterprise and applied socialism to the extent of establishing governmental control over the economy with his Reich Economic Chamber: cf. Lenin's Supreme Economic Council. Also, like Roosevelt's New Deal, Nazi economics functioned equably with both socialism and capitalism. Like Stalin's Five-Year Plans, it flattered and exploited a regimented labor. More generally, Hitler was providing a useful model for emulation by nonrepressive regimes: central control of the economy, encouragement for free enterprise, and a measure of comforts for labor. Having solved the conundrum in what sincere believers in socialism or free enterprise thought was an absolute contradiction, he could go on to address the practical policy problem. Bread, work, and now arms: how could Germany pay for it all, rising as it did out of depression?

A great proportion of the answer lies in Hitler's political genius, which was able to extend over the economics *an sich* he never understood. Like Roosevelt, he managed his economics by political instinct and simply needed technical economic help. If Roosevelt, as we have seen, found it in the institutional economists of the Brain Trust, Hitler had the inspiration to seek it in Hjalmar Schacht, an adeptly political banker. In the 1920s, the president of the Reichbank—a true central bank unlike the American Federal Reserve System at the time—Schacht, had prudently resigned when the Weimar Republic got entangled in the pathetic Young plan. This was in March 1930, before the hapless Brüning government took over. On March 17, 1933, shortly after assuming power, Hitler established Schacht at the Reichsbank as a guarantor of his government's questionable credit to the international financial community. Had Schacht been a straw-stuffed dummy, he would have been invaluable, but his range of abilities made him worth much more than that.

Schacht collected more responsibilities, becoming economics minister on August 2, 1934, and, presently, "general plenipotentiary for the war effort" in May 1935, this last too vague to be more than marginally effective. In these overlapping positions, nevertheless, Schacht also provided Hitler with additional funds to finance the increasingly expanded rearmament program. The banker had found his way to a Keynesian inflationary solution. The means was his mysterious Mefo-Bill operation, which, as a well-schooled banker, he conceded in a letter to Hitler was "an ingenious and risky structure."[11] The Mefo, the Metallurgische Forschungsanstalt, was a dummy corporation created by armaments firms, which drew commercial bills—discounted by the Reichsbank—on future or, better put, futuristic income. The bills, totaling 12 billion Reichsmarks, thus $3 billion at the rate of four marks to the dollar, functioned as paper money; they permitted Germany's money supply to double in six years and painlessly finance rearmament. The general improvement of the economy and a wage and price freeze in November 1936 secured the Mefo currency and prevented excessive inflationary effects. From 1932 to 1938, while industrial production rose 89 percent, the price index increased only 4 percent. Schacht did more than that.

Beyond finance, Schacht helped manage economic substance better. He could, of course, take advantage of the Hoover Moratorium of 1931 and the Lausanne Conference of 1932, which eliminated reparations. With the nation free of an external debt burden, he maximized economic power with the so-called New Plan of 1934. To an extent this permitted him to reduce the need for pure finance as such by concluding barter agreements with other nations, often impelling them to take less than desirable German products to sell Germany their products. Again Germany became a great economic engine on the continent.

Such rational management began to inhibit Hitler, who was thrusting beyond mediocre sense into the boundless regions of his ambitions. Still in 1935, three months after bestowing the "plenipotentiary" title on Schacht, Hitler gave the carelessly expansive Hermann Göring authority over him as head of the Four-Year Plan. A blatant imitation of the Soviet Five-Year plans, it was a less than efficient effort to organize the economy for war and a wild gambler's bet on a magic-lantern future. When Schacht, sincerely trying to keep to his banker's principles, began to resist these extravagances, he found himself out of his Economics Ministry in November 1937 and the Reichsbank by January 1939. He achieved internment successively by Hitler and the Allies, laughing last as a postwar financial expert and self-justifying memoirist. But he had given the Nazi economy a solid base.

Hitler could thereupon mount his military operations swiftly. In his first year in office he spent a modest 746 million Reichsmarks on armaments; in 1934 the sum leaped to 4,197 million RM. Toward the end of this second year, with unemployment falling to tolerable limits, arms spending exceeded other government expenditures, the figures rising to 5,487 million RM, 1935; 10,273 million RM, 1936; 10,961 million RM, 1937, and 17,247 million RM, 1938.[12] Managing armaments from February 1942 was his protégé Albert Speer, originally engaged as Hitler's private architect, who knew how to indulge his master's vulgar taste for the crushingly colossal, but who happened to possess great administrative talent. The Nazi war economy had found its manager.

Speer applied a rationality alien to Hitler's style, but, as he could recognize, supportive of his ambitions. The expert had to struggle against the politician's efforts to keep his Germans happy with housing construction and consumer goods, and his relegation of women to the *Hausfrau* status. While Allied employment of women had increased hugely, Germany's female labor force "remained virtually stable between 1939 and 1944, fluctuating between 14.1 and 14.8 million." Speer also had to resist the vested interests of regional Nazi leaders, who opposed his efforts to rationalize war production. Despite Allied bombing, which was not as effective as the air commanders claimed, German munitions increased from an index figure of 100 in the first quarter of 1942 to 184 in the first quarter of 1943, to 279 before the end of 1944. Besides Speer's shifting of the work force to more productive operations, this was due to the employment of foreigners and war prisoners, from 3 million in 1941, 4.2 million in 1942, 6.3 million in 1943, and 7.1 million in 1944, this last figure almost 20 percent of civilian employment.[13] Building upon Schacht's artful economics and, toward the end, deficit financing, this was a triumph of German finance, administration, technology—and the exploitation of all Germans and all foreigners within reach of German power.

At this point one should ask Hitler what he really meant to do. He explained wordily in *Mein Kampf*, which went to 994 pages in one English translation of its two volumes. He does not answer here: it is an impoverished thing. One must interpret largely from his actions, but it does tell us what he had in mind, although immediately facing the problem of the book's low-level mediocrity. The tortured repetition of a handful of themes could be expressed in two dozen retchingly vile pages. He sees Jews everywhere but then the Czechs threaten Germanness with the poison of "Slavization" and he reacts with horror to the "mixing of blood." He begins by compounding his own origins with the German problem. His "German Austria must return to the great German motherland.... *Common blood belongs in a common Reich*" (Hitler's italics). He immediately leaps into conquest: "As long as the German nation is unable to band together its own children in one common state, it has no moral right to think of colonization as one of its political aims ... the moral right to acquire foreign soil...." Innocently, he does not see that other nations might make similar claims themselves. Here we see the seamless obtuseness of the self-centered nature. Again and again he begins and ends with himself and race: "The deepest and ultimate cause for the ruin of the old Reich was found in the non-recognition of the race problem...." He condenses race into the problematic of the Jews as further tainted by Communism: "Slowly the fear of the Marxist weapon of Jewry sinks into the brains and souls of decent people like a nightmare."[14] The historian Michael Burleigh translated its significance in a lapidary sentence: "Nazi ideology offered redemption from a national ontological crisis, to which it was attracted like a predatory shark to blood."[15] Hitler's plunge into these indulgences worked in a period of skewed thoughts and feelings. The wilder he got, the more effective he was—up to a point. But one must ask: granting even tremendous victories, how could his Germany survive in a world composed of some decent people and non-Aryans?

This is not to deny Hitler's intelligence and powers coexisting with his blankness to vast areas of life and knowledge. Like Stalin, a mediocrity and a bore in his way, he had the mind of the killer on a historical scale. In the midst of his propagandist blather, which is its own justification, he gave one hard proof of his deadly practical accuracy. It was all the more effective because it is in blank contradiction of his racial philosophy and politics, indeed his raison d'être as a leader of the German *Volk*. He dealt with one of the most perfect injustices of the Paris Peace Conference treaties, the granting of the Austrian South Tyroleans and their land to Italy as a victory reward and the strengthening of Italy's Alpine defenses. Against demands for justice Hitler decried the "puffing up" of the issue. He pointed to the importance of Benito Mussolini and his fascism as "man and system who have dared to free themselves ... from the Jewish Marxian grip and to put up a nationalistic resistance against this international world poisoning." [16] Race is everything to Hitler but *Realpolitik* conquers all.

The accurately entitled *Hitler's War*, beginning with the attack of June 22, 1941 on Soviet Russia, is David Irving's clear, classic, politically incorrect account. It does not, however, make sense of it. Let us try while gratefully making use of his account. Hitler was leading, we remind ourselves, a nation of 70 million against 196 million people in a vast country covering one sixth of the world's surface. Another leader going too far, Napoleon suffered his tremendous defeat here after he first made a non-aggression pact with Czar Alexander in June 1807 and then invaded Russia, also in June, five years later. By October he was deserting his *Grande Armée* and leaving three-quarters of it behind to Russian mud and cold. Could Hitler improve on Napoleon? Even if, given a more sensible strategy, he had taken Moscow and torn out the heart of the Soviet Union, he could hardly hope to master its whole territory. He would then, in any case, be driving into the space of India and China. Then there were a still resistant Britain and United States, with its close British connection and its potential. Hitler had launched himself into an impossible effort. He had to fail hugely and make way for the United States, as we shall see.[17] Within that general disaster he went on to make the series of self-defeating decisions of a lower order—all emphasizing the bankruptcy of his whole enterprise. We shall have to make sense of it for him.

In Russia the war had begun intoxicatingly for Hitler and his generals. In early summer of 1941, sober observers thought he was right again. Assuming the present war to be in process of ending—another wild flight of the imagination—he seems to have futuristically envisaged a future war, "perhaps not in his lifetime … between the New World and the Old."[18] His armies effectively surrounded Leningrad, saw Moscow's church spires, and plunged toward the oil fields in the southeast. But then they halted in the trap of rain, mud, cold, and counterattacks by shocking numbers of fresh, winter-equipped enemy troops. A year later, Hitler's war concentrated on Stalingrad and oil, but the long line of communications and the now unsurprising wealth of newer Soviet forces prepared to die frustrated him again. In early 1943 the Soviet forces began an advance that continued until they got to Berlin in April 1945.

Hitler had shown himself to be a dangerously fallible, amateur commander. He began badly by failing to demand a coherent focused plan from his military staff. He used his forces wastefully and indeed had as fatal an effect on them as on his putative victims. His army by February 20, 1942 counted 112,627 frost victims, 14,357 being amputees, and one million casualties, including 200,000 dead. He could not defeat the Russian winter, but his response was to order the army to "stand fast" and continue to suffer and die.[19] He lost an entire army at Stalingrad. He lost his war with great determination and ingenuity.

Hitler compounded these wretched decisions by indulging in genocide, including the Holocaust. In the Ukraine, where Stalin's agents had killed five to seven million peasants by starvation and which had welcomed the Germans as an improvement on Soviet rule, these latter killed nearly seven million people, including virtually all its Jews. Here Stalin and Hitler joined hands silently in another pact. David Irving has been able to argue that no evidence proves Hitler ordered these massacres or the Holocaust. Indeed, in all his political life except for the bloody purge of the SA leaders in 1934, he characteristically avoided the specifics of killing. This was surely the intuitive politician's denial of responsibility for the effect of his actions. "It was ... these fanatical Gauleiters in the East who were interpreting with brutal thoroughness Hitler's decree that the Jews must 'finally disappear' from Europe...." Irving reports: "Yet the blood purge continued. The termination program had gained a momentum of its own."[20] The quest for more documentation becomes an evasion.

On April 18, 1945, twelve days before he committed suicide as the Russians approached Berlin, Hitler pronounced: "If the German nation loses this war, that will prove it was unworthy of me."[21] His self-centeredness had been fatal to millions of his chosen people as well as many more millions of absolutely unmourned foreigners—and himself. But then he had maneuvered himself into his only recourse from his monstrous errors.

Given the impossibility of total world conquest, only suicide makes sense of Hitler's enterprise. Among others, 7.6 million Germans had died for him, 3.2 million civilians, most of these latter in vast area bombings, and 4.4 million military casualties, including the hundreds of thousands of soldiers taken prisoners in Russia who died or were to die there.[22] To these figures should be added more thousands—boys and old men as well—sent by him, imagining fantastic auxiliaries, into more senseless fighting. Like the Pharaoh's household, all these deaths would join his own. His life purpose reveals itself: Hitler would die on the grandest funeral pyre of all history, his people serving as fuel. We note for the sake of proportion, although beyond the range of his concerns, that a total of 50 million or more died in World War II.

It is not extraordinary that Nazism left so little behind. Here and there dwarf imitations have stirred a little and died. The old political parties, keeping their prescriptions, returned and operated not much better than before, but modestly, sanely. Communism, even in its worst embodiment as Stalinism, has left operative structures and usefully trained personnel behind, Red China adding bulk and rationality to the Soviet Russian precedent, all subject to future improvement. Nazism left only vacancy. "The regime established by what have been called 'armed bohemians' produced nothing of any lasting moment," Michael Burleigh thus ends his just *Third Reich* with more justice. "Their leaders embodied the negation of everything worthwhile about being human; their followers demeaned and shamed themselves." He concludes: "In this sense, the lower register, the more pragmatic ambitions, the talk of taxes, markets, education, health and welfare, evident in the political cultures of Europe and North America, constitute progress...."[23]

We return to another sense of the exercise. Hitler became the ultimate facilitator of American ascendancy. Without him the rise of America would have taken longer, although it was implicit in the proportions of world power. The United States, with the largest, most efficient political economy, had the capacity for world leadership. Part of that, contrasting with Hitler's boundless objectives, was its modest ambition. Although it had not thought so far in the 1940s, the war was training it in its leadership role. This meant not mastery as seen by A. J. P. Taylor, but general agreement in the American manner as noted by Tocqueville (granting past exceptions like the treatment of Native Americans and blacks). An important element of the role of the United States as superpower was its setting of limits on itself. These were expressed in the Marshall Plan and its sponsorship of the related Organization for European Economic Cooperation (later ... Development) in which the consent of the aided was required, and also in the North Atlantic Treaty Organization, where agreement was the rule. America's friends and Allies were content, whatever incidental blows to their amour-propre, to accept help on such terms. Of course the United States would go on to make new mistakes as well.

Notes

1.   Maddison, *The World Economy,* population and GDP: 38, 96, 82; 98, 50, 85.
2.   See Joachim C. Fest, *Hitler,* trs., Richard and Clara Winston (New York: Vintage, 1975; 1st ed.: 1973). On Hitler's mother, 28-29; the niece, Geli Raubal, 321-27; Eva Braun, 744-49; quotation (Magda Goebbels), *ibid.,* 523.
3.   Anastas Mikoyan, Poliburo member, quoted, Robert Service, *Stalin: A Biography* (Cambridge, MA: Belknap Press, 2005), 34.
4.   Official figures, Karl Hardach, *The Political Economy of Germany in the Twentieth Century* (Berkeley: University of California Press, 1980), n. 60 (citing "official figures"); "formidable" and estimate of 8 million, R. J. Overy, *War and Economy in the Third Reich* (Oxford: Clarendon Press, 1994), 3. Besides these on the economy see also V. R. Berghahn, *Modern Germany: Society, Economy, and Politics in the 20th Century* (Cambridge: Cambridge University Press, 1982).

5.   Hardach, *The Political Economy of Germany*, 59.
6.   Overy, *War and Economy,* 6; the projects in general, 3-11.
7.   Holborn, *A History of Modern Germany from 1848 to 1945*, 723-24.
8.   Hardach, *The Political Economy of Germany,* 61.
9.   *Ibid.,* 53; Overy, *War and Economy,* 4.
10.   Overy, *War and Economy,* 13.
11.   Quoted, Edward N. Peterson, *Hjalmar Schacht: A Political-Economic Study of Germany 1923-1945* (Boston: Christopher, 1954), 178.
12.   Avraham Barkai, *Nazi Economics: Ideology, Theory and Policy* (New York: Berg, 1990; 1st German ed.: 1985), table, 260. By 1939 Germany had spent 60 to 90 billion RM on the military. In those years the annual American GNP was $60-$90 billion, equivalent, thus to 240 to 360 billion RM. German expenditures seem tiny in comparison but the lower European living standards permitted Hitler to buy more arms and personnel for the money.
13.   *Ibid.,* 239.
14.   Adolf Hitler, *Mein Kampf.* Tr. supervised by Alan Johnson, 2 vols. originally (New York: Reynal and Hitchcock, 1939), 388, 447.
15.   Michael Burleigh, *The Third Reich: A New History* (London: Macmillan, 2000), 13, 12.
16.   Hitler, *Mein Kampf,* 699-700.
17.   See the vast story in John Keegan, *The Second World War* (New York: Viking Penguin, 1990).
18.   David Irving, *Hitler's War* (New York: Viking, 1977), 284-85; quotation, 285.
19.   *Ibid.,* 368, 468.
20.   *Ibid.,* 332.
21.   *Ibid.,* 798.
22.   Berghahn, *Modern Germany*, 171.
23.   Burleigh, *The Third Reich,* 812.

9

Reluctant Empire

One person, a frail and insecure vessel, created the strategy that defeated—annihilated—the Soviet Union and established the United States as the one global superpower, the American empire. The strategy is expressed in the word "containment," as George Frost Kennan conceived it. He put its pure theory in the famous long—8,000 words —telegram from Moscow, where he was chargé d'affaires, on February 22, 1946. He later defined it in an article, written in the United States, in the publication *Foreign Affairs* of July 1947. The article put it: "[T]he main element of any United States policy toward the Soviet Union must be that of the long-term, patient but firm and vigilant containment of Russian expansive tendencies."[1] Accurately prophetic, Kennan promised that containment would lead to "either the break-up or gradual mellowing of Soviet power." He proposed and shaped all but one of the main policy elements that immediately transformed thought into historic action. Indeed the speed of it appalled him and he resisted inserting the last component of the containment action.

The long telegram had resulted in Kennan's return to the United States in 1946 and his becoming head of the Policy Planning Staff of the State Department from April 1947 through 1949. While he remained as counselor in the State Department until September 1950, he was preparing to leave it. By then the containment policy was completely established in principle and affecting the world. This meant the creation of the Marshall Plan (announced June 5, 1947), the Central Intelligence Agency on September 18, 1947, "the greatest mistake I ever made,"[2] and, again to Kennan's regret, the North Atlantic Treaty Organization on April 4, 1949. Thus, perhaps cynically seen, the Marshall Plan carrot, the CIA stick, and the NATO bundle of sticks. More neutrally, if one can use the word, it meant financing Europe's recovery from a devastating and depleting war, and the Cold War defense against continuing Soviet aggressions, which included such intelligence operations as spying out atomic bomb data. Without shooting, the United States effectively declared war once again, now against its comrade of yesterday's war.

The complex of postwar actions, now defined by the theory and action of containment, meant perforce the creation and expansion of the American global empire. Unlike the British Empire, which it succeeded, it was based on power alone and not territory. The United States had no desire for more land except hundreds of military bases in strategic points. This was to complete the process, which began as the economic invasion of world markets by American goods in the nineteenth century, the entry into the European conflict and the shaping of the peace after World War I, the founding of the League of Nations and its abandonment as the United States partially withdrew from Europe after 1919, the export of the Great Depression to the world, in sum the actions leading to World War II, and, now, the newer acceptance of international responsibility for war and peace. Defensively, without realizing it, the American people, reluctant imperialists, had formed themselves as the world's greatest empire, that defense, as dictated by strategy, ineluctably moving into aggressive initiatives.

Few, including the experts, fully appreciated the logic of it: international power required a balancing responsibility. The American experience had argued this logic negatively, the United States earlier wreaking vast damage when it failed to exercise its full power. The Soviet aggressions had given definition and point to the new American policy. Arguing the morality of it would be futile.

The theory of containment deserves closer examination, particularly because Kennan himself soon softened it. He had begun his 1946 telegram bluntly, excerpted here, in his first book of memoirs of 1967: "The USSR still lives in antagonistic 'encirclement' with which in the long run there can be no permanent peaceful coexistence." He quoted Stalin speaking to an American workers' delegation in 1927: "'Battle between these two centers for command of world economy will decide fate of capitalism and communism in entire world.'" The United States was a facing total hostility disguised only by "lip service" to cooperation, thus total war. The Soviet danger, as Kennan saw it, also comprised an "[i]nner core of the Communist Party in other countries" functioning as an "underground directorate of world Communism." The implication, again, was of a war to the death, with Soviet Russia "seemingly inaccessible to considerations of reality." Nevertheless the threatened war was not inevitable. "T]he problem is within our power to solve—and that without recourse to any general military conflict." Kennan concluded with insecure optimism: "[I]f the adversary [of he Soviet Union] has sufficient force and makes clear his readiness to use it, he rarely has to do so."[3] Under the pseudonym "X," his *Foreign Affairs* article, "The Sources of Soviet Conduct," saw the Soviet Union operating negatively with a "sense of insecurity" and aggressively on the "principle of infallibility." The article emphasized, rather than qualified, the sense of the long telegram, its major contribution being the word and conception "containment."[4]

George C. Marshall, following his impeccable performance as army chief of staff, had become secretary of state and served in that position for almost two years from January 1947. Confronting Stalin's impossible demands, he spent six frustrating weeks at the inconclusive Moscow Conference of March 10 to April 24, 1947. That decided him, in accord with Britain's foreign minister Ernest Bevin, to concentrate on European recovery as the essential response to Stalin's presumptions.[5] On the day after his return he assigned Kennan to develop measures to that end. With five experts Kennan began drafting the main features of what would be called the Marshall Plan. The secretary of state first proposed it in a speech at the Harvard University commencement on June 5.

Kennan's memorandum, submitted on May 23, emphasized two factors, the importance of European initiatives and the integration of the various nations within the recovery program, requiring thus a greater unity than Europe had ever known. Of course this European action would take place within the grander range of the American initiative.[6] Kennan was particularly grateful that Marshall adopted these ideas without change. But then this great military man, who had created an army of fourteen million out of a peacetime force of 200,000, had a sense of the political economy. In his speech, which Kennan then drafted with the help of his experts, Marshall pointed to the "dislocation of the entire fabric of Europe,": "Raw materials and food are in short supply. Machinery is lacking or worn out." He told the Americans that "the consequences to the economy of the United States should be apparent to all." He told the Europeans: "The initiative ... must come from Europe."[7] Bevin, who heard a broadcast report of the speech, urgently called Georges Bidault, the French premier, and went to Paris on June 17 to concert their part in the aid program. With Congress increasingly accepting, opinion-leaders active, and President Harry S. Truman driving hard, the Marshall Plan legislation, overcoming isolationist sentiment, was expeditiously passed. Before the end of 1947 the Marshall Plan had become a substantial part of Cold War reality.

Earlier, indeed two days before Secretary Marshall left for Moscow, the president had articulated his Truman Doctrine, a counter-aggressive financial response to Soviet-aided aggression in Greece and the danger to Turkish security. This was a year after Winston Churchill had begun to awaken the Americans to the Soviet danger in his famous Iron Curtain speech in Fulton, Missouri, on March 5, 1946. The British government had now emphasized Churchill's warning by informing the United States that it could no longer subsidize the Greek government's defense. At the moment the National Liberation Front of the Greek Communists, aided by Marshal Tito, was threatening to overwhelm it. Aroused to the danger, Congress gave Truman a generous $400 million for Greece *and* Turkey. Before the end of 1948 the Greek Communists had been defeated.[8]

In the early period back in Washington Kennan was an intense, multi-faceted Cold Warrior. He was effectively a deputy to both Secretary Marshall and James V. Forrestal, Navy secretary and then, as a result of the consolidation of the military forces on July 6, 1947, defense secretary. The consolidation law had created the National Security Council to coordinate security operations, and Kennan, teamed with a colonel representing the Joint Chiefs of Staff, was the NSC representative for covert affairs. This meant the CIA. He found himself planning four types of CIA action: political, psychological, and economic warfare; paramilitary operations; covert actions; and secret intelligence. While he would presently regret these military and paramilitary aspects, Kennan collaborated on them vigorously at the start.[9] In a "top secret paper," he called for "the inauguration of organized political warfare." He saw the Marshall Plan, the Truman Doctrine, and the CIA's secret operations as "interlocking parts of a grand strategy." On June 16, 1948 the "NSC directive 10/2 called for covert operations to attack the Soviets around the world."[10] One of the first CIA actions, however, was a soothing application of American cash.

In February 1948 Soviet Russia had carried out a coup against the insecure coalition government of Czechoslovakia, the loyal Communists eliminating the non-Communists. Among the latter was Foreign Minister Jan Masaryk, who fell mysteriously or not to his death from the window of his third-floor office on March 10. Meanwhile the Communists had been trying vigorously to take over the governments of Italy and France. Defense Secretary Forrestal, drawing upon private sources as well as the CIA, lavishly funded the campaign of the moderate Italian Christian Democrats, who won a great election victory over the Communists and their near-allies, the Socialists, in April 1948.[11] In the next month the

State Department impelled the dismissal of Communists from the cabinets of both Italy and France.[12] In the French instance it had delayed a large loan until France would "correct the present situation first." As the Marshall Plan aid took effect, the stability of the non-Communist Italian and French governments strengthened.

Sneakily aggressive, the economic action of the United States was stiffened by other more combative acts, thus the early operations, covertly or openly ruthless, of the CIA. The Italian election of 1948 was a paradigm for other successful CIA undertakings. The CIA went on to spend $65 million over the next twenty years on friendly newspapers and the election costs of non-Communist parties and trade unions. It also supported the Social Democratic Chancellor Willy Brandt in West Germany and the French Socialist Premier Guy Mollet.[13] In France, also, the CIA financed the union group competitive with the Communist-dominated French union federation, an action guided by Jay Lovestone, director of international affairs of the AFL-CIO and a recovered Communist. The CIA also backed friendly left-wing operations by providing the Congress for Cultural Freedom with $800,000 to $900,000 annually for such affiliated publications appealing to intellectuals as *Encounter* in Great Britain, *Der Monat* in West Germany, and *Preuves* in France.[14] If Kennan appreciated them, he began to be specifically unhappy about more martial matters.

In 1949, after the Soviet explosion of its atomic bomb in August, Kennan found the idea of atomic war appalling—insupportable. In a long memorandum, which he thought was perhaps "the most important of all documents I ever wrote," he advanced two ideas that led to his departure from the pure theory of containment and the State Department itself. He deplored the military side of containment, which he thought now dominated the political and economic. Specifically, he wanted to end reliance on atomic weapons and, associated with that, urged creating a neutral Germany, the United States and the Soviet Union withdrawing their forces.[15] By the latter part of 1949, while contributing suggestions of decreasing acceptability, he was no longer making policy and preparing to take leave without pay. He became a productive scholar at the Institute for Advanced Study at Princeton for the rest of his long life.

But Kennan's containment policy continued integral, with the military firmly fused with the other elements. In the face of absolute destruction he had turned away. The politically incorrect John Foster Dulles, who would become secretary of state in 1953, put the counter-argument in a magazine interview in early 1950: "The ability to get to the verge without getting into war is a necessary art. If you cannot master it, you inevitably get into a war. If you try to run away from it, if you are scared to go to the brink, you are lost."[16] This is not much different from the sense of Kennan's long telegram promising that if the "adversary" of the Soviet Union "makes clear his readiness to use [force], he rarely has to do so." But Kennan had moved on. His idea of a neutral Germany would have torn a gap in containment to let Stalin's Soviet Russia move through, as his armies had done in East Germany and Eastern Europe. Indeed, while the American policymakers had rejected Kennan's idea out of hand, Stalin himself thought so well of it that that he proposed a barely disguised version on March 10, 1952, a year before he died. He put it in the form of a four-power conference to arrange for elections in all of a united, neutral Germany. He had shown how to produce Communist results in any election he might control. The Allies quickly rejected it.[17]

Actually, as Stalin must have realized, the idea was too dangerous for the Soviet Union as well as for the West. If he had used his successful technique, he could have controlled the "neutral" German government and across the Rhine have found two countries with large Communist parties ready to assume power. With his leading supporters likely to be dazzled by the prospect, Stalin might have been forced to put his ideology above his prudence and accept the risk. The United States and Britain would surely have resisted, and the United States had the bomb. Otherwise Stalin had shown his caution in the early postwar period by following a policy of appeasement in the West (see below) while taking over East Europe.

The Kennan case, characteristic of the intellectual, is worth reflection in the Cold War circumstances. Like many other intellectuals, sicklied o'er with the pale cast of thought, he had wanted to deny the confrontation, which John Foster Dulles had coolly accepted as the ultimate act of statesmanship. In the fall of 1957, as scholar, Kennan returned to his idea when he gave a series of six talks in the distinguished Reith lecture series on the BBC. The reception in all of Western Europe, as well as the United States, was roundly negative, although respectful and even understanding. Accepting his failure to convince, he "came away in a state ... of intellectual brokenheartedness," as he put it.[18] He was admitting that his heart had displaced his head.[19]

Without his lead Kennan's containment was institutionalized in the National Security Council's report, labeled NSC-68 and dated April 14, 1950. The report was drafted by Kennan's successor as head of the Policy Planning Staff. Becoming the "blueprint for waging the Cold

War for the next 20 years," according to the Cold War historian Walter LaFaber, it characterized the policy of Dean Acheson, succeeding the ailing Marshall as secretary of state.[20] War, breaking out in Korea on June 25, 1950, seemed to validate the American policy as so affirmed. The United States, supported by other United Nations members, defended South Korea with its military as part of the UN's forces.

The remaining part of containment policy, the North Atlantic Treaty Organization, had been snapped into place on April 4, 1949. Containment had impelled its birth as a necessary military complement to the economic assistance of the Marshall Plan and the specialized covert labors of the CIA. West Europe, granting its general need of American support and resources, easily accepted the value of a substantive fighting force. Great Britain had articulated the desirability of a regional alliance with Canada and the United States, and the continental Europeans quickly extended the conception. One argument was the self-evident necessity of a ground force as counter, less absolute than the atomic bomb, to the massive Soviet army. In the United States bipartisan support was assured by the Senate resolution of June 1, 1948, as initiated by Arthur Vandenberg, the influential Republican chairman of the Senate's Foreign Relations Committee, who had been a supporter of the Marshall Plan as well. NATO began with twelve nations, presently adding Greece and a balancing Turkey, and, by 1955, West Germany. A validating choice, General Dwight D. Eisenhower, the triumphant but pacific World War II commander, became its first head.[21] The United States was well-positioned to balance off the Soviet threat, NATO proving its value by never being called in to fight during the Cold War.

At the same time the Western and Central European countries were integrating themselves economically to receive the Marshall Plan aid in the Organization for European Economic Cooperation of 1948. The OEEC would be transformed into the more independent Organization for Economic Coordination and Development (OECD) of 1961 while leading to the European Coal and Steel Community of 1951, the European Economic Community (called the Common Market) in 1957, the European Union of 1992, and the European Monetary Union with its Euro in 1999—all this to joint United States and European advantage. With the Marshall Plan the United States had impelled a great advance in European economic and political unity.

During the Truman period and beyond, with the economy functioning so well, much of the political energy lavished on it was wasted. A natural politician of the second order, Truman first tried to replicate

Roosevelt's New Deal with an ambitious civil rights program, an increase in minimum wages, expansion of Social Security, slum-clearing, housing, and a national health program. Although Congress passed the Keynesian Employment Act of 1946, the law could not assure the full employment its backers wanted, and the legislators rejected most of his program, including its civil rights ambitions, in its first response. Truman countered by desegregating the military, a great advance of itself and leading to the successful civil rights effort by the blacks in the 1960s. Later, in Truman's second term, Congress conceded a minimum-wage increase along with more Social Security benefits. Meanwhile, union labor had to accept a bill denying the closed shop, which required union membership as an employment condition. But then reasonable persons agreed that this would have given labor unions too much power, with negative economic effect. The issue, generating much heat, was presently abandoned. Indeed, a deeper consensus in the nation accepted a general compromise. As Truman's Republican successor, Eisenhower extended Social-Security benefits to 10 million more workers. He also created the new Department of Health, Education, and Welfare in 1953, naming a woman to head it. The nation was more united politically, socially, and economically than its rhetoric sounded. All this expressed the solidity and resilience of the American political economy, permitting an effective foreign policy addressing the exigencies of the Cold War. The economy could respond generously and variously to the varied new needs.

The major instrument of the United States in the Cold War was its economy, with the Marshall Plan as its advance guard. In an ad hoc way the nation had been helpful from war's end to the early period of the plan. President Truman had ended Lend-Lease too soon in August 1945, but the United States gave $7 billion in nonmilitary aid to that point. Beyond that, with the United States contributing 75 percent, but outvoted by other United Nations members, the UN Relief and Rehabilitation Association provided Europe with $2.5 billion in aid from November 1943. Under full American control Marshall Plan funds began flowing before the situation became desperate. In sum the Marshall Plan countries got $13.7 billion from June 1947 to the end of 1951, the equivalent of $100 billion today. By September 1948 European industrial output was up 10 percent over the same quarter of 1947, and success was evident from the early days. From 1947 to 1951 the aggregate GNP of the Marshall Plan nations went from $120 billion to $160 billion. The aid funds amounted to only 5 percent of their average GNP, but it was an essential factor in stabilizing their currencies by permitting them to purchase essential goods in dollars from US suppliers. From the early 1950s Europe entered a period of increasing prosperity building upon economic efficiencies underused during the Great Depression and swallowed up by the war. At war's end, speaking for many more than left-wingers, the British historian A. J. P Taylor said: "Nobody in Europe believes in the American way of life, that is, private enterprise."[22] Through its practical political economy the Marshall Plan provided the perfect response.

The Marshall Plan administration and the CIA fought the Cold War together. Their financial connection was through the "counterpart funds," a splendid device for enhancing the value of the American aid funds. A private European producer, for example, paid with his country's currency for American imports, that country's Marshall Plan agency, in turn, paying for them in aid-funds dollars. The local currency went into the agency's account to be invested at home in production-enhancing operations, thus food initially in some cases, production facilities, transportation repairs, and other postwar economic needs. These counterpart funds also paid the operational expenses of the European Cooperation Administration, the Marshall Plan's European offices—and those of the CIA. The ECA made $685 million of counterpart funds available to the CIA over five years.[23] While it is not clear how much was actually used, cash remained the CIA's best weapon. Here, again, the great American economy provided the foundation of containment.

Richard Bissell, a former economist, was the key personage in the early Marshall Plan-CIA connection as deputy to Paul Hoffman, the ECA administrator. Bissell passed on the funds to the CIA covert operations chief, Frank Wisner. According to the book *The CIA and the Marshall Plan*, already cited here, Bissell said that Hoffman disliked the action but accepted it. Bissell told the author: "Wisner came for the funds but said I didn't need to know what for…. [W]e needed this procedure because we needed a political action arm."[24] After the ECA was closed down (modest economic aid continuing under another agency) Bissell joined Hoffman at the Ford Foundation, but he was bored and accepted Frank Wisner's invitation to join the CIA.[25] At the CIA from January 1, 1959, he became chief of its clandestine service and was alleged to have responsibility for the development of the U-2 spy plane, a failed Mafia contract for assassinating Fidel Castro, and the more resoundingly failed Bay of Pigs invasion of Cuba in April 1961.[26]

A necessary weapon in the Cold War, the CIA undertook risky operations that were often outstanding failures while its successes were as often ambiguous. It successfully plotted the overthrow of Mohammad

Mossadeq, the nationalist prime minister of Iran in July-August 1953, after he had nationalized the Anglo-Persian oil company. This defense of old-style imperialism gave United States a suspicious character in the minds of many in the old colonial lands.[27] It would have a long trail of after-effects leading to the Iran Revolution of 1979, the taking of American hostages, and other distresses continuing into the new century. Perhaps more directly relevant to the Cold War was the CIA's part in the overthrow of Salvador Allende, the left-wing leader of Chile, in 1973. Allende was aided by the Chilean Communist Party and Soviet intelligence, and might well have led to, or been succeeded by, a Communist regime in the Fidel Castro manner. But to many Latin Americans and Third World people this was another example of a new imperialism; of course the United States was speculating in money and murder. So were the Soviets, who gave the lead in professional ruthlessness. The magnitude and successes of the great American economy, its ultimate strength, were the ultimate response.

In Western Europe, American and CIA success had been aided at first by Stalin's appeasement policy. At war's end the Communist parties of Italy and France could mobilize a third and a quarter, respectively, of their electorates. Yet "Stalin … in 1944-45 reminded the more hot-minded among the French and Italians that this was no time for revolutionary adventures, that Allied unity took priority over narrow political interests of their own."[28] He sent back Palmiro Togliatti, a Comintern operative and the Italian Communist leader, to join the bourgeois cabinet and develop a "kind of New Deal" for Italy. Under Stalin's command in Moscow, on September 14, 1944, Maurice Thorez secretary-general of the French Communist Party, broadcast the order that the party cooperate with the non-Communist resistance groups.[29] This policy ended abruptly after the announcement of the Marshall Plan, the creation of the Communist Information Bureau (Cominform for short) on October 5, 1947 signaling uninhibited Cold War. (The Cominform was a revival of the old Communist International—the Comintern—dissolved as an appeasing gesture to the Allies in October 1943.) There followed such aggressive actions as the Czech coup of February 1948, the blockade of Berlin from June 24, 1948 to May 11, 1949 as an effort to starve out the Allied forces there, and the launching of the Korean War on June 25, 1950. These spectacular operations can be seen as admissions of weakness in their straining efforts to counter American superiority. The Czechoslovak action in Central Europe was easy enough, that distant location preventing any Allied response. When the Allies, led by the United States, successfully, if expensively, provisioned Berlin by air, Stalin simply admitted defeat and ended the blockade. In Korea the fighting for the Soviet Union was done by North Koreans and, later, Chinese troops, the Soviet Union remaining safely above that fray. Stalin was functioning as statesmanlike coward at minimal risk.

The most dangerous episode of the Cold War occurred when Nikita Khrushchev, Stalin long interred, put missile sites on Cuba, an American U-2 spy aircraft discovering them on August 29, 1962. On October 22 President John F. Kennedy demanded that the missiles be withdrawn and announced a blockade of Cuba under the euphemism of "quarantine." The Cold War historian John Lewis Gaddis explained the probable motives as a romantic-revolutionary yearning to make Communist revolution in all of Latin America or at least to deter an American attack on Cuba. The first was an expression of mad Leninist ideology and the other could be seen as a saner reaction to the mad American Bay of Pigs attack on Cuba in the year before. Kennedy's measured response recalled the Kremlin leadership to reason and Khrushchev's colleagues were realistically frightened. On October 28, after the United States mollifyingly promised to remove its missile emplacements in Turkey, Khrushchev agreed to withdraw the Cuban missiles. The episode cast a lightning flash of clarity on the Cold War. The Soviet Union was admitting it was overmatched as a military force and a political economy.[30] Two years later Khrushchev's colleagues voted him out of office, the Soviet Union setting course for annihilation as absolute as threatened by a nuclear war.

With the Soviet Union producing a bare third of the American gross national product (GNP), Stalin knew that his country was too weak to challenge the United States. Unlike him, Khrushchev had momentarily forgotten that proportion under the force of the Marxian ideology. The old master had used the ideology to make up part of the difference between American and Soviet power, but knew it was not enough. After all, Lenin's miniscule band of conspirators had seized vast czarist Russia with little else than that ideology, but Stalin could calculate his chances in his time. This does not mean that the Soviet Union was not a danger, but it was more of a danger to itself than to its enemy. Still, as such, it was capable of causing more loss of life than any rational opposing leadership would want to provoke. If the Cold War was no contest for the United States, the Soviet Union was still a serious adversary and merited containment according to Kennan and Dulles. Its end, we might remind ourselves, gave the right to Kennan's policy *and* prophecy.

Khrushchev and the Soviet Union had been taking advantage of the American embarrassment in Vietnam. The French had departed that colonial empire after their great defeat at Dienbienphu in 1954. The colonial episode, however, had merged with the West's Cold War defense, the nationalist movement of Ho Chi Minh, strengthened by Communist ideology and aid, exercising a powerful attraction there and elsewhere in southeast Asia. For the American leadership the imperialist stigma of its action paled before the imperatives of the Cold War.

The administration, as led by Presidents Eisenhower, Kennedy, Johnson, and Nixon, regarded Vietnam as a central component in the policy of containment against George Kennan's opinion that it was stretching American power too far. But, again, he had no good arguments that could combine *Realpolitik* considerations and military facts.[31] Long before American troops entered into it, Eisenhower gave his reasons in a statement to the press on April 7, 1954: "[Y]ou have ... a dictatorship that is inimical to the free world ... the 'falling domino' principle ... the possible sequence ... loss of Indochina, of Burma, of Thailand, of the [Malay] Peninsula, and India following ... millions and millions and millions of people ... [and speaking as military man] it turns the defensive chain of Japan, Formosa, of the Philippines, and to the southward it moves on to threaten Australia and New Zealand."[32] He might have mentioned a real event filling out the "domino" abstraction; after Pearl Harbor the Japanese, launching out from China and threatening Australia and New Zealand, swept through that area, including Thailand, Burma (today's Myanmar), and Indonesia, to the border of India by May 1942—in less than six months. This was the same logic accepted then and now for American action in Korea in 1950. No one, from Kennan to Robert McNamara, has directly rebutted it. McNamara, Kennedy's and Johnson's defense secretary until the latter dropped him, was injected with guilt and persuaded to regret. The best he could do was: "They might be correct, but I seriously question such judgments." He could only weakly doubt that the Soviets or Chinese would have acted differently if the United States had left Vietnam in the mid-60s.[33] The pattern of Soviet and Soviet-aided expansion, on the other hand, provided strong countervailing arguments.

One has only to look at the map of southeast Asia to see the dominoes in the light of what we securely know. Vietnam is a perfect example of the forces of world Communism allied with self-respecting nationalism. Both Laos and Cambodia would fall with Vietnam, Cambodia succumbing with perhaps a million and a half of its people murdered by the fanatical leadership of Pol Pot. Thailand also had an ambitious and threatening Communist Party. India had two lively Communist parties. Indonesia was nearly taken over by Communists in 1965 until its army massacred a vast number of them, ranging, according to estimates, from eighty thousand to a million. Enough survivors remained as a serious threat in Indonesia. One cannot say that all of these countries would have fallen—India was probably too big and religious to succumb—but the others were clearly vulnerable. Later, in a 1997 book, one expert had indeed proposed that "it is…hard to see that … Vietnam had anything much to do with the demise of the Soviet Union."[34] It is hard to see his argument. In its later period, needing foreign-policy victories to impress and distract them, the increasingly rachitic Soviet Union was making its people and its satellites increasingly unhappy. A vast advance in southeast Asia would have given it longer life. Containment, peacefully helping cause the Soviet collapse, was more successful that its agonized author would admit.

Of course the war was a bloody Machiavellian interlude lasting too long, an agony for all. It killed 58,000 Americans (about 50 percent more than are killed annually in automobile accidents) and perhaps two million Vietnamese, whose lives, we should say, were worth as much. These were the merciless realities of *Realpolitik*. As a central part of the world peace process, the Americans paid the price for world leadership and the Vietnamese paid for their dignity. This is not to claim that it was a "just war," whatever that might be.

Like Korea, Vietnam represented a stalemate, although the United States had to decamp as if defeated. But it remained there long enough to prevent the Soviet Union, having lost its élan, from taking advantage of the situation. Meanwhile the American economy, having corrected its major weaknesses, was continuing to generate more productivity, prosperity, and sheer power. After falling to $56.4 billion in 1933, its gross domestic product (GDP) rose steadily from the pre-Depression height of $103.6 billion to $293.8 billion in 1956, to $526.4 billion in 1960, passing $1 trillion to $1.03 trillion in 1970, and going on to more than $11 trillion in 2004.[35] Inflation (a Keynesian heritage requiring some correction) averaged about 3 percent annually and imparted a considerable buoyancy to the GDP while reducing its value. But the real increases were large. The Employment Act of 1946 provided for the Council of Economic Advisers to guide policy, but it had a modest role because the major economic dislocations had been eliminated. Thus the Federal Reserve System was now a fully effective central-bank organization, and economic advice now attempted a better balance between inflation and deflation than heretofore. The move toward free trade prevented the United States from beggaring its good neighbors in the Great Depression manner. While problems remained, they did not upset the nation's economic stability. With its 5 percent of the population and its 49 percent of the industrial capacity in 1945, the United States was well positioned to lead the world economy, hence the American Empire.

American science, technology, and management combined had shown their greatness in World War II. From industrial accomplishment the nation had made a quantum leap into radioactive power (and its destructiveness) with the atomic bomb and was under way to produce the hydrogen bomb by 1952. Another comparable leap was the computer, the basis of the revolution in information technology (IT). In 1943, following British conceptions and driven by military aims, Americans created a huge, room-sized computer to calculate values for artillery tables. Its potential was then exponentially expanded in 1947 when its forest of vacuum tubes was replaced by transistors, solid-state devices for amplifying, controlling, and generating electrical signals. This permitted miniaturizing the whole and led, from the 1970s, to the now familiar personal computers of the desktop or laptop size, among many other computing instruments. The miraculous IT revolution took the form of a flow of electrical signals regulated by transistors, the signals saying nothing more than 1 or 0 in their digital language. Their simple alternation expressed all the communicable information: words, sounds, colors, shapes, mathematical formulae, photographs of body parts, workings of the brain ... a flood of information at virtually instantaneous speed. From the early postwar years the United States found the computer, connected by the boundlessly extensible Internet network, eerily appropriate to its style and economic management—and, inevitably, power. The computer and information technology were made for America, but America made them together in its image of Taylorean efficiency.

Against this the Soviet Union offered the promise of Marxian ideology developed into a formidable structure by Leninist-Stalinist social and industrial engineering. "We will bury you," Khrushchev boasted to Western representatives before he disappeared. He meant, as he explained, not nuclear war but the historically determined victory of communism over capitalism, proletariat over capitalist.[36] Granted that the ideology had its practical attractions to working and intellectual classes, Khrushchev had nevertheless given it too much work to do. A few figures permit a realistic comparison of the competitors.

Begin with postwar 1946 when the USSR had a per capita income of $1,913 (in 1990 dollars), rising to a $3,013, thus by more than a third, when Stalin died in 1953, and $4,439 when his successor Nikita Khrushchev was dismissed in 1964. Again we remind ourselves of the inherent inaccuracies in Soviet statistics, possible deceptions and lack of a free society's correctives, and, in the case of per capita income, the fact that the Soviets spent a greater proportion of national income on the military than the Western nations by a multiple of four or five. The low levels and the great proportional increases are, however, credible from what we know of the place and time. In those years, 1946, 1953, and 1964, the United States had a per capita gross domestic product (GDP) of $9,197, $10,613, and rising to $12,357 in Khrushchev's terminal 1964. Increasing its lead, the American per capita GDP was $27,948 in 2001. Soviet Russia, ascending from a very low base figure, had barely more than one fifth of the American per capita income in 1946, somewhat less than one third in 1953, and somewhat more than one third in 1964. Against 5 percent in the American case, calculate 20 percent of the national income going into military expenditures, the Soviet government having mercilessly deprived its proletarian society for the sake of pure killing power.

To this record we append the final figures in the USSR's life and afterward, when near-stasis began by the mid-1980s. Its per capita GDP was at $6,703 by 1984, struggled to $7,098 by 1990, and then fell to $6,409 in 1991, the last year of its life. The GDP of the post-Soviet area then fell to $3,854 at its lowest point in 1996, to rise to $4,844 in 2002, in its somewhat free-enterprising new life.[37]

We can add another layer of meaning by a transparent overlay showing the leadership, thus Khrushchev from 1953/54 to 1964, Leonid Brezhnev until 1982, and, following the virtual interregnum of Yury Andropov and Konstantin Chernenko to 1985, ultimately Mikhail Gorbachev to 1991. Vulgar, ruthless within bounds, Khrushchev, son of a miner and grandson of a serf, survived Stalin's purges and attempted a middle course between Communist ideology and common sense. This led to the "Thaw," relaxing Stalin's rigors and horrors without fundamental change. Brezhnev, a trained engineer and party *apparatchik*, built his power on the Soviet industrial system while limiting his vision to it. His leadership meant a slow decline descending into a swifter disintegration. From 1985 to the end, Gorbachev, at 54 representing a newer generation and trained as a lawyer, attempted to reform the system. His policy of glasnost (openness), however, undercut the accompanying perestroika (restructuring) and ended in a collapse of the whole structure of the Soviet Union. The system depended too much on repression and, as we shall see, died of freedom or the suggestion of it.

We return to the banal sense of our economics lesson. The Soviet Union had tried to substitute governmental administration for the purposefulness of Adam Smith's invisible hand. Free competition operating by supply-and-demand uncannily determines a satisfactory solution to the infinite problems. Lenin's all-responsible apparatus had to make all the economic decisions from the building of a steel complex to the selection of a given number of colors for a given number of fabrics of given qualities. Of course the Great Depression showed practical limits to Smith's theory, but just a pinch of Lenin's or Roosevelt's socialism could be sufficiently therapeutic. Lenin's complete system, while effective for the military operation of revolutionary war, lost the peace, its forcibly drafted personnel eventually rebelling. Most persons got poor pay for undemanding work, which they could scamp almost to taste and interrupt according to need, for example, to run out to buy goods always in short supply. Their rulers, the *nomenklatura*, monopolized the good things, the best housing and education for their children, for example, in an order that was infinitely more hierarchical than any aristocratic or bourgeois society. The incentives for honest work lacking, the motif for the unprivileged was: "You pretend to pay us, and we pretend to work." Hence the accumulating wretchedness, dishonesty, bullying, sadism, sleaze, inefficiencies—the self-destruction of the Soviet state. "Certainly, the perceptions of the population by the late seventies were that economic conditions were actually becoming more difficult, and scarcities getting worse."[38]

Khrushchev and Brezhnev inherited the ideological thrust into all the world, a physical project that became more absurd with every additional kilometer. Obliged to expand everywhere, they saw their power splintering and attenuating as it departed from their Eurasian land mass. One need only look at the globe to see the impossibilities. In their hopeless mission they sent widely scattered aid to the Third World, including India, Afghanistan, Iraq, Turkey, Egypt, Ghana, and Guinea, with little advantage and contradictory effects, Somalia and Egypt resenting their support in Ethiopia, for example, and the Ethiopian government and others eventually overthrown. In Latin America they committed general failure around the small, tightly encapsulated Cuban success. Brezhnev then entangled the Soviet Union hopelessly in Afghanistan after invading it on Christmas Day 1979. But even if all of these actions had suc-

ceeded, they would have totaled to the trivial. They had been pursuing
Lenin's ideologically driven, wrong-headed thesis, derived from Marx,
that great colonial wealth was propping up capitalism. Marxist addition
has seldom added up.

The contest between the Soviet Union and the United States was also
fought out on the terrain of the other nations from France and Italy to
North Korea and Japan, and even Red China and somewhat socialist
India. Like the Third Republic with a weak executive and overeloquent
legislature, the Fourth Republic of France (1944-58) nevertheless defeated
Communist efforts, greatly improved its postwar economy, freed Morocco
and Tunisia, and soberly accepted its ejection from Indo-China. But it
tried to retain Algeria, the resolution beginning with a war between France
and Algeria and a simultaneous civil war between the French government
and the 3 million *colons* (French settlers with an infusion of Italians and
others) aided by a mutinous French army. Charles de Gaulle, who had
given up on the Fourth Republic after leading the Free French, was called
in to apply magic and did: he tamed the Army, resettled the colons in
France, and organized the Fifth Republic with a stable presidential system. In 1947 the Fourth Republic had begun by making enough sense to
support Jean Monnet's organization of his economic planning authority
on the American model. Encouraging the economy variously, President
de Gaulle retained the Monnet Plan and stabilized the currency at the
old rate of five francs to the dollar. In 1979 a book by a former Monnet
Plan official celebrated thirty prosperous postwar years, thus *Les Trente
Glorieuses ou la Révolution de 1946 à 1975*, recalling the "three glorious days" of the Revolution of 1830. He recorded: infant mortality per
1,000 going down from 84.4 to 13.8, average life span up from 61.9 to
69.1 years, and average well-being (1932 = 100) from 87 to 320.[39] All
this was in the context of American aid and influence, the Ministry of
Finances in 1947-48 abolishing subsidies, and letting the market laws
operate.[40] "After 1978 liberalism was the order of the day."[41]

Italy, similarly responding to the postwar challenges with American
help, plunged into liberal capitalism. Luigi Einaudi, governor of the
Bank of Italy, later budget minister and Italy's first president (1948-55),
adopted a "quasi-liberal line … not shared by the majority of politicians,
who nevertheless were still in no position to intervene directly, and so
let the liberalization of the economy take place."[42] Becoming the world's
fifth largest industrial power, Italy improved her economic situation
more than any other leading nation in the century. In the period 1950 to
1980, approximately sharing the growth of France and West Germany,

her GDP rose 5 percent annually, cumulatively a magical rate. In war-shattered 1945 her GDP had been down to $87.34 billion (1990 dollars) from $154.7 billion in 1939. It rose vigorously to $114.42 billion in 1946 and, without a single relapse, continued in that pace upward every year to the end of the century, thus $165 billion in 1950, $293 billion in 1960, $521.5 billion in 1970—and more than $1 trillion from 1997.[43] Odd evils attended the production of this wealth, including an ever wealthier Mafia and enough scandals to annihilate or reduce the leading political parties of the postwar era before the century's end. But Italy had become an active partner of the United States and the free world in the Cold War.

Germany's two parts became the great champions of either side of the Cold War. Between 1951 and 1976 West Germany increased its population from 47,456,000 to 61,531,000, and East Germany saw itself reduced by 2 million from 18,355,000 as they fled its prisonlike character.[44] In West Germany, the Federal Republic of Germany from 1949, constructive changes building upon the Weimar Republic created a remarkably easy economic and political order—a political economy pacific within and without. With these proportions remaining approximately the same, the fractionally leading Christian Democratic Union (CDU), and its Bavarian ally, the Christian Social Union (CSU), got 31 percent of the vote in the first elections, the Social Democratic Party (SPD) 29.2 percent, and the liberal middle-class Free Democratic Party (FDP), balancing the two, was at 11.9 percent; the Communist Party, the electorate reacting to the atmosphere from the East, remained insignificant at 5.7 percent.[45] The CDU, uniting Catholics and Protestants, buried their historic hostility to each other. At a party conference in 1959 the Social Democrats formally gave up both their anti-clericalism and the pure socialist theory and class-ideology of their origins.

Economic leadership was provided by the research economist Ludwig Erhard, who propounded the theory of the "social market economy," thus an approximation of the consensual idea of a mixed economy. Given the Marshall Plan financing, Erhard could introduce the currency reform of June 18, 1948, which started with a stable mark (at about four to the dollar) that stayed stable in a context of economic freedom. He then worked the repeal of some 90 percent of the price regulations the next month as Allied and German officials trembled. The West Germans rose to economic well-being on the escalator of the 1950s, notably the 1952-58 "Golden Years," an early accompaniment of the French *Trente Glorieuses*. Industrial production, indexed at 100 in 1950, was at 248 in 1960, 435 in 1970, and 486 in 1974. Unemployment began at 8.1 percent in 1950, fell to 4.2 percent in 1955 and to 1 percent in 1960; it dropped .7 percent in 1971.[46] These last figures suggested the need for additional labor and the FRG began to import more and more *Gastarbeiter* from Spain, Italy, and Turkey: 80,000 in 1955, 300,000 in 1960, and, in 1970, 2 million, a tenth of the labor force. Income was increasing in the decade after 1960 at an annual rate of 5 percent, the per capita average rising from 4,331 marks in 1960 to 8,790 marks in 1970 and 16,281 marks in 1978.[47]

East Germany, becoming the German Democratic Republic a few weeks after the Federal Republic was formally founded, was a laboratory example of sovietization. The appeasing Stalin played democratic social-ist for the moment, permitting the existence of the Social Democrats, the Christian Democrats, and the Liberal Democratic Party of Germany along with the favored Communist Party. First, on April 20-21,1946, the Social Democrats were forced to join the Communist Party to form the Socialist Unity Party (SED). Then the two other parties were eliminated when the SED failed to win the election in October 1947, the resistant leaders being imprisoned. The SED became the one party of a one-party state. From 1947, after some 1,900 plants were dismantled and shipped to the Soviet Union as reparations, the remaining firms were nationalized over the next two to three years. A new economic administration moved upon the private shops, which were doing 82 percent of the business in 1948, and soon took them over. The last sector to submit to socializa-tion was agriculture. The government had quickly broken up the great estates, thus annihilating the conservative landowning class, and created some 500,000 small farm holdings. Beginning in 1949 they were then impressed into collectives, the now classic sovietization process.

W. R. Berghahn, the German historian cited here, saw "East Germany … as a barely dispensable cornerstone of Soviet-dominated Eastern Europe…." The most successful of all sovietized economies, thus jus-tifying Lenin's respect for German efficiency, the German Democratic Republic was in eighth place among the world's industrial nations; its industry was growing at an annual rate of 6 percent from 1966 to 1975, the GDP doubling from 1960 to 1975. Still Berghahn found a gap of 30 percent to 50 percent between East and West German real income; some staples in East Germany were cheap but eggs, butter, fruit, and coffee were "several times more expensive." He did not factor in the housing stock, which except for what was built for show or the habitation of the elite, was shabby and steadily deteriorating.[48] East Germans could live in shabby semi-comfort with no fear of unemployment. But then one should also factor in the pervasive spying and the humiliation of life as servants of alien masters and an alien dominating idea. In the end, the East German authorities would open the Berlin Wall and the people freely celebrated Free Germany's victory by joining it en masse.

And yet, reviewing the achievements of the new united Germany at century's end, one can be disappointed. Consider the culture of the short-lived Weimar Republic: the scholarship of historian and sociologist Max Weber; the scintillating cynicism of Bertolt Brecht; the egregious cracker-barrel philosophy of Oswald Spengler; the great, overphiloso-phizing novels of Thomas Mann; the Nazi-adoring philosopher Martin Heidegger; the aristocracy-adoring, philosophizing businessman and government minister Walther Rathenau; Albert Einstein; the architec-turally pioneering Bauhaus and its leader Walter Gropius; the Frankfurt School with its creatively wrong-headed Marxian sociology and thought; the quantum theorist Werner Heisenberg; and the poet Stephan George. The reasonable Federal Republic of Germany failed to match the Weimar Republic's cultural creativity. One need not ask why the GDR failed in every way.

If the two Germanies incorporated two opposing statements about free enterprise and socialism, and the United States and Soviet Russia, then Great Britain, America's partner in the Cold War, expressed an oddly contradictory one. She inconsistently represented a theoretical and op-erative Trojan horse in the area of American influence by plunging into unqualified socialism and denial of the morality of free enterprise. For she formally and democratically denied the social justice of a free-enterprise society, her own as well as the glaring example of the United States. She would apply socialism to take back the surplus wealth expropriated by the British capitalists and distribute it fairly to the people. This was explicitly articulated in the Labor Party program of 1918 and promised in the campaign for the election of July 5, 1945. The electorate agreed although most voters did not quite realize what it meant.[49]

Labor's electoral victory made Great Britain the only democratic nation possessing a clear mandate to carry out an unqualified socialist program—a revolution, if in the unviolent British style. The election had produced a majority of 393 seats in Parliament for the Labor Party against 213 for the Conservatives; the votes were 11,995,152 against 9,888,306. Labor had been committed to socialism by its "Labour and the New Social Order," a report by a party subcommittee submitted in January 1918. It proposed to reconstruct "society itself" to escape "the decay of civilization itself" by means of the "democratic control of industry." This would assure "the sharing of the surplus wealth for the common good." The method would be the "scientific reorganization of industry no longer deflected by individual profiteering on the basis of the common ownership of the means of production."[50.] The British program had been conceived by a party minority. Nevertheless, the Labor Party set out to nationalize major industries and control the economy more tightly in a socialist sense. It took over coal and communications in 1947; railroads (already public corporations or closely supervised) on January 1, 948; electricity, April 1, 1948; gas, May 1, 1949, and iron and steel, February 15, 1951. Between 1945 and 1958 a vast administrative action merged 800 mines, 550 electrical firms 1,000 gas authorities, and 5,800 trucking operations. "For a reform ... so widely heralded as the triumphal realization of socialist progress nationalization turned out to have been vaguely conceived...." In the 1950 election Winston Churchill charged: "Socialism with its vast network of regulations and restrictions and its incompetent planning ... is proving itself everyday to be a dangerous and costly fallacy. Every major industry ... has passed from the profitable or self-supporting side of our national balance sheet to the loss-making debt side."[51] Statistics measured generalized inefficiency and crippled production. This failed revolution later convinced the government to reverse itself and begin a comparably huge privatization action. In one of many examples, during the late 1980s, the British Steel Corporation doubled productivity with half the work force. By the year 2000, in sum, only six nationalized industries, some operating with private subcontracts, were left. Labor had given up on privatization, which was "no longer a mainstream political issue in Britain."[52]

Two other related policies intensified the negative effect of British socialism. One was the mindless application of Keynesian low-interest policy, a practical antidote during the Depression-era deflation but toxic in the postwar inflationary period. The effect was a great currency drain to other countries offering higher interest rates and a further devaluation of the pound. At the same time the precipitous introduction of the Beveridge Plan for health and welfare, however excellent and even necessary in the long-run, added greater burdens to the budget. The effects of socialism, Keynesian economics, and Beveridge's welfarism protracted the war deprivation. While food rationing ended in her neighbors by 1950, Britain continued it, an instructive example of equality, until 1954, when the Conservatives finally stopped it. Britain remained hungry, shabby, and dingy too long.

Recall the annual growth figures for the other European nations during the postwar years, thus for the period 1949-59, 4.5 percent for France,

7.9 percent for West Germany, and 5.9 percent for Italy. Against this the United Kingdom had a 2.4 percent annual growth rate: half, less than half, and a third of her European competitors. The British figures were not much better for 1959/60-1970/1. Clearly, Great Britain was not growing enough, improving only to 2.9 percent in the second period while France improved all the more and the others slipped back only slightly.[53] Britain had begun the twentieth century with the world's highest per capita as well as GDP, higher even than the American. While her national income remained greater than her European competitors in the years following World War II, the French and German GDPs exceeded it by 1970 and even the Italian was ahead by 1980.[54] In the 1980s the British economy would, however, be shaken up by privatization and the vigorous policy of Prime Minister Margaret Thatcher, the most virile leader in British politics since Churchill. Once more Adam Smith's invisible hand would prove itself in the American manner and Britain would, whole-heartedly or not, rejoin the American Empire.

Pursuing and refining the principles of political economy that had made it great, its one rival vanquished, the United States bestrode the globe later in the twentieth century. Without wanting to do so, without even being aware of it, the United States had created a global empire of the most economic kind. It had not burdened itself with the responsibility for managing land mass or other people. It could exercise its influence sufficiently by the cool measuring out of cold cash. This was the best kind of empire. Of course the nation would not get all that it wanted, but then it could be led into the unwise exercise of its tremendous power.

Notes

1.   George F. Kennan, "The Sources of Soviet Conduct," reprinted in his *American Diplomacy 1900-1955* (Chicago: University of Chicago Press, 1951), 566-82; quotations, 576-77, 582.
2.   Quoted, John Lukacs, *George Kennan: A Study of Character* (New Haven: Yale University Press, 2007), 98. But this comment was later in Kennan's career.
3.   Excerpts from Telegraphic Message from Moscow of February 22, 1946, quoted, George F. Kennan, *Memoirs 1925-1950* (Boston: Little, Brown, 1967) 547, 553, 554, 557, 557-58.
4.   Kennan, "The. Sources of Soviet Conduct," 110, 116.
5.   John Lewis Gaddis, *The Cold War: A New History* (New York, Penguin, 2001), 34-35.
6.   Kennan, Memoirs 1925-1950, "The Marshal Plan," 325-53.
7.   Marshall's speech, annex 2, reprinted, Charles L. Mee, Jr., *The Marshall Plan: The Launching of the Pax Americana* (New York: Simon and Schuster, 1984), 271-73.
8.   Walter LaFeber, *America, Russia, and the Cold War* (New York: McGraw-Hill, 1993: 7th ed.), 51-65.

9.   Sallie Pisani, *The CIA and the Marshall Plan* (Lawrence: University Press of Kansas, 1991), "Coordinating Intervention," 58-80.

10. Tim Weiner, *Legacy of Ashes: The History of the CIA* (New York: Doubleday, 2007), 28-29; quotations, 29.

11. John Ranelagh, *CIA: A History* (London: BBC Books, 1991), 53-55.

12. Mee, Jr., *The Marshall Plan*, 118.

13. Weiner, *Legacy of Ashes*, 298-300.

14. Ranelagh, *CIA: A History*, 53-55.

15. Gaddis, *Strategies of Containment* (New York: Oxford University Press, 2005), 77-86; quotation, 77.

16. Quoted, *ibid.*, 149.

17. Gaddis, *We Now Know: Rethinking Cold War History* (Oxford: Clarendon Press, 1997), 126.

18. Kennan, *Memoirs 1950-1963* (New York: Pantheon, 1972), "The 1957 Reith Lectures," 229-66; quotation, 261.

19. Kennan's not-quite extinguished diplomatic career confirms his decreasing affinity for diplomacy. He was ambassador in Soviet Russia from May to November 1952. On a stopover to Berlin under way to London for a conference, he unburdened himself to reporters on the dank Soviet Union atmosphere, comparing it to that of Nazi Germany. Stalin was so offended by the comparison that he declared Kennan persona non grata and refused to let him return to Moscow. In 1962-63 Kennan was ambassador to Tito's Yugoslavia, where he enjoyed good relations. But he was so distressed when Congress refused to grant Yugoslavia an agreed-upon financial concession that he resigned his post. He happily returned to scholarship at Princeton.

20. LaFeber, *America, Russia, and the Cold War*, 96-98; quotations, 96; see also Gaddis, *Strategies of Containment*, "NSC-68 and the Korean War," 87-124.

21. See especially Lawrence S. Kaplan, *NATO and the United States* (New York: Twayne, 1994; 1st ed.: 1988), William Park, *Defending the West: A History of NATO* (Brighton, UK: Wheatsheaf, 1986), and Andreas Wenger, ed., *Transforming NATO in the Cold War* (London: Routledge, 2007).

22. Greg Behrman, *The Most Noble Adventure: The Marshall Plan* (New York: Free Press, 2007), 4, 200, 333; quotation, 29.

23. Weiner, *Legacy of Ashes*, 28.

24. Quoted, Pisani, *The CIA and the Marshall Plan,* 73.

25. Behrman, *The Most Noble Adventure*, 329.

26. Weiner, *Legacy of Ashes*, 160, 161, 173-77.

27. *Ibid.*, 81-92, 315-17.

28. Adam Ulam, *Stalin*, 66.

29. Marc Lazar, *Maisons Rouges: Les partis communistes français et italiens de la Libération à nos jours* (Paris: Aubier, 1992), 42 ("New Deal"); Joan Barth Urban, *Moscow and the Italian Communist Party* (Ithaca: Cornell University Press, 1986), 191, 197.

30. Martin Walker, *The Cold War* (New York: Henry Holt, 1994), 170-82.

31. John Morton Blum, *Years of Disorder: American Politics and Society, 1961-1974* (New York: Norton, 1991), 282.

32. Quoted, David L. Anderson, *The Columbia Guide to the Vietnam War* (New York: Columbia University Press, 2002), 257-58.

33. Robert S. McNamara, *In Retrospect: The Tragedy and Lessons of Vietnam* (New York: Random House, 1995), 319, 320.

34.   Robert D. Schulzinger, *A Time for War: The United States and Vietnam 1941-1975* (New York: Oxford University Press, 1997), 335. On Vietnam see also Leslie H. Gelb and Richard K. Betts, *The Irony of Vietnam: The System Worked* (Washington: Brookings Institution, 1979), and Stanley Karnow, *Vietnam: A History* (New York: Penguin, 1984; 1st ed.: 1983).

35.   U. S. Department of Commerce, Bureau of Economic Analysis, US Gross Domestic Product, *bea.doc.gov*. These figures express current dollars.

36.   Quoted, Gaddis, *The Cold War: A New History* (New York: Penguin Press, 2005), 84.

37.   Maddison, *The World Economy*, tables, 100, 101. The military proportions of the national income, Nove, *An Economic History of the USSR*, 321.

38.   Quoted, Geoffrey Hosking, *The First Soviet Society: A History of the Soviet Union from Within* (Cambridge, MA: Harvard University Press, 1985), 387, 382.

39.   Jean Fourastié, *Les Trente Glorieuses ou la Révolution invisible de 1946 à 1975* (Paris: Fayard, 1979), table, 36; 267.

40.   François Caron, *An Economic History of Modern France*, tr. Barbara Bray (New York: Columbia University Press, 1979), 273-76.

41.   Robert Gildea, *France since 1945* (Oxford: Oxford University Press: 1996), 98.

42.   Vera Zamagni, *The Economic History of Italy 1860-1990* (Oxford: Clarendon Press, 1993), 322.

43.   Maddison, *The World Economy*, tables, 50, 52. See also Zamagni, *The Economic History of Italy*, 321-78.

44.   V. R. Berghahn, *Modern Germany: Society, Economy and Politics in the 20th Century* (Cambridge: Cambridge University Press, 1982), table, 284.

45.   *Ibid.*, table, 45.

46.   Karl Hardach, *The Political Economy of Germany in the 20th Century* (Berkeley: University of California Press, 1976), 186; Berghahn, *Modern Germany*, tables, 258, 266.

47.   Hardach, *The Political Economy of Germany*, 195; Berghahn, *Modern Germany*, 226, 227; tables, 262.

48.   Berghahn, *Modern* Germany, 192-97, 226-49; quotations, 230.

49.   Leslie Hannah, "A Failed Experiment: The State Ownership of Industry," in Roderick Floud and Paul Johnson, eds., *The Cambridge Economic History of Modern Britain*, 3: *Structural Change and Growth, 1939-2000* (Cambridge: Cambridge University Press, 2004), 94-96, 107-11; quotations, 107.

50.   Labour Party (Great Britain), *Towards a New World: Being the Reconstruction Programme of the Labour Party* (Microform: New York: W. R. Browne, 1918), 6, 19, 13.

51.   W. N. Medlicott, *Contemporary England 1914-1964* (London: Longman, 1976; 1st. ed., 1967), 478; Churchill quoted, 508.

52.   Hannah, "A Failed Experiment," 91, 99, 107-11; quotations, 94, 107.

53.   Gildea, *France since 1945*, table, 86.

54.   Maddison, *The World Economy*, tables, 62, 88, 64, 65, 89.

10

Disorder and Early Sorrow: The Sixties

The spirit of the Sixties cuts perpendicularly across the simple line of progression of national and world events. As articulated by the New Left, aggressively correcting the present order *and* the old left, this sense dominated the ideology, as distinct from rational thinking, of the period. The New Left denied the past and angled away from its promised future. Its activists, turning their backs on the Cold War, deceptively cleared a space in the murk of that conflict, which had another generation to run its course—long after the New Left itself had disappeared.

The period's denials affected the officially recorded political logic of events profoundly. By those denials the New Left would change the character of the struggle with Soviet Russia and give the United States unexpected new strengths. It would transmute its self-conscious perversity and become a constructive episode in American and world history.

The new movement expressed the urges of a minority of a minority, only one of many contradictions. Another was the comparable and solider importance of the black civil rights movement, a grander minority, which antedated the New Left and gave it much of its will and force. Vastly raising their political and economic situation, the blacks achieved a social revolution during the first half of the Sixties. The black movement was purposeful, conservative, legal, logical, based on religion as community and hope, and administered with American managerial efficiency. The New Left, denying antecedents and seeing visions, swathed itself in an anarchistic freedom from government, laws, economy, and history. But American pragmatism made the collaboration between New Left and black community possible.

Under impulsion of the black actions, with a measure of New Left support and eloquence, other groups suffering discrimination organized themselves and fought for *their* rights: Latinos, women, homosexuals, the handicapped, and younger people and students generally. The social revolution rippled through American society and beyond.

The American operations of the New Left's whites and the less specifically politicized blacks also stirred Europe to spasms of associated demands and protests, indeed intimations of revolution. Once again Americans had seized world leadership. This was contemporary with the revolution in information technology and even culture generally. Since the 1940s the New York school of painters, such luminaries as Jackson Pollock, Willem de Kooning, and Mark Rothko, had begun to dominate painting. Now in the persons of its students, a traditionally revolutionary France, a feebly socialized Britain, an Italy cured of fascism, and a (West) Germany virtuously free of Nazism essayed imitative protests during the 1960s into the 1970s. Like the American left, the Western Europeans did not quite know what they were protesting against. The American blacks would show both the way. Cravenly absent from this action, apprehensive of undirected revolution, were the Soviet Union and its satellites.

The protests curved back against the land of their origins. Increasingly powerful and transgressive, the United States invited them in its Cold War maneuvers, the new situation given point through the Sixties by the war in Vietnam. Succeeding French hegemony, the United States was presenting itself as a greater imperial power. The European protestants, moreover, could ally themselves with the American New Left against American policy. Other contradictions followed.

In the United States radicalism launched itself into the unspecified latitudes of what it called "participatory democracy." It was a purer political society than the radicals had felt themselves experiencing, but it remained unspecified, an anarchistic vessel containing yearnings rather than ideas. The blacks, for their part, were proceeding under the leadership of their civil rights organization, the National Association for the Advancement of Colored People (NAACP), founded in 1909, supporting other more precisely purposeful civil rights groups. The others often got more attention for their tactical actions than the NAACP, established in New York City, got for its grand strategic role. The major allocation of functions derived from the North-South division of the nation and its civil rights. The South, defeated in the Civil War, but reluctantly and half reconstructed, remained resistantly alien, "like another country within the United States, locked into its own massive apartheid system, implacably enforced by legal and political authorities," a biographer of Martin Luther King, Jr., began his study.[1]

The Supreme Court had earlier rationalized the South's separate position in its decision Plessy *v.* Ferguson of 1896, which upheld "separate but equal facilities" for the races. This was an expression of generalized prejudice and a recognition of the South's obduracy. The NAACP's strong legal staff assailed this decision with the common-sense argument that separate could not mean equal, and the court finally succumbed in Brown *v.* Board of Education of Topeka, Kansas on May 17, 1954, after more than a half century. "From Brown *v.* Board flowed a robust civil rights torrent that, in time, became a great wave of the legal equal-rights legislation that even a Congress disproportionately influenced the by old-guard Southerners, could not resist," as a New York *Times* editorial saw it.[2]

The action of the NAACP and the black community thus proceeded in strict legality, one of many instances of the distinction between their operations and the ethos and acts—the principled anarchism—of the sympathetic New Left. Of course this did not prevent black groups like the Black Panthers or unorganized blacks from committing overt violence, nor the New Left from hiring the best legal experts to defend themselves against the law's sanctions.

The first significant action, both spontaneous and organized, to realize the Supreme Court's decision occurred in the year of the 1954 decision. A forty-two-year-old seamstress, who was secretary of the Montgomery, Alabama, branch of the NAACP, and trained in defending social rights, decided she was too tired to move to the segregated back of the bus. She refused and was arrested. Protesting, the local blacks staged a one-day local boycott of the bus system. This led to an extended boycott lasting nearly a year. Montgomery's blacks organized a car pool with 200 drivers giving 20,000 daily rides, the Supreme Court effectively sanctioning the boycott with the decision that confirmed the unconstitutionality of bus segregation. This marked the beginning of the historic civil rights action revolutionizing the position of blacks in American society.

Out of the boycott emerged the unlikely figure of the young Martin Luther King, Jr., as his biographer thought, to become a perfect example of charisma. Son of a powerful Atlanta preacher, assisted by a plagiarized trial sermon and Ph.D. dissertation, young King became, first, a valedictorian graduate of a Pennsylvania seminary and then a doctoral graduate of Boston University. He had begun his pastoral career in 1954, the year of the Supreme Court's decision, at the age of twenty-five as Baptist minister in Montgomery, Alabama. He immediately showed that the charisma and a personally developed philosophy were authentic, the latter associating itself fluently with Mahatma Gandhi's principle of nonviolence. He also demonstrated the marvelously effective union of courage and caution of a statesman of social revolution.[3]

When the black ministers of Montgomery formed an ad hoc group to organize the boycott, King found himself leading it with inherited and natural skill. Suddenly he was a national leader. In Montgomery the whites reacted with violence and he learned to fear for his life. A bomb blew up, harmlessly as it turned out, on the porch of his home. He was arrested for allegedly speeding; a black group freed him. King quieted three hundred indignant supporters with knives and guns: "We want to love our enemies—be *good* to them."[4]

At first the NAACP, under executive secretary (1955-77) Roy Wilkins, another great black leader, was doubtful of King, but the clear-headed, secure Wilkins repressed a sense of rivalry and found more reason to support him. King, taking advantage of the organizing talents of Ella Baker, a field representative of the NAACP, created the Southern Christian Leadership Conference of ministers, priests, and rabbis in 1956. The SCLC became King's personal instrument, but he had to accept help not only from the NAACP but also from two other ad hoc organizations, the Congress of Racial Equality (CORE) founded in Chicago in 1942 to attack discrimination, and the Student Nonviolent Coordinating Committee (SNCC, called "Snick"), emerging in April 1960 from meetings held in North Carolina by the indefatigable Ella Baker following sit-in actions at segregated lunch counters. The SNCC functioned as a "kind of commando strike force for deep-country operations."[5] Challenging segregation, CORE organized the often dangerous Freedom Rides to invade the South, SNCC also joining on Freedom Rides and undertaking many more sit-ins. In New York Roy Wilkins managed the national strategy. From Atlanta, where he had joined his father as co-pastor of Ebenezer Baptist Church in November 1959, the younger King led the SCLC in direct attack on segregation in the heartland of the South.

In Atlanta King was joined by four figures who would help him achieve his national dimension. A. J. Muste, a former pastor of Dutch origins who had become a radical and passionate pacifist, expressed his ideals in founding the Fellowship of Reconciliation, a position sympathetic to King's. Bayard Rustin was an openly gay former Communist and the frequent associate of Muste's. A. Philip Randolph, a socialist and president of the Brotherhood of Sleeping Car Porters, was a leader of many progressive actions. Another was, like Rustin, a public embarrassment to King, but an indispensable ghost-writing colleague: Stanley Levison, a wealthy attorney connected to the Communist Party. All four were essential in shaping King's strategy.

Guided by his advisers, backed financially by the NAACP, King functioned as point leader in a series of civil rights actions from 1962 to 1965, the SNCC and CORE operating as outriders at risk of violence and death. They were sending volunteers, including whites, on Freedom Rides to end segregation in transportation, an action of greater demonstrative than practical effect at first. Then, following the definitive success in Montgomery, King joined the SNCC in an eight-month general desegregation campaign in Albany, Georgia, during late 1961 and early 1962. He had to give it up as a failure, Albany retaliating by closing the officially desegregated library and parks.

The year 1962 was the birth year of the New Left as an identifiable movement. On June 11-15 the SDS, the Students for a Democratic Society, gathered itself at its national convention in the educational camp of the United Automobile Workers in Port Huron, Michigan, some fifty miles north of Detroit. There it produced the Port Huron Statement with its conception of participatory democracy, (which will be examined here later). Warmed by the blacks' actions, the SDS took fire quickly. Another revolutionary statement, Betty Friedan's *The Feminine Mystique*, appeared on February 19, 1963.

The year 1963 was the annus mirabilis of the civil rights movement, but at a mortal price. On June 12 Medgar Evers, state field secretary of the NAACP, was shot dead at his home in Jackson, Mississippi. On September 15 four black girls were killed in the bombing of a Birmingham, Alabama church. In the resulting disorder two black youths were killed. At their funeral King stubbornly insisted, "We must not lose faith in our white brothers."[6] The next year, on June 20, three civil rights volunteers, two white youths and a young black, were murdered in Mississippi. In 1963 *Time Magazine* named King its man of the year and in 1964 he was awarded the Nobel Peace Prize.[7]

King and colleagues were trying to move President John F. Kennedy, who was cautiously sympathetic but mindful of the Southern white vote. Against his political instincts, the president had been obliged to send federal troops to assure the admission of the University of Mississippi's first black student. Riots killed two persons. But King and his people, the civil rights movement taking on more momentum, overwhelmed Kennedy's reluctance.

Like his admired Gandhi, King showed his greatness in humiliation. He was attacking rigid segregation in Birmingham. Also, in April and May 1963, he had to contend with the public safety commissioner, one Eugene, called Bull, Connor, a classic Southern police personality, in a classic action. At one point Conner used hoses and police dogs against children. Marching on City Hall, King was himself dragged into a police vehicle and jailed nine days with no outside contact for the first two days. There, on the borders of a newspaper, he wrote the famous twenty-page "Letter from Birmingham Jail."

King was addressing the white ministers wanting more forbearance in dealing with injustice: "But when you have seen vicious mobs lynch your mothers and fathers at will … when you are fighting a degenerating sense of 'nobodiness,' then you will understand why we find it difficult to wait." He cited St. Paul and Martin Buber. The action and the words brought the world's attention to the "miracle of Birmingham."[8] As many as 758 demonstrations in 186 towns demanding open public accommodations were counted. They forced a reluctant President Kennedy to call for a comprehensive civil rights bill.[9]

Bayard Rustin and A. Philip Randolph then organized the March on Washington for Jobs and Freedom. This gave King another opportunity to use his preacher's charisma and skills at the Lincoln Memorial on August 28, 1963. A crowd of 200,000 to a quarter of a million, a third of them white students or whites encouraged by the SDS and New Left generally, listened to him: "We will not be satisfied until justice runs down like waters and righteousness like a mighty stream…. I have a dream that one day on the red hills of Georgia the sons of former slaves and the sons of former slaveholders will be able to sit down together at the table of brotherhood."[10] Viewing and listening on television John F. Kennedy said: "He's damned good. Damned good."[11] Three months later Kennedy was assassinated. Lyndon Baines Johnson found it politic to carry out the agenda that Kennedy had not quite achieved.

Functioning powerfully in the White House, using his great legislative connections and experience, President Johnson drove the Civil Rights Act of 1964 to realization on June 10 after a 75-day filibuster requiring cloture. Now definitively, with the federal government to enforce the laws, discrimination was legally ended in education, employment, and public facilities. There remained the vote, which Southern laws and procedures, embedded in Southern prejudices, still nullified.

On March 7, 1965, leading some 600 demonstrators on a march from Selma toward the state capital in Montgomery, Alabama, a radicalized leader of the SNCC took an initiative suggesting that King was faltering. The group got no farther than the bridge leading to the Montgomery highway, where state and local police used clubs and tear gas to drive them back. Two days later King himself led a symbolic march to the bridge but replied with prayer when the troopers blocked the march. King and colleagues then took recourse to the law and a judicial opinion supporting their avowedly peaceful demonstration. On March 21, protected by active agents of the law, three thousand marchers set out for Montgomery, the number increasing to 25,000. They arrived five days later in Montgomery after sleeping in the fields. To King, Selma meant "the end, benediction," the Voting Rights Act becoming law on August 6, 1965.[12] In 1965 three million black Americans had registered to vote; by 1990 the number exceeded twelve million. The number of black elected officials went up from 500 to 7,200, thus by a factor of fourteen; two thirds of them in the South.[13] Once again a peaceful gesture of King's had produced grand national substance.

The struggle for racial justice then began escaping King's mastery and moved toward the sense of the New Left and its anarchistic suggestions. Young blacks questioned his temporizing conduct at the famous bridge in Selma. The Black Panther Party, created in 1966, flourished guns and sought open warfare. In 1966 the SNCC (we remind ourselves: Student Nonviolent Coordinating Committee) would be captured by Stokely Carmichael, an advocate of black power, which he interpreted as a corollary of the New Left's ideology. Less structured objections expressed themselves as riots. On July 16, 1964 a series of violences erupted in New York City and, in emulation, other cities. During the next three summers much more destructive urban riots took place. The first, in Watts, in south central Los Angeles, raged over six days from August 10, 1965. Uncontrollable looting and arson devastated an area of 50 square miles, 35 persons died, 600 buildings were destroyed or badly damaged, and 4,200 arrests were made. In 1966 riots swept through 16 cities. In 1967, after Cleveland anticipated matters on April 16, a great riot killed 26 in Newark, and on July 27-29 the worst one, in Detroit, killed 43, injured 2,000, and destroyed or damaged 1,300 buildings, while 2,700 businesses were looted. Victims included black businesses, while middle-class blacks and their children were seen exuberantly participating in the looting. The responsible black leaders, King prominent among them, condemned the actions as self-harm.

The emerging leaders of the SDS found the black actions exhilarating and undertook their own expressions on a new level of their own violence. The white community, furthermore, granted that the blacks had real grievances, and indicated a willingness to help ghetto persons and areas. In 1968 a presidential advisory commission chaired by Governor Otto Kerner of Illinois warned that the nation threatened to split into two societies, "one black and one white—separate but unequal." To correct the socioeconomic injustices "programmes on a scale beyond anything hitherto envisaged were vital…." So emphasized, the protests had positive effects to be set beside the restrained statesmanship of Martin Luther King, Jr.[14]

In 1967 King tried to transcend both the unhappy results of three summers of black violences and the limits of his efforts for his cause. He undertook to lead the Poor Peoples Campaign, a union of white and black poor, but he failed to win the usual collaboration he had received from church-based Christian churches in the south. In March 1968 he also tried to help 1,800 black garbage workers demanding union recognition in Memphis, Tennessee, but a march of protesters got out of control and disintegrated. In the evening of April 4, preparing a new march, he went out on the balcony of his hotel and a white supremacist shot him fatally. Riots erupted in Washington and a hundred other cities.[15]

King had achieved all that was possible at the time. His more radical associates faltered. Stokely Carmichael, taking over the SNCC in 1966, resigned in the next year, joined the Black Panthers, but later settled in Guinea in Africa. The SNCC dissolved. So did CORE (Congress for Racial Equality) under another leadership after expelling its white members. His achievement perfect, King left a great and real heritage. In the real world the NAACP, under the sober leadership of Roy Wilkins and his successors and with its membership of a half-million, has carried out the substance of that heritage.

The black civil rights movement served as a remarkably secure fulcrum lifting the other actions of the Sixties. That stability tended to keep the more extravagant proponents of revolution grounded in the American reality they despised or thought they despised. The new revolutionaries, as we have seen, were revolutionaries doubled, rejecting the old capitalistic society but also the structured opposition to it in the form of Marxism. Of course all this was not as pure as pure belief would have it. There was, on second thought, no alternative to Marxism's great ideological wealth, and the New Left began to draw upon its renewable fount of thought.

A contemporary context was provided by an army of French thinkers beginning with Jean-Paul Sartre although, like Marx, he was beginning to be old hat while being continually renewed. They were best designated as structuralists shading into post-structuralists, the structural component provided by the anthropologist Claude Lévi-Strauss, who saw kinship patterns as providing a social structure dominating society and history and canceling out Sartre's individualistic existentialism. But then Lévi-Strauss's view associated itself with Marx's massively structured ideology. In mixed agreement and disagreement intellectuals like Jacques Derrida, Roland Barthes, and Michael Foucault moved on to poststructuralism, which emphasized the cultural context of structuralism and its capacity to overwhelm structure itself.

In the United States the émigré professor Herbert Marcuse had uncannily interpreted the mood of the Sixties and provided a precisely calibrated thought mechanism for appropriate action. One began with denial, moved on to contradiction in Marxian style, and debouched into a puddle of quasianarchism, the shallow end station of all these rivulets of ideas and velleities. Besides Marcuse, the practiced professional, the practiced amateur Thomas Emmett—"Tom"—Hayden, the former editor of a student newspaper, served as a link to minor minds like his own.

Marcuse, as a graduate student and a Social Democratic activist in Germany, had learned to manage Marxian politics and ideas along with Hegelian thought. He was using Hegel and the contemporary Martin Heidegger to historicize and philosophize Marx. Marcuse developed his ideas in two major works, the first adding Freud to harmonize these thinkers in his *Eros and Civilization: A Philosophical Inquiry into Freud* (1955).[16] He gave all this contemporary point in his *One-Dimensional Man: Studies in the Ideology of Advanced Industrial Society* (1964).[17]

Marcuse was using the dialectic in the Marxian (and thus the Hegelian) manner to homogenize reality into easily manageable ideational units. He went on to communicate his sense in a series of dialectical dyads that were self-canceling oxymorons, thus "democratic unfreedom," "free competition at administered prices," "liberty ... a powerful instrument of domination," "a police-universe," and, in a concluding thought, "the realm of the irrational becomes the home of the really rational."[18] To persons intensely but vaguely dissatisfied with their world, these verbal contradictions seemed to suggest higher truths than "is" as an irreducible statement. One purpose of all these impossibilities of meaning was to dispose of Marx's proletariat. Marcuse condemned it as the "'people,' previously the ferment of social change [having] 'moved up' to become the ferment of social adhesion." Now Marcuse proposed to substitute "the outcasts and outsiders," who could function as an improved proletariat, the rebellious university students of the Sixties encouraged to apply for the role.[19]

Marcuse's texts were the metaphysics, but Tom Hayden's Port Huron Statement of June 15, 1962 was the working document of the Sixties, mentally unburdened, superlatively jejune, simplistic, vacuous, and innocently self-centered in the American manner. It began: "We are people of this generation, bred in at least modest comfort, housed now in universities, looking uncomfortably to the world we inherit." Grandiosely, "we may be the last generation to experiment with living." The statement, while enjoying the union's hospitality, dismissed organized labor as tending to apathy and prosperity. Proffering a scattering of incomplete suggestions, it admitted to a general lack of ideas: "[W]e have no sure formulas, no closed theories." Its one solution was encapsulated in the term "participatory democracy," a phrase that circulated in the New Left of Europe as well. No one, certainly not Hayden, was able to fill "participatory democracy" with secure meaning. It suggested that "decision-making of basic social consequence [should] be carried out by public groupings."[20] Its general discussion implied that protest actions could correct the decisions of the electoral lawmakers, a kind of redundant and self-contradictory democratic chaos. Surely the idea, in the context of the Sixties, rationalized protest to the point of using force.

The SDS was the party of the New Left to the extent that the movement had an identity and to the extent that the SDS was sufficiently organized to call itself a party. Many adherents of the New Left had not consciously or even dreamily joined the SDS, but they let it represent them, more or less, until the decade ended. The parentage went back to 1905 and the Intercollegiate Socialist Society, with such members as Jack London, Clarence Darrow, and Upton Sinclair; it was renamed the League for Industrial Democracy in 1921, and revived as a left-wing anti-Communist leftist organization in the 1930s. In 1959 one Alan Haber, entitled field secretary, led it as the Student League for Industrial Democracy, thus SLID. In 1960 it had three campus chapters and changed its name to Students for a Democratic Society. In 1962 at Port Huron, Hayden made his presence felt in the drafting of the statement and his election as president for 1962-63. The anarchistic SDS had to fight off the intrusion of Communists, whose organizing skills were seductively useful. It defended itself against them by giving its individual chapters complete autonomy to escape possible Communist control. At the same time, against charges of Red-baiting, it professed a policy of anti-anti-Communism. This permitted the SDS members to be friendly to revolutionary Cuba, Nicaragua, and the Vietcong while denying that the USSR was a threat to the free world and dismissing the Cold War from their minds. The result was an insecure compromise while marking an eventually fatal fault line. Yet, in the fertile field of the Sixties, the SDS grew apace, in 1962-63 claiming 1,000 members in nine chapters and toward the end of the decade it had perhaps 100,000. Two influences led it into sometimes purposeful action, the black movement, as we have seen, and the war in Vietnam. The counterculture of the Sixties provided a nurturing context.[21]

The rationally organized and purposefully focused blacks provided the saving structure for the loose SDS operations. "For northern supporters were swept into SNCC's force field, " Todd Gitlin, an SDS leader, wrote in his chronicle of the period, continuing with renewed feeling, "From 1960 on SDS felt wired to the staggeringly brave, overalled, work-shirted college students.... SNCC was there, bodies on the line, moral authority incarnate." In 1966, nevertheless, the radical black power advocate Stokely Carmichael succeeded a moderate leader and expelled the whites.[22] Similarly, other blacks like Black Panthers chose to turn away from them. Indeed, all blacks found the whites patronizing. The SDS organization, which was becoming more radical itself, found another purpose in the Vietnam War, but it owed much to the blacks, who were modestly indebted to it.

While the black civil rights movement, except for its radical associates, aimed at a reformed order, the New Left, approximately led by the SDS, lusted toward a denial of order. If it was convinced of the general social injustice, its remedy was not justice, but mockery of bourgeois justice. Anything standing was a target. In a prophetic film in 1953 a Marlon Brando character replied to "What are you rebelling against?": "Whadda ya got?" Todd Gitlin, the personal historian of the Sixties, felt that marijuana ("grass") and, more powerfully, LSD ("acid") "open[ed] up an *inner* space, so that you could *space out*, for the sheer exultant point of living." In 1965 the cashiered Harvard professor Timothy Leary and Ken Kesey, author of the popular novel *One Flew Over the Cuckoo's Nest* (1962), arrived with like-minded friends in a psychedelically painted bus in the San Francisco Bay area. The mad hero of Kesey's novel was a paradigmatic figure of the period, and professor and novelist joined in a paradigmatic moment with the poet Allen Ginsberg who chanted Hindu phrases while Leary pronounced, "Turn on, tune in, drop out." Gitlin recorded: "[T]wenty thousand young people ... reveled, dropped acid, burned incense, tootled flutes, jingled tambourines, passed out flowers, admired one another, felt the immensity of their collective spectacle."[23]

Many, calling themselves hippies, heads, or freaks, entered into thousands of communes from California and Washington to New England, New Mexico, the East Village of New York City, and Bayswater in London and other foreign locales. There were Asian-type religious groups, experiments in group marriages, "Jesus freak houses," centers of radical politics, and back-to-the-land experiments in agricultural self-sufficiency. One commune, dominated by the petty thief Charles Manson, achieved a greater fame by murdering, according to its members, some thirty-five persons. Most of the communes disintegrated, leaving a few to struggle into the twenty-first century.[24] In 1970 the Yale law professor Charles A. Reich celebrated the counterculture in his best-selling *The Greening of America* as achieving the recovery of "self": "The Corporate State will be ended as miraculously as a kiss breaks a witch's enchantment."[25] But the New Left and the SDS were dead certain about Vietnam. In the end the United States had two and a half million troops there.[26] The commitment required the draft, an issue particularly acute for military-age college students.

The first overt protest action began in the University of California at Berkeley in September 1964 as a general operation against the university for serving reaction. On December 2, when the university tried to forbid it as a political operation, some 6,000 students and radical sympathizers, identifying themselves as the Free Speech Movement, joined a "sit-in" in an administrative building. Police arrested 700 demonstrators the next day, but the movement, gaining faculty support, won its point in establishing the right of political activity on the campus. With President Johnson's escalation of the Vietnam War, the SDS's general activity became antiwar agitation.

On March 24-25, 1965 faculty and students of the University of Michigan began the first "teach-in," an unbounded colloquium permitting unending protests, in imitation of the Berkeley sit-in. This inspired the National Teach-In in Washington two months later and hundreds of imitations. The agitation now had its modus operandi, as led by an increasingly radicalized SDS.

Washington, as the black civil rights leaders had shown, was an important stage for demonstrations. The National Mobilization Committee to End the War in Vietnam ("Mobe"), composed of SDS members and sympathizers, put on a grand march to the Pentagon on October 21, 1967. It could attract 100,000 demonstrators and the eloquent presence of Dr. Benjamin Spock, Noam Chomsky, Robert Lowell, Dwight MacDonald, and Norman Mailer, the last writing *The Armies of the Night*, a classic of sorts on it. Female hippies inserted flowers in the barrels of soldiers' guns and more aggressively bared their breasts. A group of males urinated in unison in a direction of the Pentagon. Abbie Hoffman and his Yippies (from Youth International Party), a wilder fringe, collectively thought elevated thoughts to levitate it.[27]

In 1968, the year of the barricades (as one book title put it), the great protest climaxed. In April Martin Luther King was assassinated; in June Robert Kennedy, seen hopefully by the New Left as a possible presidential candidate, died similarly. The effect was a "rage released in us," as Todd Gitlin put it in the subtitle of his book, *Days of Rage*.[28] Of course the SDS had been seeking disillusionment and despair, the end station of the utopian dream. But rage had erupted into disorder at Columbia University before Kennedy's death. It would, however, be much greater in August, when the SDS would make a stand for peace at the Democratic presidential-nomination convention.

The Columbia University episode, enduring from April 23 to 30, was the appropriate opening. Tolerated or supported by the other students, SDS militants were objecting to various university-military connections, thus a renewed consortium on government projects, the Naval Reserve Officers Training Corps, and CIA recruiting. They also fell upon a fine black issue. Columbia, needing space in its urban location, was tactlessly planning to build a gymnasium in a park serving a contiguous black neighborhood. SDS members demonstrated at the gymnasium site and, taking a dean hostage, occupied Hamilton Hall, a student dormitory and classroom building. The SDS thereupon seized the old Low Library, now the university administrative center, smoked the president's cigars and trashed two manuscripts of Orest Ranum, an outstanding scholar of early modern France. After various violences and trashings, the police charged Low Library and cleared the university, injuring several students, one policeman suffering permanent injuries when a student jumped on him from a window ledge. They arrested 705. The university president resigned. The gymnasium remained unbuilt. The students won some concessions in the form of slightly more influence on the university administration. It took Columbia University a year and more to reduce the bad feeling.[29]

The best account of the Chicago convention action is provided by Todd Gitlin, a participant able to retain a sense of the real. While the deaths of King and Kennedy generated unrelieved feelings, Vietnam had loosed massive events. The Viet Cong's Tet offensive of January 1968 threatened American strategy and, on March 31, a suddenly disheartened President Johnson, having been told the truth by realistic advisers, broadcast to the nation that he would not run again. He put forward his loyal vice-president, Hubert Humphrey, a northern, labor-friendly liberal, as his successor. That made the convention in August a strait gate of decision and gesture.

Todd Gitlin expressed the double sense of the situation and the SDS's highest hopes: "How stop the war, or (as a growing segment of the new Left was putting it) make the revolution?" This called for Gitlin's "rage" to act out "participatory democracy." The objective was to halt the convention unless it voted to stop the war. He was, however, appalled to hear the usually temperate Tom Hayden "speak in chillingly cavalier tones about street actions that would run the risk of getting people killed." SDS and its allies fought—trashed—in actions centered around Lincoln Park on the North Side, Grant Park across from the Hilton Hotel housing the convention delegates, and the Amphitheatre housing the convention. Protestants broke police-car windows, hurled rocks, bombs, obscene insults, and bags of urine and feces, and built barricades. The powerful and unintimidated Mayor Richard J. Daley mobilized 12,000 police, some of them enraged, clubbing demonstrators at the Hilton. The convention delegates voted down a peace plank by 1,569 3/4 to 1,041 1/4 votes.[30]

Humphrey was nominated and underwent defeat by Richard Nixon. In Vietnam the war went on. Yet the New Left had enforced better policy than it demanded or realized. It had helped drive President Johnson from the White House. It constrained the government to a policy leading to our humiliating defeat, but a defeat, as it turned out, better than a victory, the fighting proving too difficult in the circumstances. The New Left helped prevent extending it unnecessarily. President Richard Nixon covered the defeat skillfully with the policy of Vietnamization, a euphemism for fleeing Vietnam by 1973. The hopeless Vietnamese government could not on its own withstand a patriotic movement, however ruthless to its own people.

Containment in southeast Asia, however, lasted long enough to succeed, the craven American departure not altering the sense of it. By 1975, when the Viet Cong entered the capital, the Soviet Union had become too rigid to make much of the victory and only four years later stumbled into the trap of Afghanistan. In the Sixties the New Left had served its country well. This is a reminder of the Cold War, which the radicals and many other Americans preferred to forget. But the movement had even more to contribute to the Cold War victory.

The New Left had been usefully jejune in its thinking about the sense of American policy in Vietnam. But it had based itself on reality for black civil rights and women's rights. In his *Sixties*, often cited here, Arthur Marwick moved fluidly: "From Civil Rights and Student Protest to Women's Liberation and Fundamentalist Feminism," as his subheading read. Women "were brought together in stimulating interaction in a period when all authority systems, all power relationships ... were subject to the most intensive scrutiny...." This was a natural context for Betty Friedan's moderate feminism, which saw that "the American dream was in many ways a nightmare for American women." The solution, appearing obvious to men as well as women when even suggested, was a truly equal partnership of the sexes. Inevitably, the women "could not avoid taking on the defining characteristics of the other protest movements of the Sixties, anarchic anti-authoritarianism and ruthless fundamentalism."[31]

A mother of two and wife (until her husband took to beating her after the book's success), Betty Friedan was a capable radical journalist and magazine writer. Communicating her sense with ruthless skill and unrecognized heartbreak, she spoke of "the problem that has no name [which] lay buried, unspoken for many years in the minds of American women." Pathetically, "it was a strange stirring ... a yearning that women suffered in the middle of the 20th century in the United States. Each suburban wife struggled with it alone." The old leftist Friedan seemed unaware that, like Herbert Marcuse, she was excising the working class and its wives from her world. The suburban woman, disposing probably of two automobiles, "matched slip-cover material ... chauffeured Cub Scouts ... lay beside her husband at night afraid to ask herself the silent question—Is that all?" The problem was "the feminine mystique," which as Friedan explained in her introduction to a 1997 edition, resulted "when women were defined only in sexual relation to men." She saw them existing only "as childlike dolls" in the excessively male imagination of Sigmund Freud.[32] It had been a powerful statement, particularly because it was so measured. As she recognized in herself, she could not help agreeing with him that women wanted, *needed*, husbands (or lovers at least), and children. But, she insisted, they had to have work and the accompanying dignity.

The success of her book thrust Betty Friedan into a position of active leadership. The result was the National Organization for Women (NOW), proposing to achieve a "truly equal partnership with men [and] take the actions needed to bring women into the mainstream of American society." NOW began life on October 29, 1966 with three hundred members. The objective was to "break through the silken curtain of prejudice and discrimination against women in government, industry, the professions, the churches, the political parties, the judiciary, the labor unions, in education, science, medicine, law, relationships, and every field of importance in American society." In the tranquillity of the century's end, Friedan recalled, "This was a period when everybody was liberating themselves and liberation was news. You had SDS, the student movement; you had the Vietnam War, the peace movement, you had the grape pickers striking ... you had SNCC...." She had tried and failed, however, to recruit black women against the resistance of their men; she quoted Stokely Carmichael's words, "'The only position for women in SNCC is prone.'" Like the SDS and other reform organizations, except for the NAACP, NOW became radicalized. Giving up the presidency in 1970, she remained at a benevolent but prudent remove from the organization, finding NOW "wracked by divisiveness" in 1975. In 1999 she saw it and "the other women's organizations ... stuck a little in the time warp and rhetoric of earlier years."[33] The internal conflict weakened a NOW campaign for the Equal Rights Amendment to be added to the Constitution, which failed by the ratification deadline of 1982. Some of NOW's promise had dimmed, but like the black rights action, it was part of a broadly successful drive for greater dignity and functionality in American society.[34]

The SDS, after its passionate assault on national and urban authority in Chicago, gathered itself meanwhile for its climactic effort the next year. The student movement had become not only radicalized, but variously radicalized. In 1965, such was the power of Marxism as thought and action structure, that the SDS had formally repudiated its anti-Communist position. It was not so much Marxism as Marxism-Leninism in the sense of direct revolutionary action. The Weatherman group of the SDS took its name from the song by Bob Dylan, the premier rock troubadour, "You Don't Need a Weatherman to Know Which Way the Wind Blows." The accelerated developments moved through the SDS convention in Chicago in June 1969, the events known vaingloriously as the "Four Days of Rage" in October, and the Weathermen's National War Council in Flint, Michigan at Christmastime that year—and explicit action promptly thereafter.

Meeting in the Chicago Coliseum in mid-1969, 1,500 SDS delegates fought over control, destroying the organization in the process. A third were Weathermen and their allies, a third were members of the Marxist Progressive Labor group, and a third were uncommitted. The effective leader of the Weathermen was Bernadine Dorhn, an attractive and imperious lawyer. Using a Communist reversal of reality tactic, she excommunicated the Progressive Labor faction as "objectively anti-Communist and counterrevolutionary." She led out her people, proclaiming, "Long live the victory of the people's war" and chanting the then popular radical slogan: "Ho, Ho, Ho, Chi Minh."

In Chicago in October, to make their point, the Weathermen went on to practice their "Four Days of Rage." Some 200 to 300 of them trashed cars, broke windows, and assaulted and injured 75 police, 250 being themselves arrested. A dynamite blast destroyed a police monument in Haymarket Square. Baffling the indifferent students, this was part of their policy of "kicking ass," which also had squads invading blue-collar high schools attacking teachers in Pittsburgh, Boston, and Detroit. Other bombings followed the Chicago explosion, some 250 from September 1969 to May 1970 in ROTC and draft board buildings, induction centers, and other federal offices, but the Weathermen's bombs failed to kill anyone (except for three Weathermen who died in an accidental Greenwich Village explosion on March 6, 1970).

At the seriously meant National War Council at Christmas 1969 the Weathermen imploded. Gitlin recalled Bernadine Dohrn saying, "That's what we're about, being crazy motherfuckers and scaring the shit out of honky America." Referring to the Charles Manson group, she celebrated: "Dig it! First they killed those pigs, then they ate dinner in the same room with them, then they shoved a fork in the victim's stomach. Wild!" But that was nearly the end. The few activists went underground, most of them, including Bernadine Dohrn, surrendered in the late Seventies. On October 20, 1981 three holdouts, including a female survivor of the Greenwich Village blast, killed a guard and two police when they demonstratively robbed a Brink's truck north of New York City. They were captured and sentenced to long prison terms. It remains to balance out what the New Left and the SDS had done.[35]

As in postwar painting, Western Europe followed the American pattern of revolutionary action, plunging into para-anarchism and extending to purposeful murders. Similarly, futility of performance accompanied extremity of belief. This is not to exclude positive as well as negative side results. The most important result was what did not happen, namely, revolution.

The French students had real grievances expressing, however, the inconvenient side of their good fortune, the democratization of European education in American style. With her increasing prosperity France, consciously endeavoring to create a greater class of educated elite, was graduating many more university-level secondary students and building universities for them. In the 1960s the universities of Nanterre and Orsay appeared in the outer suburbs of Paris and others in the cities Amiens, Orleans, Rheims, and Rouen. The Nanterre faculty of letters, rising on the dismal stretch of land, began with 2,300 students in 1964, reaching

15,000 by 1968. In 10 years France's student population had increased from 170,000 to 514,000. In Nanterre as elsewhere facilities and faculty were inevitably flawed. Another grievance, reflecting the spirit of the times, was the denial of entry of male students into female dormitories.[36] Action had begun with demonstrations in Nanterre against the Puritan restrictions on February 14; by March 22 *"incidents graves à la faculté des lettres."* The students of the Sorbonne, the core of the University of Paris, responding sympathetically, the rector got the police to evacuate it on May 3. Classic Parisian violence followed in the tradition of the Revolutions of 1789, 1830, 1848, and the Paris Commune uprising of 1871.

With workers also validating the action, Paris was acting out its revolutionary tradition almost to the ultimate. All the elements were in play in Paris and elsewhere in France: streets torn up, paving zones and other missiles hurled, thousands of students traversing Paris singing the *Internationale*, automobiles and the Bourse (the financial center) torched, high barricades built of commandeered vehicles, battles between young rebels and forces of order, 1,500 demonstrators and 1,900 police injured, 10 million workers out on general strike, eight persons killed, an aborted seizure of the Ministries of Finance and Justice, a government very nearly overthrown, indeed, on second thought, the great leader of that government effectively overthrown. Yet the country quieted down so fast that France made the long Whitsunday weekend of June 1-3 the usual holiday. Some 150 persons were killed on a mid-August weekend in the usual highway accidents.[37]

It had all been not quite serious. Appearing on walls and buildings through central Paris, slogans expressed the students' self-mocking sense of the rising: "It is prohibited to prohibit/The dream is real /Be realistic, demand the impossible/I am a Marxist, Groucho tendency/Long live de Gaulle (signed, a masochistic Frenchman)."[38] Herbert Marcuse, who happened to be in France participating at a Unesco symposium, blessed the revolutionary suggestions he saw, but a student leader dismissed him as unknown to French students.[39] Indeed they were too intelligent to take themselves quite seriously. Unlike the American "Days of Rage," these were days of exuberance. This may suggest why the revolution never came.

If the old revolutionaries Paris and France had failed to make revolution, why had the newer revolutionary, the Soviet Union, symmetrically failed the opportunity? Certainly the machinal Leonid Brezhnev, succeeding the risk-prone Khrushchev only four years earlier, was representing a very mature revolution. Lenin, straining to believe in the revolutionary Germany in 1923 and willing to risk so much to join it, had expressed the true Bolshevik spirit; the Soviet Union in 1968 accorded with Brezhnev and did not. Clearly, a pacific message went out to the national Communist parties, as the actions of the French Communist Party showed. The French workers, aroused by the student uprisings, joined solidly with their strikes and factory occupations, but the leadership of the General Confederation of Labor, controlled for years by the Communist Party, kept them separate from the students and their uproarious actions. As a chronicler cited above has it, this was the "contradiction of May.... [T]he students had set automobiles on fire; the strikers wanted better pay to buy one—or replace what they already had.... Around the occupied factories [the union organization] maintained a *cordon sanitaire* in order to prevent students from entering." Protecting them from infection, their leaders insisted that the workers "had no need of instruction, they had their own responsible chiefs." David Caute, a British leftist historian and activist cited above, quoted a French leftist intellectual on Soviet policy: "'[T]he USSR feared that a revolution sparked by a generational conflict and fired by democratic aspirations in Paris would spread east as well as West and hence the essential congruency of interest between the Kremlin and the Elysée.'" By June 6 the strikes were ending. Caute himself concluded: "The trade union leaders and the Communist Party saved de Gaulle [temporarily, as it turned out] by driving the strikers back to work and swimming frantically into familiar waters like sharks offered a rotting carcass."[40] So ended the revolutionary crisis in France.

The resolution secured all the more firmly the stable order, which Charles de Gaulle had so magically created for his unquiet countrymen. As premier, Georges Pompidou was his adept deputy. Taking the initiative, Pompidou let the rebellious students reoccupy the Sorbonne on May 13 and two weeks later, on May 27, concluded agreements highly favorable to the workers. With that the basic conditions for civil peace were in place. In a television talk, de Gaulle warned of the danger of a Communist dictatorship and got the nation's approval in elections on June 23 and 30. On June 30 a tremendous demonstration of 500,000 supporters marched for de Gaulle on the Champs-Elysées. The French nation, appalled at the thought of losing him, voted hugely for his party. The president however, could not abide Pompidou for saving his government and got his resignation on July 10, but then de Gaulle could not abide his own weakness despite the voters' support. With his profound political instinct he may have felt that his time was over. He demanded a vote on an unpopular and unimportant measure reforming the regional govern-ments. He lost the vote and took that as a signal to resign on April 28, 1969. He died on November 10, 1970. Pompidou was elected president on June 16, 1969, remaining in office until his death (by cancer) on April 2, 1974. France was at peace.[41]

The spirit of the American Sixties had flashed throughout Europe, even in sober Britain, the Soviet Zone, and the Spain of the aging dictator Francisco Franco. In the Soviet Zone the Polish police acted with restraint within zonal imperatives and in January 1968 gently arrested 50 of 200 persons protesting the closing of a play with anti-Russian lines. This was as far the protests were permitted. In Czechoslovakia, also, the students expressed general unhappiness. In 1967 they were clashing with the po-lice, and the minister of the interior mollifyingly apologized to them for police brutality in December. This led to the Prague Spring after a milder Communist became de facto leader and by June was supporting a reform program. The result was a Soviet counterattack. On August 20 Soviet, East German, Polish, Hungarian, and Bulgarian armed forces entered the country and the reform movement was strangulated, the Soviet Union refusing to permit even a suggestion of Western freedom.

The radicalized Western students had approached the spirit of Marx-ism-Leninism but in a free manner more alien to the Soviet Union than to their own governments. The Spanish and British students agreed on moderation. By 1967 and 1968 Francisco Franco was letting his power slip into the hands of efficient subordinates. As early as February 24, 1965 a students' silent march confronted the government with a protest against its control of the major student organization; there followed a cycle of "repression and protest" from December 1967 and four days of "heavy rioting" from April 30, 1968. The University of Madrid was closed on March 28, but reopened on May 6, four days after the govern-ment disarmingly responded that it would build three new universities and two polytechnics.[42] If unrest persisted, students and government had sagely compromised until a better day.

British students, further removed from internal violence, acted in char-acter and carried out a few sit-ins in London and one in Oxford University, the latter calling up a manifesto signed by a thousand others deploring the action. In London, on June 15, 1968, the Revolutionary Socialist Student Federation, representing 2,500 students, was organized; its first conference, in November, heard "ritualized speeches about imperialism." As David Caute saw it, "The vast majority of British students continued to believe that revolution was appropriate for France and points farther afield, but not for Britain."[43]

The most ferocious radicalism, transcending the Weathermen's murderousness, was contributed by Germans and Italians, the Germans expressing themselves ultimately in withdrawing from humanity, and the Italians seeking to improve on Stalinist deadliness. In both cases, as in France, protestants began reasonable campaigns against obviously bad, if understandable, conditions.

In Germany the universities were dominated by the archaic dictatorship of tenured professors. The student population had grown from 80,000 in 1913 to 384,000 in 1965, and by 1966 an alliance of leftist students and faculty was demanding reform, which the government was not unwilling to grant. A radical group, the SDS, the Socialist German Student League (by chance it had the same initials as the American SDS) combined reform demands with a denunciation of American policy in Vietnam. A radical magazine pronounced: "In a society overfed with butter-cakes and baked chickens, German secondary-school students, undernourished with regard to love, are rehearsing revolution." [44]

Out of these predispositions and events arose a tiny movement calling itself the Red Army Faction (RAF). The leaders were German SDS members, two women and a male arsonist and robber of drunks. The RAF killed forty-seven persons in actions over seven years during the 1970s, including the president of an employers' association after his kidnapping and an American lieutenant-colonel. All three Germans were arrested later in 1972 and tried from May 1975 to April 1977. One of the women wrote in her isolation cell: "The feeling that one's head explodes.... Naturally, no lifting of a finger for them...nothing but enmity and contempt.... Suicide is the last act of rebellion." All committed suicide. [45]

In one aspect the Italian action was not so sacrificial, exhibiting a purposeful, indeed a calculating, mad logic. It began upon the rational protests of those groups who wanted and needed more for themselves, workers and university and secondary-school students. While the workers demanded a larger share of the nation's increasing wealth, the students, like those elsewhere, wanted better facilities and more freedom of choice to improve their rigid, uncaring instruction. From November 1967 Italy experienced a wave of university occupations and strikes, accompanied by secondary-school actions. Virtually all of Italy was on educational strike by 1969, cities so engaged including Genoa, Naples, Rome, Florence, Venice, Bologna, Modena, Pisa, Padua, Siena, Perugia, Lecci, and Messina. The Italians were more serious and less ironic than the more anarchistic French while the factories joined the schools in riots and strikes. Italian society was becoming much more radicalized but also reformed. [46]

Italian activism deposited substantial reforms but dragged behind it a death-dealing tail. In the Communist manner the Potere Operaio (Worker Power), among other violent groups, attempted to lead the workers as the rigid Italian Communist Party itself failed to do. It acted only after the general agitation, mollified by the reforms, began to subside in 1969. In a tremendous advance for Catholic Italy, also, a proposed divorce law was introduced in 1970 and confirmed by a vote in 1974.

By a dramatic stroke on March 16, 1970 the Red Brigades kidnapped Aldo Moro, a left-wing Christian Democrat, who had been prime minister five times, and was concluding a deal with Enrico Berlinguer, the Communist Party head, for a unitary government on March 16, 1970. A well-managed action killed his five guards and captured Moro, who was held fifty-five days until 9 May when he was shot after the government refused to exchange thirteen incarcerated terrorists for him. The Red Brigades people, who were sooner or later arrested, knew they would not suffer capital punishment and tried to make their trials, enduring from 1982 to 1994, theaters of accusation. The first trial, with some forty defendants, brought out information on seventeen other murders. The other trials dealt with more than 200 defendants still trying to live in their conspiratorial imagination. This had been "a twilight phenomenon of an epoch now formally ended with the convulsion and radical reduction of Communist culture in Italy. ...."[47]

What was the sense of the Sixties? How *sensible* were the rebellious spirits? What meaning can we give to the whole episode? Avoiding such moral certainties as good and evil, we should try to apply mediocre common *sense* to the cockeyed actions. First, we should rule out an emphasis on the period's more vicious acts as here recounted. We have to live with the spillover, as history records, of murderous acts from virtuous motives, thus, as history reminds us, sixteenth-century church reform and religious civil war, Danton's and Robespierre's—the French Revolution's—incitement to murder and massacre, American genocide in the winning the West, Soviet liquidations and Gulag, and Mao's trashing of tens of millions of lives. What was the sum of what the Sixties had wrought?

We have seen that one advance of the Sixties was unambiguously positive, the revolutionary improvement in black civil rights. It enhanced life for all in marking a great step toward dignity of an important part of the American populace while leading to a greater equality elsewhere as well for other disadvantaged groups: women, young people, children, male and female homosexuals, and physically and mentally handicapped persons. For them this meant more ease as well as dignity, physical facilities for the handicapped like self-propelled vehicles, leveled curbs, and mechanical bus platforms, legal recognition of quasi-marital relationships; and more tolerant attitudes toward the beneficiaries to improve their lives generally. The total is a kinder world for everyone to the extent that it extends.

The moral improvements have brought with them substantial economic benefits. Blacks, women, and the handicapped have been given vastly greater opportunities to function. This has meant a profitable economic revolution for society. Formerly excluded from many occupations, millions of blacks have been flowing into higher professional reaches and the middle class: bank tellers to bank officers, providers of skilled services from store clerks to department managers, technicians repairing computers and lawn mowers, and trainees to corporate presidents. Similarly, women have been rising higher in *their* occupations, as have the handicapped. One result has been a major increase in wealth creation in the United States. But this has been true of other nations in the West, with their growing Muslim population of immigrants, civic virtue being rewarded in dollars, pounds, and euros.

The positive changes affected the course of the Cold War positively. They gave the United States and the West generally greater strength to deal with the last feeble, but still dangerous, aggressive thrusts from the Soviet area. The Soviet Union, more and more suffocated in its thickening ideological carapace, was increasingly limited in matching performance with mendacity. The West met the challenge of the youth and other rebels with remarkable flexibility, tolerance, and even understanding; in Herbert Marcuse's turned inside-out language it co-opted them for the good of all. The result had been a considerable relaxation of the structural impediments to action. While permitting disruptions of administrative efficiency, the Western authorities gave more opportunity to individual and group initiatives, leading to a more efficient administrative process. In the longer run the result was a healthier, more productive society, and one happier with itself. This is not meant to be a picture of the ideal; great errors and injustices persist despite corrections. Nor is this a happy ending of the story. The next episode could end in more annihilation, like that of the World Trade Center towers. We can, however, trust our sharpened senses to anticipate whatever. The West's advantage is its ability, helped by the impulse of the Sixties and now built (but how much?) into the system, to repudiate its worst and change for the continually needed better. In the process the Cold War was won without resort to killing, the most perfect victory in a war. With the radicalism of the Sixties swung away from its perpendicular denials, the period has joined in the movement forward of history.

Notes

1. Marshall Frady, *Martin Luther King, Jr.* (New York: Lipper-Viking, 2002).
2. Rather later, on December 24, 1999, quoted, Gilbert Jonas, *Freedom's Sword: The NAACP and the Struggle against Racism in America, 1909-1969* (New York: Routledge, 2005), 31. The outstanding NAACP lawyers were Charles Houston, William Heny Hastie, and Thurgood Marshall.
3. Early years, Frady, *Martin Luther King, Jr.,* 11-28; Taylor Branch, *Parting the Waters: America in the King Years 1954-63* (New York: Simon & Schuster, 1988).
4. Frady, *Martin Luther King, Jr.,* 36-54; quotation, 46.
5. *Ibid.*, 72.
6. *Ibid.*, 126.
7. *Ibid.*, 125-53; Klaus P. Fischer, *America in White, Black, and Gray: The Stormy Sixties* (New York: Continuum, 2006), 112-20. See also Taylor Branch, *Parting the Waters*, 272-491.
8. Taylor Branch, *Parting the Waters*, 737-40; quotation, 739; Branch, *Pillar of Fire: America in the King years 1963-65* (New York: Simon and Schuster, 1998), xiii ("miracle").
9. Brady, *Martin Luther King, Jr.,* 119.
10. Quoted, Branch, *Parting the Waters*, 881-82.
11. Frady, *Martin Luther King, Jr.,* 127.
12. *Ibid.*, 159-64; quotation, 164.
13. Jonas, *Freedom's Sword*, 226-27.
14. Arthur Marwick, *The Sixties: Cultural Revolution in Britain, France, Italy, and the United States, 1958-1974* (New York and Oxford: Oxford University Press, 1998), 563-65, 572-83; quotations, 581; John E. McWilliams, *The 1960s Cultural Revolution* (Westport, CT: Greenwood, 2000), chronology of events, xvii-xxxvii.
15. Marwick, *The Sixties*, 575-77, 647-56; Frady, Martin Luther King, Jr., 170-205; Fischer, *America in White, Black, and Gray*, 125-36; John Morton Blum, *Years of Disorder: American Politics and Society, 1961-1974* (New York: Norton, 1991), 287-318.
16. See his intellectual biography, Barry Katz, *Herbert Marcuse and the Art of Liberation* (London: Verso, 1982), especially the chapter "Heidegger and Concrete Philosophy," 58-86.
17. Boston: Beacon Press.
18. *One-Dimensional Man: Studies in the Ideology of Advanced Industrial Society* (Boston: Beacon Press, 1964), 7, 84, 120, 124, 247.
19. *Ibid.*, 256.
20. *The Port Huron Statement* (Chicago: Charles H. Kerr, 1990; 1st ed.: 1962), 7, 8, 28-30, 11, 13.
21. See Todd Gitlin, *The Sixties: Years of Hope, Days of Rage* (New York: Bantam, 1987), 81-126; Dominick Cavallo, *A Fiction of the Past: The Sixties in American History* (New York: St. Martin's Press, 1999), 186-249. The SDS history has been carelessly thrown together.
22. Fischer, *America in White, Black, and Gray*, 129-30.
23. Quoted, Gitlin, *The Sixties*, 32, 45, 50, 202, 210.
24. Timothy Miller, "The Sixties-Era Communes," in Peter Braunstein and Michael W. Doyle, eds., *Imagine Nation: The American Counterculture of the 1960's and '70s* (New York: Routledge, 2002), 327-51; Marwick, *The Sixties*, 480-86, Gitlin, *The Sixties*, 404-5.
25. David Caute, *The Year of the Barricades: A Journey Through 1968* (New York: Harper & Row, 1988), 453; the Reich quotation, 454.

26. David L. Anderson, *The Columbia Guide to the Vietnam* War (New York: Columbia University Press, 2002), 43-62.

27. Gitlin, *The Sixties*, 187-88; Marwick, *The Sixties*, 545; Blum, *Years of Disorder*, 280.

28. Gitlin, *The Sixties*, 311.

29. Marwick, *The Sixties*, 656-65. I observed an anguished Lionel Trilling, the distinguished critic and a mild leftist, trying and failing to negotiate with the students in Hamilton Hall.

30. Gitlin, *The Sixties*, 285-340; quotations, 285, 320, 327, 330; see also, Marwick, *The Sixties*, 666-70.

31. Introducing his chapter, "Women's Turn," *The Sixties*, 679-724; quotations, 679.

32. Betty Friedan, *Life So Far* (New York: Simon & Schuster, 2000), 177, 179, 285, 377.

33. Betty Friedan, *The Feminine Mystique* (New York: Norton, 1997; 1st ed.: 1963), ix, xix, 113, 109.

34. See also Maryann Barasco, *Governing NOW: Grassroots Action in the National Organization for Women* (Ithaca: Cornell University Press, 2004); Debra Michaels, "From Consciousness Expansion to Consciousness Raising," in Braunstein and Doyle, eds., *Imagine Nation*; Eleanor R. Klein, *Feminism under Fire* (Amherst, NY: Prometheus, 1996).

35. Extended account in Gitlin, *The Sixties*, 377-444; quotations, 400; "Four Days of Rage," 393-95; National War Council, 399-40. Another account, Peter Collier and David Horowitz, *Destructive Generation: Second Thoughts about the Sixties* (New York: Summit Books, 1989), 95-98 (National War Council). See also Paul Berman, *A Tale of Two Utopias: The Political Journey of the Generation of 1968* (New York: Norton, 1996); Roger Kimball, *The Long March: How the Cultural Revolution of the 1960s Changed America* (San Francisco: Encounter, 2000); Cavallo, *A Fiction of the Past.*

36. Marwick, *The Sixties*, 555-56; Caute, *The Year of the Barricades*, 251 (quoting André Glucksmann in *State and Revolution in France).*

37. Michel Winock, *Chronique des Années Soixante* (Paris: Éditions du Seuil,1987), 235; chronology: 14 February, 22 March; 3, 6, 7 May; 18 August.

38. Caute, Quoted, Marwick, *The Sixties*, 611.

39. Caute, *The Year of the Barricades,* 171.

40. *Ibid.,* 255. See also for the major occurrences of May, Marwick, *The Sixties*, 602-18.

41. Gildea, *France since 1945,* 51-53: quotation, 55. On the events of 1968, see also Geneviève Dreyfus-Armand, *Les Années 68; Le temps de la contestation* (Brussels: Éditions Complexe, 2000).

42. Caute, *The year of the Barricades*, 81-85.

43. *Ibid.,* 345-88; quotations, 345, 354.

44. N. b. the ch. "Domestic Policy in the Era of the New Left," in Dennis L. Bark and David R. Gress, *A History of West Germany*, vol. 2: *Democracy and its Discontents 1963-1988* (Oxford: Basil Blackwell, 1989), 118-36; quotation, 130.

45. Stefan Aust, *Der Baader-Meinhof Complex* (Hamburg: Hoffman und Campe, 1997; 1st ed.: 1985), 658, 272; quotations, 270, 389.

46. Marwick, *The Sixties*, 586-602, 618-32; quotations, 600, 619-20 (Marwick himself). See also Sydney Tarrow, *Democracy and Disorder: Protest and Politics in Italy* (Oxford: Clarendon Press, 1989).

47. Richard Drake, *The Aldo Moro Murder Case* (Cambridge, MA: Harvard University Press, 1995), quotation, 256.

11

Third Way

In his State of the Union Address opening the year 1998, President William Jefferson Clinton saw a solution to the "sterile debate between government is the enemy ... and government is the answer." He proposed, "[W]e have found a Third Way ... the smallest government in thirty-five years, but a more progressive one." For him it meant "a smaller government but a stronger nation." In 1998, also, the Labor prime minister Blair pronounced: "The 'Third Way' is the best label for the new politics which the progressive left is forging." Upon its "passionate ... commitment to social justice" it now ventured beyond "an Old Left preoccupied by state control, high taxation, and producer interests."[1] Against the Old Left he proudly claimed to lead New Labor. Both highly sensitive politicians, Clinton and Blair had learned their political-economic lesson of the late twentieth century.

At issue was the problem of achieving a proper balance between "public investment," expenditure for the immediate common good, as against "sound public finance," the maintenance of balanced budget for the long-run common good. Of course political elements entered into the determination of that balance. Robert B. Reich, Clinton's first labor secretary, responding to his labor constituency and passionate about social welfare, insisted on favoring public investment more and public finance less than did a consensus, which his chief had joined. In 1997 Reich resigned after the president rejected his advice on increasing public investment and continued to follow that of Treasury Secretary Robert E. Rubin, who had been director of the National Economic Council and who preferred a more conservative financial balance.[2] Clinton went on to achieve that rarity, a budget surplus, the United States having risen from a deficit of 3.9 percent of the gross domestic product (GDP) in 1993 to a surplus of 2.4 percent in 2000. Reich believed that such a policy had sacrificed the common good and found a champion in a British-American political economist of leftist leanings.

In his *Clinton and Blair: The Political Economy of the Third Way*, Flavio Romano insisted that their "Third Way [depended] only on technological innovation."[3] In this he was denying what he had just quoted Clinton and Blair as saying. Both were emphasizing the interrelatedness of the many nontechnological factors as well. Moreover, while he might have argued for another balance, as Reich had vainly done, Romano was also simply and arbitrarily denying the reality of a modern economy where public investment and private finance are inextricably interrelated. Of course no policy can claim to be the perfect response to national need, but certain visible factors can suggest better rather than worse solutions, thus the inflation rate, unemployment figures, and comparative production levels. He might have dealt with the contemporary experiences of France and Germany, with their generous social welfare programs and high unemployment rates, not to mention the past experience of Prime Minister Margaret Thatcher.

Indeed Margaret Thatcher had made the Third Way a reality although the American example was an inspiration to her. Enduring Britain's experience of Labor Party socialism, she could see the vigor of the American economy. The situation was ready for her. At her moment, the elections of May 3, 1979, the British wanted to change from the drear days of interminable recovery from the war and socialist-and-Labor hegemony. Returning to power in 1951, the great Winston Churchill had to yield to the Old Left's arrangements. This led to the policy of Butskellism (named for a Conservative and a Labor chancellor of the exchequer), a fused first-and-second way that compromised left and right aims to the benefit of neither. In effect the Trades Union Congress, directing the British unions, could veto laws opposed to Labor's perceived interests. Balancing off Parliament, the TUC was one of two heads of a double-headed government. This was an approximation of the 1917 situation in Russia, with the Petrograd Soviet frequently blocking or paralyzing the actions of the Provisional Government. Margaret Thatcher, an authoritative grocer's daughter calling herself a Conservative revolutionary, changed all that. She won the election of 1979 on the issue of trade union power. She destroyed it. Edward Heath, Conservative prime minister from 1970 to 1974, had started the process by somewhat limiting the political impact of the trade unions with his Industrial Relations Act; Thatcher followed through with laws against sympathy strikes and picketing in 1980, 1982, and 1984. She went on to defeat the miners' union, which capitulated after an eleven-month strike begun in March 1984. Her "main objective ... was to remove [Labor] from the realm of government."[4] She succeeded.

Thatcher's grandest objective was the correction: end socialism. She wanted a "property-owning democracy," the property including capital shares. Using the word "privatization," on July 1, 1981, she privatized forty state-owned concerns, including British Airways, British Steel, British Gas, and British Petroleum. She increased the number of share-holders in Great Britain from 2 to 11 million.[5] Her example was so successful that while Tony Blair, her Labor successor, "was eager to continue the Thatcher policy of privatization ... there was not much left to sell."[6] While the British growth rate in the early postwar years was humiliatingly lower than that of her European rivals, it rose to a level nearly equal to theirs in her stewardship from 1979 to 1990, and better in 1990-99, under the conditions she had created. In the last period the rate was 1.9 percent, compared with France at 1.6 percent, Germany at 2.1 percent, and Italy at 1.2 percent.[7] By 1996 Britain's unemployment was, at 6.7 percent, lower than unemployment rates in the other major European nations, where it hovered at the 10 percent level or higher at a price dictated by their generous social-welfare policies. In 1983-86 Britain's GDP rose by 8 percent, industrial production by 7 percent, and productivity per worker by 13 percent; exports were up 21 percent while inflation was reduced to 5 percent from the peak of 21 percent in 1980. The per capita GDP for her whole period in office increased from $13,167 to $16, 430 (1990 international dollars).[8] Of course Margaret Thatcher had to be punished for her excellences.

Thatcher's powerful purposefulness led her perhaps too far. While thrashing Labor and socialism so thoroughly, she abraded Conservative skins as well and, like the great de Gaulle, made herself superfluous. Indeed, like him, she faltered on a minor local-government issue and fell out of office. John Major, her Conservative successor in 1990, continued her policies, and, as noted above, so did Tony Blair for Labor from 1997. In 1994, confirming her anti-socialist policy, the Labor Party formally dropped its nationalization principles of 1918 in a reform of the party's constitution. Peter Mandelson, theorist of Blair's New Labor, announced: "We are all Thatcherites now."[9]

Here, we return to the United States and its Third Way of economic policy and act as developed by the presidents from Lyndon Baines John-son to William Jefferson Clinton, and hélas, beyond. Within the American economy the corrective Third Way ruled, even under its imperial presidents. Lyndon Johnson, as we have seen, leaned leftward with his Great Society program, a revival of New Deal promises and dreams, but Richard Nixon, that redoubtable anti-Communist warrior, was a seeker, if not always a finder, of the Third Way. Detested by many liberals for aggressive anti-Communism of the early postwar years, Nixon pursued a complex policy that could best be described to his and the liberals' discomfiture as ... liberal. This derived from his political emphasis, which saw every economic act translated into political essence. It 1964 he reasoned: "I remember '58. We cooled off the economy and cooled off fifteen senators and sixty congressmen at the same time."[10] Expanding government services variously, he accepted the resultant deficit, announcing: "We are all Keynesians now."[11] At the time he sought counsel from Milton Friedman, now winning more adherents for his non-Keynesian monetarism, but the political Nixon had to stay with deficit-financing. In that sense he felt he had to impose price and wage controls, a favorite prescription of the populist economist John Kenneth Galbraith, while indexing Social Security benefits to keep up with the burgeoning inflation. Indeed, Nixon had to find himself ejected from the postwar prosperity into the insecure 1970s, when Keynesianism was working rather badly as stagflation unreasonably joined unemployment and rising prices together. In two steps by 1973, also, Nixon found himself ending the Bretton Woods system to give up on the last remnants of the gold standard and letting the dollar float.

Yet in foreign affairs, adventuring far from Republican dogma, Nixon showed himself to be a much better president than suggested by his use of underhanded methods. Here his unerring sense and management of the ultimate realities prevailed. Thus he carefully initiated the détente with a Red China on the principle of your enemy's enemy is your friend. This led to his carefully prepared (by his security adviser Henry Kissinger) five-day visit to China in February 1972. His agreement with Mao Zedong began the normalization of relations with China and the end of American restrictions on trade with her. It meant a tacit strategic alliance against Soviet Russia, another victory in the Cold War. It was more: the beginning of constructive relations between the United States and China into the next century.

Nixon also showed great skill in Vietnam. While bombing Cambodia, he prepared to quit the country under cover of his Vietnamization policy. In the Middle East, however, the problems defeated any good solution. American support of Israel in the Yom Kippur War of 1973 resulted in the oil embargo by the Arab states and, by December, the quadrupling of oil prices by the Organization of Petroleum Exporting Countries (OPEC). Economic results were painful but American power had its limits. Nixon's successors, the moderate Republican Gerald R. Ford and the idealess Democrat James (politically "Jimmy") Carter, could only try to keep balance during the economic distresses of the rest of the 1970s. Absorbing the worst blows, they had to see Ronald Reagan, after countering the lingering recession, lead the nation to newer heights. Of course another fortunate factor was the healthy underlying economics of the United States. During all these years the nation's terrific productivity asserted itself, the age of computers and information technology generalizing more and more material well-being.

It was Ronald Reagan, a half-step in the rear chronologically, and Margaret Thatcher, who established the Third Way's political economy. Both, consciously working against their predecessors' policies, revived the arguments for laissez-faire as preached by Milton Friedman in contradiction to the depression philosophy of John Maynard Keynes. This was the time when Friedman came into his own. He was a member of the president's Economic Policy Advisory Board, where he supported Reagan's efforts toward cost-cutting and minimal government. But then these efforts did not go terribly far. Neither Reagan nor Thatcher, nor the libertarian Friedman, could be called reactionary. A former New Deal Democrat and president of the Screen Actors Guild, Reagan maintained his populist posture and achieved an artful but sincere compromise. He was benefiting the common man even when he was taking measures against the trade unions. Mild in manner, Reagan could be granitic in principle. Union membership had been about 35 percent of the labor force in the immediate postwar years, but the American economy, moving into the service and information age, was reducing the number of its industrial-worker members; in Reagan's time membership was 20 percent and moving further down toward 12 percent in the early 2000s. Reagan's harshest act was to break the air traffic controllers organization (PATCO) for an illegal strike in 1981. Soon after taking office he acted to oppose the reemployment of the union's 13,000 members.[12] That was a brutal warning that drove the unions into passivity and made his economic policies easier to implement. Reagan, however, was inviting labor to enjoy the general benefits of his economic policy. During his administration federal payments to individuals rose. Housing and urban development spending increased from $14.8 billion in 1981 to $28.8 billion in 1985; the number of low-income households receiving subsidies rose from 3.2 million to nearly 4 million.[13] If some of the effects of his economic policy were contradictory, the general rise in GDP made good for most of the cost-cutting and labor-mauling.

One major issue was the remains of stagflation, which was resolved by the policy of Paul A.Volcker, appointed chairman of the Federal Reserve System by Gerald Ford. His method was to restrict the money supply rigorously instead of targeting interest rates. Inflation peaked at 13.5 percent in 1981, when Reagan arrived in office, but leveled to 3.2 percent by 1983 with Reagan's firm support. Of course this meant more unemployment but Reagan took the responsibility and firmly backed Volcker: "Stay the course." The country fought through a recession in 1981-82. Later Reagan got Volcker, the deed done, to loosen the money supply while he increased taxes for his expanded defense program. (Volcker's successor named by Reagan in 1987, was the even more successful Alan Greenspan, FRS chairman until 2006, who continued much in the same manner.) This was Reaganomics, producing a burst of economic activity. From August 1982 stocks rose in the longest bull market in history, the Standard and Poor index of 500 stocks increased about 300 percent from 1982 to 1989 as inflation remained damped. Most of the other numbers scintillated.

The economic reality behind the figures was firm. The GDP was up 3.6 percent in 1983 after a 2.5 percent drop in 1982, but then its growth shot up to 6.8 percent in 1984 and held mostly in the range of 3, although dropping to 2.5 in 1989. Something had to give, and this was the budget, which produced deficits from $73.8 billion in 1980, $207.8 billion in 1983, and similarly negative figures throughout Reagan's administration—to a deficit of $153.4 billion in 1989. But then the American economy was generating 18 million new jobs in the 1980s. Unemployment, which had been higher than in the major European nations until the late 1970s, slipped to half of the European figure in 1980: 5.2 percent in 1989, against Italy at 14 percent, France at 11 percent, and West Germany at 9 percent.[14] This was the substantive part of the Third Way: the United States had manufactured a prosperity engine.

Reagan matched his domestic program with a similarly simple and even more powerful foreign policy. He could be egregious while his amiability diluted the effects, thus in terming the Soviet Union "evil empire."[15] He was dead serious about the danger and the cure. He meant resolute power, increasing military spending close to $1.5 billion in the first five years. On March 23, 1983 he proposed the more than imaginative Strategic Defense Initiative (SDI), called "Star Wars" by critics. It was a plan for a defense umbrella to intercept nuclear missiles directed at the United States, but on the basis of futuristic technology. One major effect, however, was to frighten the Soviet Union leaders and cause them to undertake unbearable expenditures to defend against the imaginative or imaginary danger. From 1985, at the same time, Mikhail Gorbachev as new leader took Reagan's dire purposes as seriously as he took Soviet Russia's vulnerability. Their negotiations maintained the peace while driving Gorbachev into measures intensifying the strains on the Soviet Union's economy and its satellite empire. The Berlin Wall fell a few months after Reagan left office in 1989, and the Soviet Union itself dissolved in 1991. So Reagan won the Cold War. In its moderation and general spirit one can see his policy as an aspect of the Third Way.

Within the stricter confines of economics, and in a purer sense, one must credit Margaret Thatcher, Reagan's companion in spirit and act, with being the prime agent of the Third Way. If Reagan had to deflate Johnson's Great Society program, all social welfarism generally, Keynesianism, and one recalcitrant trade union, Thatcher had to do all that and more: overcome a much more powerful labor movement organized under the Trades Union Congress *and* unqualified socialism. On the domestic front she had a revolution to carry out. Together, creating the great compromise of governmental management and free enterprise, Thatcher and Reagan dominated the economics of the 1980s, indeed of the rest of the century and more as well.

With Thatcher acting as a bridge, the Thatcher-Reagan effect conquered continental Europe as well. All nations were expressing the same need for freeing their economies from the insufficiently restrained growth in social services and the insidious creep of inflation. In all cases the resistance to change guaranteed that the economic freedom would not go too far, that a given nation would not circle back to the economic license that had permitted the Great Depression. The beneficiaries of social welfare were reluctant to see it diminish, even if their economies would benefit from higher incomes and lower unemployment. On the other hand the force of circumstances drove them away from too much dependency. In all major cases, each European nation expressed its uniqueness and variously found a comparable third way.

One acute British student of French political economy, already cited here, entitled his chapter on the issue of this period, "The Problem of the Centre." He sketched the outline: "France has developed a stable constitution, pluralist democracy, national consensus, and the convergence of the major parties on the centre ground of politics."[16] President de Gaulle, as we have seen, established the fundament of the new stable order. But a few unintegrated exceptions, products of France's profound divisions arising in the great Revolution of 1789, remained to be planed down. The process occurred under the generalship of President François Mitterrand, the consummate French politician.

Mitterrand's career shows precisely the complex compromises and hypocrisies of the nation's political history. He got his start on the right, indeed in a manner that required a collective act of amnesia. In a nation where "collaboration" was the dirtiest of words Mitterrand lived down an early career as a Vichy official. He then attached himself nimbly to the Socialist Party. De Gaulle disappearing politically in 1969, following the less-then-consequential exuberances of 1968, his deputy Georges Pompidou had carried on ably as president until his death in 1964. His successor, the aristocratically named Valéry Giscard d'Estaing, led the small Independent Republicans in a continuation of the moderate conservative policy. In 1981 Mitterrand won election to the presidency by allying himself with the Communists. In the 1986 general election the Communists, crippled by their rigid philosophy, lost more votes in the National Assembly. So did the Socialists, but they were still winning 30 percent of the vote, and Mitterrand resolved the issue by naming Jacques Chirac, a Gaullist, Pompidou protégé, and founder of another small conservative party, as premier. "For a Socialist politician this was as bad as Hindenburg summoning Hitler."[17] The Socialist Party disagreed. The Communists dropped out of the government and into impotence. So began a period of the "cohabitation" of a leftist president and a conservative premier, Chirac introducing a new policy of privatization. France, joining Great Britain and the United States, had shifted to the center. With that correction toward continuing collaboration of the left and right, de Gaulle's revolution of the center was consolidated: the Third Way *à la française*.

Of course the French resolution was far from ideal. Something had to be sacrificed in all the compromises with reality. One loss was economic efficiency. The resolution, as suggested by Pompidou's concessions to the strikers in 1968, was to bribe the workers and the left generally with unaffordable wage and social-support levels. France as welfare state increased its social transfers from one fifth to a third of the GDP. The workers themselves were giving up on their unions, which went from 35 percent of employees postwar to 10.9 percent in 1993. Following upon the "thirty glorious years," France was entering the thirty "pitiful years of stagflation and bungled opportunities," in the opinion of one French economist. But that was one expert's opinion. Unemployment, as employers found help more and more expensive, went from 5 percent in 1979 to 10 percent and above from 1980 through century's end (plus 2 to 4 more percentage points for categories defined away as "in training").[18] Still, per capita GDP rose from $15,106 in 1980 (1990 international dollars) to $18,093 in 1990.[19] Either as plainly hedonistic or unemployed, the French were democratically demanding more free time and security generally at the cost of "economic dynamism," the popular feeling "heavily skewed toward inactivity and leisure." The French expert cited here found "the ongoing demotion of the French economy" dispiriting, but France's solution could not be seen as unrelievedly bad.[20] Secure in its government and economy, France was enjoying life. With a measure of nonchalance she could even contemplate the Union of West and East Germany into an unqualified Germany—from a population of some 66 million to 82 million—as a firm part of the European Union.

Seen up closely, Germany's economic performance since the 1960s, like that of America's, Britain's, and France's, appears much worse as magnified by the trained perceptions of the experts. All nations were enjoying increased incomes while falling short of their potentials. A German expert had to record six decades of strong growth in the GDP, making a multiple of six since 1950. To this he added that the East German rising of 1989 was "a quantum leap in Germany's postwar development ... a final blow to the Communist approach." But then he felt obliged to add that economic growth was not as great as it could have been, that the unemployment rate of 10.5 percent, like France's, excluded the 4 percent of "jobless...hidden in government schemes," and that a "timid approach to the market" had somewhat "eroded the ... social market economy."[21] With half of the GDP passing through the government, a third of that GDP was devoted to the social budget. Prosperity was thus being shared with the less fortunate.

Of course the strains were greatly intensified with the incorporation of East Germany into the united Reich. Unification was indeed "a shock to the German economy." The rusted, rigid East German production plant simply could not contribute equally to the unified economy. Most of the nationalized firms were downsized or destroyed. A trustee administration, taking over 90 percent of the East German economy, reduced the state-owned firms from 11.5 percent to 7.5 percent of productive capacity, transferring 500,000 persons to private sectors. West German companies took over the best firms, but many others vanished. The East Germans, despite their loudly suffered pains, found themselves in "one of the most dynamic economic regimes in Europe."[22] Helmut Kohl, the West German chancellor and continuing as such for the unified country to 1998, made the handsome political gesture of permitting the East Germans to trade in their low-valued East German marks for West Germany's currency, a terrific but costly gift. The East German area began at 33 percent of the West German GDP, but with this kind of help got to 62.7 percent of the GDP of the unified country by 2002. This required the transfer of 2 percent of the West German GDP annually, but most observers thought the sense of German unity made it more than worthwhile.[23] Indeed all the agony of unification was far secondary to the thing itself, achieved with the help of Chancellor Kohl's great tact. After the Berlin Wall fell one of his great coups was to get Gorbachev's guarantee permitting the unification when he made a visit to the crumbling Soviet Union in February 1990.

In the longer economic record, the economic costs of unification were easily absorbed. The united Germany continued to gain in the post-unification years. The growth rates from 1991 to 2003 were a positive, if modest, 1.25 percent of GDP, not much lower than the average rate of the other European Union countries without such extra problems.[24] All shared the pains of high unemployment as the cost of their social programs. They were agreeing upon a braver approach to the free market, thus the Third Way for Germany (and Italy) as well. In that sense, in 2005 Angela Merkel of the Christian Democratic Union like Kohl, but raised in East Germany, became chancellor with a pro-market program.

While Russia, no longer Soviet Russia, was the center of the most drastic change, Italy rivaled Great Britain in achieving the greatest change among the Western nations. The Italian consummation was another aggressive act of the Third Way, emphasized, furthermore, by its centrist and remarkably American manner. Much of this radiated around one man who was overbearing in a manner some people found reminiscent of Mussolini. But then Silvio Berlusconi, the richest Italian as media proprietor and entrepreneur, was eloquently pro-American in a laissez-faire sense to the point of supporting the younger Bush in his Iraq adventure. In a more home-styled accusation, the periodical *Economist* alleged without perfect proof that he had a Mafia connection and anyway had been committing fraud in his accounts and tax payments. Berlusconi emerged into political prominence during the Italian Time of Troubles that destroyed all the major parties. Tarred more definitively with a brush of corruption, the Communist, Socialist, and Christian Democratic parties all disappeared by 1992. Berlusconi carried through a revolution the Marxists had dreamed away for themselves.

Through it all the Italian economy roared up in continual triumph. Extending its rise, the per capita GDP went from $9,719 (1990 international dollars) in 1970, the year the five-times prime minister Aldo Moro was murdered by the Red Brigades, to $13,149 in 1980, $16,313 in 1990, and $18,740 in 2000 and was still moving upward.[25] The political destruction was related to the new wealth by way of specific and general corruption, the latter an aspect of the temptations for all. The specific corruption had attainted the leaders of the Christian Democrats and Socialists, specifically sending the Socialist leader Bettino Craxi to legal safety in Tunisian exile.

A long-serving prime minister, Craxi had a constructive period in office from August 1983 to April 1987. He frustrated the Communists by allying himself with the Christian Democrats and had the fortitude to abolish the measure automatically increasing wages with prices, inevitably a generator of inflation. But such positive achievements were overwhelmed by the corruption scandal. Berlusconi, who had enjoyed many favors from a friendly Craxi, found his discomfiture to his advantage and replaced him in office by 1994.

Berlusconi founded his own political party, Forza Italia (a sports slogan: "Go Italy!"—appropriate for the proprietor of a soccer team) in February 1994. He became prime minister in April, enduring eight months in office as head of a coalition of parties that also included the regional Northern League and the somewhat neo-fascist National Alliance. This frustrated the hopes of the former Communists who had transformed themselves into the Democratic Party of the Left (splitting off from some of the more stubborn old members calling themselves the Communist Reformation). But Berlusconi could not hold his coalition together. In 2001, however, he regained office, this time keeping it for nearly five years, the longest duration of any government of the Italian Republic. In office and managing his media properties, which included three television channels, Berlusconi persuasively advocated free-market reforms, including privatization, that produced an annual growth rate of 2.5 percent and a reduction of inflation from 6-7 percent in 1990-91 to 4 percent in 1993, while interest rates fell from 14 percent in 1992 to 7 percent in 1994. However odd his rhythm, Berlusconi marched in step with the other European leaders, and despite all of their national and unique differences, Britain, France, Germany, and Italy united in a policy of moderation: the Third Way throughout.[26]

With surprising rationality, given the commodious empire of the irrational, these leading nations of the Atlantic world had responded with a common strategy to global problems. Other nations, from a continuingly moderate Spain to a resistantly bourgeois Chile, were joining them.

This included the other Atlantic powers, thus approximately the NATO nations. The general agreement was a factor, along with the other more urgent ones, that meant a growing counterforce against the last thrust of the Soviet Union. But then that nation under Mikhail Gorbachev was also seeking and finding its Third Way—more or less.

The Soviet Union had been becalmed in slack interlude from the last years of the mentally and physically enfeebled Leonid Brezhnev, who died on November 10, 1982, the moribund leadership of the former intelligence chief Yuri Andropov (to February 9, 1984), and the general nonentity Konstantin Chernenko (to March 10, 1985). Andropov, characteristic of his police mentality, attempted anti-corruption and anti-drunkenness campaigns but committed one sensible action. Aware that more had to be done, he brought forward Mikhail Gorbachev, representing a new generation of leaders. Gorbachev, at fifty-four, expressed the consensus of the younger, more open-minded party officials: the Soviet Union required drastic therapy. With uncanny accuracy his prescribed *glasnost* (political openness) and *perestroika* (economic restructuring) at the same time promised rational reform and worked the annihilation of the Soviet Union. The rigid system could endure neither the freer thinking permitted by glasnost, which found too much unacceptable, and sensible economic efficiency, which threatened too many officials' vested interests, privileges, and incompetence. The solution was collapse. Gorbachev's great accomplishment was to asphyxiate a powerfully armed tyranny without violence, the openness of glasnost weakening the organs of repression and perestroika opening the way for non-state economic enterprise. Individuals and groups discovered they could express themselves, thus the correction of the politics of the center in freely electing democratic bodies and of the economics of the center in taking the initiative to survive by buying, selling, and stealing: free enterprise.

Within the Soviet Union reforms proceeded in sudden spurts. In January 1987 Gorbachev called for more democracy; at the end of the next year the old Supreme Soviet, the mock legislative body, proposed establishing a Congress of People's Deputies as an elected and indeed a real lawmaking body. Elections followed in March and April 1989, and Gorbachev was elected president, the first and last of the Soviet Union. Earlier, in May 1988, a law was enacted permitting private ownership of businesses. By 1989, thus, the country was plunging into economic and political freedom, or license at least.[27]

These internal Soviet events were inevitably and quickly accompanied by actions among the Soviet satellites. Early in 1989, as part of the general reform program, Gorbachev, acting through the old Politburo, repealed the Brezhnev Doctrine, which threatened intervention should any nation of the Soviet Union act independently. This was an opening to freedom. Similarly the old ethnic identities, which Lenin had sought to eradicate, announced their life as powerfully as ever. In April the independent Polish labor union Solidarity, repressed since the end of 1981, was legalized and went on to participate in free parliamentary elections. The result, in June 1989, was its total domination of the new legislature. In October the Hungarian legislature, besides providing for the free election of different political parties, opened its border to Austria. Some 31,000 East Germans escaped to the West: the dike to freedom had burst open. In October, also, Gorbachev visited East Germany and told its leadership to accept reform. When it resisted, a new leadership was named and the new men opened the Berlin Wall (and the East German border) on November 9. With that, and accompanying revolutions elsewhere in the Soviet zone, the Soviet empire had vanished. The next month, on December 3, Gorbachev met President George H. W. Bush in Malta and the two agreed that the Cold War was over. We should pause for a moment. The old nightmare of a global holocaust had disappeared, if not definitively.

Back in the old Soviet Union a chain of mostly nonviolent revolutions tumbled after each other. At one point, during the first half of 1991, Gorbachev found the movement too fast and tried to resist the loss of the Baltic states, but the Lithuanians, Latvians, and Estonians refused to be deterred. The process continued in and out of the Soviet Union. Gorbachev, meanwhile, had helped create a rival to himself in Boris Yeltsin, a former construction engineer and aggressive party politician. Holding the equivalent to the mayor's position in Moscow, Yeltsin then quarreled with Gorbachev, was exiled to the provinces, but reappeared as newly elected president of the Russian Soviet Republic on June 12, 1991. The nations of the Soviet zone having already freed themselves, Yeltsin took the lead in dissolving the Soviet Union itself. On August 19 hard-line Communist officials including the Soviet Union prime minister and head of the KGB seized Gorbachev, then on vacation in the Crimea, and attempted to take Yeltsin in Moscow as well. But sympathizers defended Yeltsin and the coup collapsed in three days. Back in Moscow the liberated Gorbachev found himself fatally weakened, Yeltsin using the new Russian government to take over the Soviet Union's government. With the Soviet economy deteriorating rapidly, Yeltsin as Russian president arranged a meeting with the leaders of the Ukrainian and Belorussian republics on December 8, 1991; the three declared the

Soviet Union dissolved and replaced by the 15-unit Commonwealth of Independent States. The other states agreed, the Baltic countries going their way to their independence. Gorbachev himself resigned as president of the dying Soviet Union on December 26. On December 31, 1991 all its operations had ceased.

Still a vast area, the Russian Republic struggled painfully with the manifold problems it had inherited. Most of the nations of the Soviet Zone snapped back into more-or-less operative democracies with social services. The Russian Republic and the Soviet Union area, with less democratic antecedents, lurched into mixed democratic-authoritarian solutions. Defeating another coup on October 3-4, 1993, Yeltsin wielded power authoritatively, if not quite autocratically, while showing himself erratic and alcoholic. Unfortunately, expectedly, the Russian legislature was less than effective in developing its democratic capabilities. The economy, the old compulsions gone and the new freedom lacking self-discipline, plunged into disaster. In the whole area, including the old Soviet Zone, the per capita GDP had peaked at $7,098 (1990 international dollars) in 1989, slipping down each year to $6,878 in 1990, then down to $3,854 in the nadir year 1996, then painfully rising to a bare $4,844 in 2002.[28] Pensioners went hungry, government services failed, and workers found themselves unemployed or often mock-employed for vestigial wages as inflation exploded. It was a period of renewed suffering. In self-defense Russia fell into private enterprise, a privatization operation from 1992 taking over the great firms. Suddenly party and government officials became entrepreneurs, robber barons post-Soviet style. A mechanism of free vouchers to workers and employees permitted the transition, but as usual, the poor man stayed poor, and the well-connected, capturing the vouchers, became the hugely rich "oligarchs." Exhausted and in shaky health, the now wealthy Yeltsin was persuaded to resign on December 31, 1999, to be succeeded by his recently named young prime minister, the intelligence officer Vladimir Putin. With a silently obedient legislature, Putin, becoming president, had succeeded at least in establishing a stable government and a recovering economy. Three economic sectors can be identified: a rational area operating outside of legality with links to crime, big business too big to be illegal and capable of manipulating the market, and the old Soviet economy requiring subsidies to function. A poor country endowed, however, with substantial oil and other reserves, Russia has since begun to assert herself as a significant, politically major power.[29] But the Cold War is history.

With the disappearance of the Soviet Union the United States, while enjoying its broader global command, had the embarrassment of redefining its position. Its new power seemed excessive in view of its smaller defense needs. It soon augmented NATO by enrolling seven new members from the Baltic states eastward, but all this rendered the organization's mission all the more ambiguous, while the surviving Russia, which the United States was trying to help as a friend, could hardly be called an enemy. Herself excluded from NATO, she could not look upon its expansion as friendly. This is one of the many confusions in the new American global role. The appearance of an aggressive global terrorism in the Middle East failed quite to define the American mission.

The United States had indeed accepted its imperial responsibilities, but both President George H. W. Bush and the American people were loath to exercise all the powers they demanded. Lacking an imperial ego to match his imperial presidency, Bush, with governmental experience that included service as vice president as well as ambassador to the United Nations and director of the CIA, easily apprehended the risks. He was presently challenged to use his powers in moderate and virtuous fashion. Saddam Hussein, the Iraqi leader, emerged in 1988 from a murderous eight-year war with Iran desiring more advantages. Tempted by the vast oil reserves and weakness of Kuwait, a small state at the head of the Persian Gulf, he manufactured an excuse and invaded it on August 2, 1990. Besides helping a small power, the United States was defending its interests in an oil-rich area. Bush diplomatically got the support of thirty-three nations as well as congressional approval and led an international coalition in ejecting the Iraqi army. In six weeks of operations the mission was accomplished without unseating Saddam Hussein. If Bush mollified critics of imperial America with his moderation, he felt obliged to defend his toleration of the man's dangerous and vicious rule. Indeed Bush's policy toward Iraq fit comfortably within the political economy of the Third Way as well as the historically successful containment policy. His good deed was condignly rewarded. The failure to win much glory from that uninspiring victory plus a mild recession defeated his second campaign for the presidency.

Arriving in office in 2001 after the Democratic interregnum, George W. Bush essayed to expand the Clinton Third Way both to the right and left. In 2003 he supported the Medicare Act providing prescription coverage to its elderly recipients. He had a more conservative agenda in mind, however, and his first major movement, achieved in June 2001, was to put through a program cutting taxes $1.35 trillion over the next

10 years. Democrats assailed it as a benefit chiefly for the rich, with the greatest gain for the upper 1 percent of income recipients, but Bush's rationale was to enliven the economy. Indeed during his presidency the real GDP rose by 2.5 percent annually. The budget, however, was in deficit by $434 billion in 2006 from a Clinton surplus of $86 billion in 2000, an effect the left usually incurred (although Reagan had committed it as well). Another move toward business encouragement, the effort to privatize Social Security partially, also failed. The example of Chile, which had claimed to improve its economic performance by privatizing its social security program, did not convince many persons, who feared the effects of the insecurities of the private economy. Another effort, this one toward the left also failed. Bush proposed to legalize the status of 12 million immigrants, mostly Mexicans who had slipped over the southern border. Everyone agreed that something has to be done to resolve a nagging problem demanding both justice and economic sense, but disagreed about modalities. This halted the action in the last period of Bush's presidency. If all these were variations on the Third Way and older policies, the younger Bush would have much greater effect, indeed a revolutionary one, on the fundamental character of the presidency and foreign relations.

Cold War gone with the wind, the two Iraq wars, thus the two Bush presidencies, provide the perspective, *force* its use rather, to redefine the situation of the United States. This requires also a reexamination of the imperial presidency, which functioned with such efficiency in World War II and after the necessary adjustments, moved on to broader sway during the Cold War. The foundation of the imperial presidency was American economic power enhanced by experience and pragmatism. Europe's febrile left-wing intellectuals like Jean-Paul Sartre might rail, sometimes even reasonably, against the dirty hands wielding such power, but the European common man, unpersuaded, usually matched American common sense with his own.

A nation with the international responsibility of the United States, like Great Britain in its imperial period, had to act powerfully. If the Cold War justified its general operations, one can still say that the nation, led by its imperial presidents, went too far. This writer has defended it against negative criticism of its fighting policy in Vietnam, but less defensible acts can be mentioned, thus Theodore Roosevelt's detachment of Panama from Colombia, Woodrow Wilson's imposing impossible democratic idealism on Europe, Franklin Roosevelt's illegal internment (sanctioned by Congress and Supreme Court) of Japanese during World War II, John

F. Kennedy's Bay of Pigs invasion (incompetent as well as bizarre), the CIA's machinations against the would-be Soviet puppet Salvador Allende in Chile, Nixon's sanctioning of burglarizing the Democratic National Committee headquarters (this, however, bereft of national purpose), and President Reagan's presiding over the twisty use of the Iranian funds against the leftist government of Nicaragua. But all this suggests spillover rather than policy. The United States had to exercise its power.

The younger Bush's leadership in the second Iraq war represented a terrific leap even for the imperial presidency. His father's policy, fitting comfortably within the bounds suggested by containment, addressed Saddam Hussein's aggressions with the same flexible means. If one were specifically to apply the son's policy to the American-Soviet postwar position, the United States would have sent troops to Czechoslovakia against the Communist coup in March 1948 and tanks to break through the Soviet blockade of West Berlin beginning in June 1948: chilly thoughts. The younger Bush was correcting his father, but in a sense antithetical to that of this chapter. The first Bush's policy fit comfortably into the period's corrections toward the center. In the management of his office and foreign relations generally the second Bush turned sharp right.

In his own presidential time, George W. Bush, enlightened by the 2001 attack on the World Trade Center and Pentagon, found the Iraq leader guilty of storing weapons of mass destruction (WMD) in violation of a United Nations resolution, although the UN itself did not. In his State of the Union address of January 29, 2002 Bush, plagiarizing Reagan's phrase for Soviet Russia, condemned Iraq as a member of the "axis of evil." Referring to North Korea and Iran, and threatening war in those cases as well, he announced dramatically and reprovingly: "By seeking weapons of mass destruction, these regimes pose a great and growing danger. They could provide arms to terrorists, giving them the means to match their hatred." Intelligence estimates claimed that Iraq was seeking nuclear materials in Africa. The U. S. administration also charged that Iraq had active links to the terrorist organization Al Qaeda. None of these claims was proven. On March 20, 2003 the United States invaded Iraq.

In twenty-one days the United States could declare victory. The contrast to the earlier victory was thorough. The United States had accomplished it almost alone. Instead of 33 allies, it had only Great Britain with substantial forces, some 45,000 along with 250,000 Americans, and token Australian, Dutch, and Polish units. France and Germany sent none and objected to the action. Iraq was shattered but the U.S. had a mindless post-victory policy and insufficient forces to impose any kind of order;

a murderous civil war began between the old dominant Sunni minority and the old oppressed Shi'ite majority, while the Kurds in the north made themselves nearly independent. Iraq was supposed to be the laboratory for the model of Middle East democracy, another Bush objective. The U. S. had gone on from the paranoia of seeing enemies everywhere to the megalomania of imposing its governmental principles on the Middle East. The Provisional Government, its creation and dominated by the somewhat more collaborative Shi'ites, was a democratic travesty whose most decisive action was to hang Saddam Hussein. Bush's presumed counterattack on terrorism generalized it widely. After four years Iraq was a savage quagmire spilling suicidal terrorism beyond its borders into an infected Middle East.

The Iraq situation was the product of wrong-headed thinking, which had presumed to bring democracy to a culture unready for it. Islam, developing reasonably out of its history, had functioned in terms of tribal loyalties to clan-connected leaders, a context which could appreciate the leadership of Moses, the prophets, the medieval lords, or Henry VIII and Louis XIV. A democratic legislature had little meaning for it. Except for superficial Western expressions, the Middle East was still inhospitable to democracy in the early twenty-first century. This is not to foreclose its future, but that future will come much more slowly than granted American impatience. President Bush had led a children's crusade.

It had been false to equate Saddam Hussein, however vicious he was, with terrorism. Similarly, it had been self-defeating to proceed with one ally and chilled, damaged feelings in our major global partners. Announcing to the world that the United States was an incompetent bully, our Iraq policy severely crippled our leadership at a time when America might have used its unchallenged power to generalize stability for the world at large. Instead it had generalized tension.

With surgical accuracy the operations of September 11, 2001 had shocked the world into a confusion of a thought and action. Suicide groups had seized four American transport aircraft and, one crashing harmlessly perhaps as a result of passenger action, piloted three of them into the two towers of the World Trade Center and the Pentagon. At the Trade Center they killed 3,000 persons besides themselves. We know that some 40,000 Americans die, unshockingly, each year in automobile accidents. For young Bush this was a call to counterattack that terrorism, a first step in self-destructive thinking. He simplified the problem by equating Saddam Hussein in Iraq with worldwide terrorism. The sane strategy would have been to mount a meticulous, long-term, cooperative counter-terrorist action making the best of Western technology.

The great mistake had been to see terrorism as a serious enemy. In Afghanistan's defense against Soviet forces, and with America cooperating, the Saudi Osama bin Laden (b. 1957), son of a very rich construction magnate in Saudi Arabia, established Al Qaeda (the base) as a center training forces for military action against all that the West represented. He was influenced by an Egyptian theologian preaching a militant global jihad (that is, struggle) as a Muslim duty to conquer all Islamic lands from Palestine to Indonesia. "Jihad and the rifle alone; no negotiations, no conferences, and no dialogues."[30] With his vast funds bin Laden financed what he called in the year 2000 the World Islamic Jihad against Jews and Crusaders. His logic suggested the West revolved around Israel as an agent of evil and extended to all who could be called crusaders, thus Western Christians.

This could be related by multiple stretches of the imagination to the thesis of Samuel P. Huntington's *Clash of Civilizations and the Remaking of World Order.*[31] With his dramatic facts, reductive reasoning, and shambling logic Huntington saw a clash taking place, the Soviet-Afghan war providing one fault line, "a war between civilizations in which the inviolability of Islam was at stake."[32] But with the United States opposing the Soviets in that area, it is hard to see the designated clash of civilizations. Huntington was right about the conflicts that did and could arise between civilizations, but history shows that most wars occur against neighbors *within* civilizations, that, accordingly, the great wars of the twentieth century occurred between Western nations and, otherwise, that effective attacks on the West used Western weapons. Recall the early Japanese victories in World War II. The central aspect of bin Laden's jihad was its futility, thus as suicide action.

What was the combined power of the Middle East with its oil reserves, Islam broadly (from Palestine to Pakistan and Indonesia), and terrorism? The first is a poor area, riven by ethnic, tribal, and religious divisions. Its Islamic culture was still medieval in thought and practice (hence the madness of imposing democracy on it), physically feeble, and incapable of fundamentally endangering the West. It simply lacks the science and technology, the rifles and nuclear bombs, although Iran might have been stretching toward them. The West, with its efficiency, has been able to prevent more harm from borrowed weapons and computers than the killing of individuals or, at best or worst, the massacres of odd groups. Even if terrorism and a rogue power joined to launch a nuclear attack and, say, incinerated a half million or one million persons, this would hardly reduce the global population of the 6 plus billion while demanding a devastating response. This is a best- or worst-case scenario, but it must be envisioned in the real world. It is, however, less likely than, say, the effects of global warming or other examples of the West's acts of self-harm.

The election of 2006 recognized the self-destruction in the younger Bush's policy. Democratic majorities in both houses, rejecting his pretensions, called for a troop withdrawal from Iraq, an action perhaps more difficult than the invasion, but this has meant an effort to return to prudent policy. Following the paternal Bush, the objective is to retreat to the proven policy of flexible containment. Only in this way, with the United States carefully keeping allies—real allies—and undertaking nothing important without them, could it begin to establish a rational, long-term course of action. The world has recognized the need for it. Of course this would not exclude danger, even extreme danger, but living is risky. With its vast resources, with companions of the road, the United States, renewing the corrections that had lately served it so well, could continue to exercise its responsibility as world leader.

Looking beyond the wretched threat of terrorism, the United States had to begin to recognize that the greatest threat to its position was China.

Notes

1.   Quoted Flavio Romano, *Clinton and Blair: The Political Economy of the Third Way* (London: Routledge, 2006), 3.
2.   *Ibid.*, 23-26.
3.   Quoted, *ibid.*, 8; see "An Introduction to the Third Way," 2-12.
4.   E. H. H. Green, *Thatcher* (London: Hodder Arnold, 2006), 117. See also Earl A. Reitan, *The Thatcher Revolution: Margaret Thatcher, John Major, Tony Blair, and the Transformation of Modern Britain, 1979-2001* (London: Rowman & Littlefield, 2003); Andrew Gamble, *The Free Economy and the Strong State: The Politics of Thatcherism* (London: Macmillan, 1994, 2nd ed.).
5.   Green, *Thatcher,* 4-6, 101.
6.   Quoted, Reitan, *TheThatcher Revolution,* 222.
7.   Chart compiled by the Organization for Economic Cooperation and Development (OECD), Jean-Pierre Dormois, *The French Economy in the 20th Century* (Cambridge: Cambridge University Press, 2004), 18.
8.   Reitan, *The Thatcher Revolution,* 53, 29; Maddison, *The World Economy: Historical Statistics,* chart, 65.
9.   Green, *Thatcher,* 188; quotation, 189.
10. Quoted, Allan Matusow, *Nixon's Economy: Booms, Busts, Dollars, and Votes* (Lawrenrce: University of Kansas Press, 1998), 22.
11. Quoted, Reeves, *20th Century America,* 200.
12. Robert H. Zieger, *American Workers, American Unions* (Baltimore: John Hopkins University Press, 1994), 100, 198; U.S. Department of Labor, Bureau of Labor Statistics.
13. Reeves, *20th Century America,* 239.

14.   John W. Sloan, *The Reagan Effect: Economics and Presidential Leadership* (Lawrence: University Press of Kansas, 1999), quotation, 227; 229-32.
15.   Quoted, Reeves, *20th Century America*, 238.
16.   Gildea, *France since 1945*, the chapter, 169-200; quotations, 178, 181.
17.   Quoted, *ibid.*, 181.
18.   Dormois, *The French Economy,* chart, 21; 77-79; quotation, 22; chart, 84.
19.   Maddison, *The World Economy*, chart, 64.
20.   Dormois, *The French Economy*, 129, 131.
21.   Horst Siebert, *The German Economy: Beyond the Social Market* (Princeton: Princeton University Press, 2005), vii, viii (preface).
22.   *Ibid*, 22; Martin Geiling, "Germany's Changing Political Landscape," in Thomas Lange and J. R. Shackleton, eds, *The Political Economy of Unification* (Providence: Berghahn, 1998), 56-71.
23.   Geiling, "Germany's Changing Political Landscape," 42.
24.   Siebert, *The German Economy,* chart, 24 (from OECD figures).
25.   Maddison, *The World Economy: Historical Statistics,* chart, 64.
26.   John Newell, ed., *The Italian General Election of 2001: Berlusconi's Victory* (Manchester: Manchester University Press, 2002); see especially Michele Capriati, "The Economic Context 1996-2001," 52-56. See also Martin Clark, *Modern Italy 1871-1995* (London: Longman, 1996; 1st ed.: 1984), 408-26.
27.   On these events, Michael McFaul, *Russia's Unfinished Revolution: Political Change from Gorbachev to Putin* (Ithaca: Cornell University Press, 2001); Mike Bowker and Cameron Ross, eds. *Russia after the Cold War* (London: Longman, 2000); Lee Edwards, ed., *The Collapse of Communism* (Stanford: Hoover Institution Press, 2000).
28.   Maddison, *The World Economy,* chart, 101.
29.   On the economy, Anthony Phillips, "Economic Reform," in Bowker & Ross, eds., *Russia after the Cold War,* 121-34; McFaul, *Russia's Unfinished Revolution,* 251-55.
30.   Quoted in an extended overview of terrorism, John L. Esposito, *Unholy War: Terror in the Name of Islam* (Oxford: Oxford University Press, 2002), 7. See also Jessica Stern, *Terror in the Name of God* (New York: Ecco/HarperCollins, 2003); Peter L. Bergen, *Holy War, Inc.: Inside the Secret World of Osama bin Laden* (New York: Free Press, 2001).
31.   New York: Simon & Schuster, 1996.
32.   *Ibid.*, 249.

12

China Rising

The greatest corrections toward the Third Way have been committed upon the two largest nations. We have seen how Russia was corrected to Communism and then corrected back again to a Western political economy with an approximation of democratic rule. In somewhat the same way, as well as uniquely differently, China moved into Communism and then toward a more nearly Western order. The one element to be emphasized here is the relation of national *magnitude* to this process, with Japan as a control. The point is that the two large countries were worlds unto themselves. The initial great change required tremendous force against the resistance of tradition, hence the Leninist and Maoist dictatorships. It had been necessary to force-march Russia and China military style to gain the necessary momentum for change. The military mode, however, was incapable of the efficiencies of a free society. Thus the ultimate correction in Russia was the annihilation of that military mode. As a small nation finally submitting to powerful foreign influences, Japan showed a way without Communism. The experience of India, moreover, will suggest another road taken by a large nation.

With a certain unhappy diversion Japan moved from a conservative royal system, Asian style, to a consciously copied Western order. This was after a United States naval force opened her up in 1854. The domestic impulse came from the educator Fukuzawa Yukichi, who organized a training center for Western learning in the late 1850s, and wrote with refreshing modesty in 1872: "If we compare the knowledge of the Japanese and Westerners in letters, in techniques, in commerce, or in industry … there is not one thing in which we excel…. All that Japan has to be proud of is its scenery." He emphasized that the correction was not an "external form," but the "spirit of civilization."[1] Effective action took place after the overthrow of the Tokugawa Shogunate, the military rule that had substituted for imperial power since 1192. Now a formally restored emperor gave authority to a group of modern-minded administrators and courtiers. In 1871-73 forty-nine of these visited fifteen countries, including the United States, to study business, industry, schools, and constitutions. The result was the Japanese constitution of 1889, modeled somewhat after the German and British constitutions, and action to carry out its sense. Japan became an efficient political economy.

Japan was presented with seductive opportunities by the sick-man-of-Asia China and challenges by the Western imperialist powers. The results were the Sino-Japanese War (1894-95), which gave Japan Taiwan (which she called Formosa), and the Russo-Japanese War (1904-05), which led to Japanese power on the mainland, the later seizure of Manchuria from China in 1931, and Japan's efforts to acquire more of China from 1937. Thus Western progress led to aggressive Japanese militarism. It was an extraordinary presumption for tiny Japan to create a vast empire on the prostrate body of China while also contending with the Western powers. The presumption ended when American atomic bombs shocked Japan into defeat in World War II. The American occupation provided Japan with another correction, indeed a model leading to the development of a rather democratic and efficient society. In the late 1990s she suffered a depression, somewhat on the American model again, but without significant unemployment and presently permitting her to recover her prosperous position. The lesson was that small had its advantages when it did not lead to delusions of grandeur. Meanwhile immense China was given the opportunity to make up for the handicap of size.

In the late twentieth century the United States found itself facing not only China, with four times the population, but the almost as populous India. How long could it maintain itself when these countries successfully adopted its efficiencies?

Consider India first, population slightly over a one billion in the year 2002. With a rich culture, an exquisite religious development and allied philosophical exercises, India had been trained in law and administration by British imperialism. When she made herself free in 1947, she had a viable legislature and a secure judiciary. She went on to adopt many Western skills from manufacturing to computer science. Yet one American student of her ethos has inquired: "Why were Indians so ingenious in scientific theory, so deficient in the practical and technological implementation of such ideas toward alleviating their own most urgent social, political, and economic problems?"[2] Among other things he was referring to the deep poverty in which "close to a fourth of the population lives on less than a dollar a day," as an Indian political scientist has calculated.[3] The other negatives included a self-crippled legislature, which permitted the government to function without its approval.[4] Tactfully he did not mention two other dominating factors, the antiscientific nature of the Hindu religion and a caste system with thousands of castes and subcastes keeping the nation profoundly divided, from the superior Brahmins to subcastes signifying feces to the others. India remains a stable but grotesquely inegalitarian democracy. In these circumstances the growth rate of 7 percent to 8 percent annually at the turn of the century had generated substantial wealth for her growing middle class but failed to lift those lower on the socioeconomic scale. Despite her growth, India's per capita GDP was at $1,957 in 2001, only slightly more than half of China's and a small fraction of the United States'.[5] With her poverty and areas of backwardness, she was hardly a threat to the West in wealth and power, although she could be a valuable trading partner and ally.

The great Jawaharlal Nehru led India into a distinctive socialism modeled on both Soviet and British socialism. While it had encouraged a measure of progress, it meant the usual inefficiencies. Finally the correction: in the 1990s, a decade after the enlivening model provided by Thatcher and Reagan, India attempted to reduce out government controls and encourage private enterprise. The results were good but the task remained colossal. Limited by caste divisions and lulled by the comforts of religion, India cannot quite challenge the United States. But China can.

China can promise to embody the ultimate correction. If she is true to her past and culture, she should be able to rise beyond the United States in power and achievement, *should* but not necessarily will. Certainly the possibility demands serious thought. We pause here to balance between history and prophecy, and lean back into history. We begin with the proportions: a population of 1.3 billion against 300 million for the United States. There is nothing substantive that Americans do that the Chinese cannot do. That does not quite resolve the question. As the Japanese educator said, spirit is also essential.

Of all advanced nations China has the richest cultural foundation. The great Confucius (551-479 BCE) did his thinking more than a century before Plato (427/28-348/47 BCE) and Aristotle (384-322 BCE). With his "unique eminence as a 'culture hero'" Confucius led and influenced many thinkers over the centuries. He speculated within the frame of morality and ethics radiating out from the family as center and moving toward a light-handed government. His "legalist" followers of the fourth century BCE emphasized the importance of laws and obedience under an impotent ruler and a powerful chief minister. With no interest in epistemology, metaphysics, and logic, simply the ethics of a rising gentry, Chinese thought did not range nearly as far as the Greek speculations. It lacked a concern about reality comparable to Aristotle's as he disassembled the world and sought to examine its moving parts before putting it back together again. Nor did Confucius indulge in the poetry of ideas like Plato. When Chinese did indeed extend thinking beyond the visibly real, it slipped into divination, harking back to the magical thinkers of a much earlier age with mysterious interpretations of symbols like trigrams and hexagrams.[6] Possibly explaining China's failure to advance in science like the West, Confucius had failed, as did his successors, to develop the "fuzzy logic" important in science, as one researcher saw it.[7] The practical importance of intellectual and cultural history is suggested by Mao Zedong's calling for a battle against Confucius and his counter-balancing praise of Shih Huang-ti, ruthless founder of the Ch'in state in the third century BCE.[8] Like Stalin denouncing Shostakovich, Mao knew exactly what he was doing: stop thinking beyond a certain point. With its fuzzy thinking the West had gone further but China can move along with it today.

Yet one cannot do justice to the wealth of Chinese thought just as China herself could not do justice to the wealth of history she had to contemplate. The Chinese, identifying themselves as such from 1000 BCE, had entered their early period in 1600 BCE. They had developed their writing somewhat later than the peoples of the Middle East and India, but they invented the wheel, protected their cities with walls, and produced stone sculptures and fine friezes. They fought and absorbed Turkic, Mongolian, and Manchurian enemies. Shih Huang-ti conquered all of the feudal states by 222 BCE to command a vast area governed by legalist principles and organized hierarchically with military discipline. From 214 BCE he raised the Great Wall. In this period the Chinese were sufficiently self-conscious to write history and indulge in Buddhism, the latter attracting many unsatisfied with the thinkers' dominant secularism.

In modern times, beginning about 1000 AD, China's middle class began to contend with the gentry. Trade, much of it with foreigners, expanded and generated such manifestations as large industrial operations employing as many as 500, strikes, artisanal guilds, and labor laws. From the tenth to the twelfth century the Sung dynasty established a firm order with medical care, pharmacies, the equivalent of "ever-normal granaries," fire protection, and geisha houses for troops away from home. For more than half the period from 1280 to 1911 China was under alien rule, although the rulers became sinicized: a century under the Mongolian Ming dynasty and then the Manchus from 1644 to the end. The population was increasing from 53 million in 1500, 60 million in 1662, 275 million in 1850, 612 million in 1953, and now more than twice that.

Given her magnitude and capabilities, why had China, enjoying a well-being comparable to the West's in the seventeenth century, become a victim of Western and an even Eastern imperialism? The best answer begins with the well-being. The size of the Middle Kingdom, as she called herself, prevented her from seeing much beyond her borders. Contrary to fable, she was indeed aggressive, defeating Turkic peoples to the west and conquering much of the Southeast Asia in 1594-1604. But the Chinese court could not be bothered with so much responsibility. In the fifteenth century Cheng Ho (1371-1435), admiral and diplomat, led fleets on seven voyages, the last three reaching Africa. But the new emperor was bored with the project and China failed effectively to exploit the area for trade and plunder.

Similarly, China failed to exploit her terrific scientific and techno-logical advances. In agriculture she was first with the iron plow, seed drill, weeding rake, and the deep-tooth furrow. Her other inventions or advances include the blast furnace, the spinning wheel, development of water power, clocks, the compass, and other improvements including ship design, paper and printing, porcelain, the wheelbarrow, kites for manned flight, lacquers, chemicals, bricks, the horse collar (about 250 BCE), the crossbow, acupuncture, matches, the umbrella, the toothbrush, and playing cards. But these were all underdeveloped. While she did create movable type, she did not generalize its use, leaving it to the Europeans. The above list was compiled by the economic and technology historian Joel Mokyr, quoted above, who comments: "The greatest enigma in the history of technology is the failure of China to sustain its techni-cal supremacy."[9] Actually Mokyr, together with another distinguished historian in the same field, David S. Landes, has explained the enigma persuasively. Mokyr mentions "social forces that for one reason or another tried to preserve the status quo." In his chapter "Why Europe?" Landes emphasized its contrasting autonomy of intellectual inquiry and conscious encouragement of science and invention, thus in the Accadémia dei Lincei of Florence (1653), the British Royal Society (1600), and the Académie des Sciences of Paris (1666). He pointed out the competition among European states, the church-state separation, and the divisions among the various churches themselves as against the all-encompassing unity of China.[10] In the seventeenth century China was on the same economic level as Europe. She was too comfortable to bestir herself just as Europe was exploding with progress. But then European progress would invade China, eventually encouraging her to build upon her unexploited culture.

In the nineteenth century the now incompetent Manchu dynasty lost complete control of the nation. Europe invaded in force and thought. The government failed to exclude Western imperialism, submitting to a British bombardment in 1840 and other attacks, for example, its failure to prevent opium sales in 1842. Another result was the great Taiping Rebellion of 1850-64, driven by Christian and populist ideas, which killed 20 million. The Boxer Rebellion of 1900 and the Japanese and Russian incursions noted above also contributed to China's humiliation. On October 1, 1949 under Mao Zedong and the Communist forces China was again a united power defying an imperialistic West. Then came the Korean War of 1950-53. One historian, already cited here, put it bluntly: "Clearly, the Korean War was the beginning of the decline of American power, in fact, it was a war which the United States lost."[11] One may disagree with that but China had become a significant power.

In the global intellectual and physical context, Soviet Russia having shown the way, Communism was China's fate. With it Mao had been able to defeat Chiang Kai-shek, only a nationalist and compromised by association with Chinese bankers and Western aid. Communism, expressing itself in Soviet technology, also promised progress. Mao had to make one obvious correction; Stalin wanted a proletarian Communism as dictated by dogma and Soviet success, but China had too little industry and hence proletariat. Mao successfully defeated ideologist and ideology to build on Chinese reality. The peasants inevitably had grievances against the landlords. Mao could base his movement upon them in the beginning and go on to create an industry and a supportive proletariat. After Stalin's death in 1953 he began to compete for world leadership with his Soviet successors. By 1960 China had outgrown Soviet Russia.

The rest of Mao's career and life consisted of his struggle against reality and his own more rational lieutenants. Uninhibited by concern for lives, he had a vision of brute power transcending that of the emperors he had succeeded. When the party congress of 1956 outvoted his group on key issues, Mao seduced the doubtful with his "Hundred Flowers" campaign of the spring of 1957, the suggestion that other opinions were permitted. He then swung around, crushed their proponents, and proceeded to the Great Leap Forward from the fall of 1957 to the fall of 1958. In less than a year yet he drove 500 million peasants into 24,000 people's communes, a process accompanied by terrific waste and kangaroo courts condemning resistants. Famine killed 20 million. After a recovery he then launched his Cultural Revolution from the end of 1965, continuing it irregularly until 1976, when he died on September 9. Less generalized than the Great Leap Forward, it killed only a half million more or less. The total was an effort to lift his world out of its hinges and hurl it to greater heights of power (and submission to him). This time he turned against the Communist Party itself while closing the schools and universities for a decade. He raised up hordes of younger people against his own party and government. Mao was able to govern against the party and the army as well, but then, seeing the anarchy the young people had wrought, used the army to reestablish order. When he and Zhou Enlai both died in 1976, the former General Party Secretary Deng Xiaoping, (1904-97), who had been shunted from power earlier, reestablished himself in 1977 and was able to give the party and country rational leadership. Avoiding formal governmental titles, he maintained his position as chairman of the Communist Chinese Communist Party Military Committee.

Deng set the pattern of China's rise to great pragmatic power and world economic leadership. He established a balance between ultimate governmental control *and* free enterprise. One of his great achievements was to silence the ideology of Communism. He would maintain party control only by way of the market and private ownership, not a contradiction as he managed it, but building upon Chinese rationality and sense of order going back to Confucius and earlier. In 1983 Deng announced to revolutionary effect against the Communist revolution just passed: "We should let some people get rich first, both in the countryside and in the urban areas. To get rich by hard work is glorious."[12]

But Deng's balance included ruthless action when an expression of democracy threatened it. In May 1989, emboldened by all of their new freedoms, students, joined by workers, began to demonstrate in the central Beijing square of Tiananmen and began to demand democracy. Hundreds of similar protests erupted throughout the country. The governmental leadership was uncertain what to do. Zhao Ziyang, the premier, mollifyingly visited the students in the square on May 19. But Deng decided that these protests endangered the state too much and on June 3-4 tanks and troop carriers attacked the crowd. In Beijing perhaps 1,000 died and 3,000 were arrested. Jiang Zemin, a strong Shanghai mayor, succeeded the mild Zhao. A moderate repression followed. The state remained secure.

Deng's solution was a "qualitative shift of economic gears which over the next decade completed China's transformation into a quasi-capitalist system." The result was a "fever of activity which changed the face of China (at least urban China) by the beginning of the new millennium." Social mobility would "compensate for a political system which could still be heavily repressive." Deng told the Communist Chinese Party Central Committee: "'Reform and greater openness [shades of Gorbachev!] are the only way out.'"[13] If destructive for Soviet Russia, this worked for Red China. One of the modalities was special economic zones, Shenzhen, in southern China near the economically lively Hong Kong, in 1992, and, soon, Shanghai and other cities, where free enterprise was encouraged, followed. China was plunging into production expansion and consumerism; she exploded into computer and online activity: by 2005 100 million Internet users and 383 million wielders of cell phones. Production needed more hands and poor peasants were moving into the cities, a revolutionary rural-urban shift. The country was undergoing a continuing revolution.

These figures of China's progress are cumulatively powerful: growth rate leaping from 7.8 percent in 1990 to 9.2 percent in 1991, then above 10 percent in 1996, when it dropped to 9.9 percent, remaining between 7.1 percent and 9.5 percent to 1994. Increases in industrial output for those years ranged from 7.8 percent to 23.6 percent, although this last figure was rather exceptional and the rate slipped down to 8.8 percent while rising to 18.1 percent in 1993.[14] And lest we forget, despite these relative figures and growing cash reserves, China was still a poor country trying to feed 1.3 billion people. During those years (1996 to 2001) the per capita GDP went from $1,858 (1990 international dollars) to $3,583 against $16,872 and $20,024 for twelve West European countries and $22,745 and $26,943 for the United States.[15] But we should note that China, even if her income was an eighth to a sixth of her Western competitors, had doubled her GDP in the period and was accelerating. Economists have surely optimistically seen her at the Western level by the year 2020.[16] That brings up another question: Can China maintain a free economy in an unfree state?

China's administration, we should note, is an extraordinary tour de force: it lacks any basis in ideology or even announced sense. No longer justified by Marxism, it is just there, a guardian of order and little more, hence its embarrassment over the Tiananmen Square events. The embarrassment could be transformed into opportunities if China's leaders move toward democracy with clearly articulated and accepted goals. But then they might move toward it with purposefully unclear goals.

The great danger for the leaders of such a powerful state is megalomania and denial. The great emperors, like Mao, could indulge their fantasies without effective controls. This had limited China in the imperial past, in thought as well as action. The only effective corrective is popular control reflecting *reality* that could prevent such extremes, thus those of a Napoleon, Hitler, Stalin, or Mao. *Could*, not necessarily would. The people are not necessarily a great beast, but they can be wrong-headed or seduced. They can also bethink itself in the long run. In any case they provide the best, the only, limits to imperial excess. At least China is experimenting with direct elections in the villages, due to a failure of party and state organizations, as the "only mechanism available." In 1996 some 900,000 villages elected leadership committees to three-year terms, "the most sweeping abdication of power since the People's Republic of China was founded." In Beijing itself the community council has been directly elected.[17] Internet, communications generally, and the concomitant contact with the outside world all have their effects of openness. China becomes more and more pervasively democratic as long as the leaders want to make money.

Can China rival the United States? Why not, with her huge and highly competent population? If it failed to develop her science and technology in the old closed imperial society, conditions are different and demand more now. Granted, she never quite had a philosophical base, Chinese thought never driving beyond visible boundaries. But it may yet. On the basis of past scientific and technical achievement, it should be able to do as well as the West. The result could be overweening power. But China is, on history's evidence, rational, if it can be aggressive. In view of this the United States must augment its own power with allies in Europe, perhaps Russia as well, and India, which has a larger role to play, and China's other neighbors. It will be a very different world, with the United States vis-à-vis the great China as Europe ranged itself with and against the United States in the past. This is another argument on the need for ultimate allies. The American position may be less distinguished, but no nation has guaranteed primacy—not even a China of the future.

Notes

1. Quoted, James L. McClain, *Japan: A Modern History* (New York: W. W. Norton, 2002), 177-78.
2. Quoted, Stanley Wolpert, *India* (Berkeley: University of California Press, 2005; 3rd ed.), 197.
3. Ashutosh Varshney, "India's Democratic Challenge," *Foreign Affairs* 86 (March/April 2007), 98.

4.   Bimal Jalan, *The Future of India: Politics, Economics, and Governance* (New York: Penguin/Viking, 2005), 6.
5.   Maddison, *The World Economy,* chart, 184.
6.   Benjamin I. Schwartz, *The World of Thought of Ancient China* (Cambridge, MA: Belknap Press, 1985), quotation, 60; see 383-406; Wolfram Eberhard, *A History of China* (Berkeley: University of California Press, 1987; 1st German ed.: 1948), 55-59, 35-40.
7.   Quoted, Joel Mokyr, *The Lever of Riches: Technological Creativity and Economic Progress* (Oxford: Oxford University Press, 1990), 229.
8.   Eberhard, *A History of China*, 35.
9.   Mokyr, *The Lever of Riches*, quotation, 209; discussion 209-18, part of ch., "China and Europe," 209-38.
10. Landes, *The Wealth and Poverty of Nations: Why Some Are So Rich and Some So Poor* (New York: W.W. Norton, 1999), 200-12.
11. Eberhard, *A History of China*, 351.
12. Quoted, Ian Jeffries, *China: A Guide to Economic and Political Developments* (London: Routledge, 2006), 15.
13. John Gittings, *The Changing Face of China: From Mao to Market* (Oxford: Oxford University Press, 2005), 251, 252 (quoting Deng).
14. Jeffries, *China*, 153-54; chart, 617.
15. Maddison, *The World Economy*, charts, 65, 89.
16. David Hale and Lyric Hughes Hale, "China Takes Off," *Foreign Affairs* 82 (November-December 2003); Paul J. Bailey, *China in the 20th Century* (London: Blackwell, 2001); Bruce Gilley, *China's Democratic Future* (New York: Columbia University Press, 2004); Oded Shenkar, *The Chinese Century: The Rising Chinese Economy* (Upper Saddle River, NJ: Wharton School, 2005).
17. Jeffries, *China*, 230-40; quotation, 230.

Bibliography

Abernethy, David B. *The Dynamics of Global Dominance: European Overseas Empires, 1415-1980.* New Haven: Yale University Press, 2000.

Adler, Selig. *The Uncertain Giant 1921-1941: American Foreign Policy Between the Wars.* New York: Macmillan, 1965.

Aldcroft, Derek H. *From Versailles to Wall Street 1919-1929.* Berkeley: University of California Press, 1981; 1st ed.: 1977.

Anderson, Clay J. *A Half-Century of Federal Reserve Policymaking, 1914-1964.* Philadelphia: FRB of Philadelphia, 1965.

Anderson, David L. *The Columbia Guide to the Vietnam War.* New York: Columbia University Press, 2002.

Ascher, Abraham. *The Revolution of 1905. 2 vols.* Stanford: Stanford University Press, 1988, 1992.

_____. *P. A. Stolypin: The Search for Stability in Late Imperial Russia.* Stanford: Stanford University Press, 2001.

Aust, Stefan. *Der Baader-Meinhof Complex.* Hamburg: Hoffman und Campe, 1997; 1st ed.: 1985.

Avrich, Paul. *Sacco and Vanzetti: The Anarchist Background.* Princeton: Princeton University Press, 1991.

Bailey, Paul J. *China in the 20th Century.* London: Blackwell, 2001.

Bairoch, Paul. *Economics and World History: Myths and Paradoxes.* Chicago: University of Chicago Press, 1993.

_____. "International Industrialization Levels from 1750 to 1980." *Journal of European Economic History,* no. 11 Fall (1982).

Barasco, Maryann. *Governing NOW: Grassroots Action in the National Organization for Women.* Ithaca: Cornell University Press, 2004.

Barber, William J. *From New Era to New Deal: Herbert Hoover, the Economists, and American Economic Policy, 1921-1933.* Cambridge: Cambridge University Press, 1985.

_____. *Designs within Disorder: Franklin D. Roosevelt, the Economists, and the Shaping of American Economic Policy, 1933-1945.* Cambridge: Cambridge University Press, 1996.

Bark, Dennis L. and David R. Gress. *A History of West Germany, vol 2: Democracy and its Discontents 1963-1988.* Oxford: Basil Blackwell, 1989.

Barkai, Avraham. *Nazi Economics: Ideology, Theory and Policy.* New York: Berg, 1990; 1st German ed.: 1985.

Barnes, Harry Elmer. *The Genesis of the World War: An Introduction to the Problem of War Guilt.* New York: Knopf, 1968 reprint of 2nd revised ed. of 1955; 1st ed.: 1929.

Barratt, G. R. V. *Voices in Exile: The Decembrist Memoirs.* Montreal: McGill-Queens University Press, 1974.

Bedford, Henry F., Trevor Colbourn, and James H. Madison. *The Americans: A Brief History.* New York: Harcourt, Brace, Jovanovich, 1972, 4th ed.

Behrman, Greg. *The Most Noble Adventure: The Marshall Plan.* New York: Free Press, 2007.

Bergen, Peter L. *Holy War, Inc.: Inside the Secret World of Osama bin Laden.* New York: Free Press, 2001.

Berghahn, Volker Rolf. *Imperial Germany, 1871-1914: Economy, Society, Culture, and Politics.* Providence: Berghahn Books, 1994.

_____. *Modern Germany: Society, Economy, and Politics in the 20th Century.* Cambridge: Cambridge University Press, 1982.

Berle, Adolf A. and Gardner C. Means. *The Modern Corporation and Private Property.* New York: Harcourt, Brace & World, 1932; revised ed.:1967.

Berman, Paul. *A Tale of Two Utopias: The Political Journey of the Generation of 1968.* New York: Norton, 1996.

Bernanke, Ben S., ed. *Essays on the Great Depression.* Princeton: Princeton University Press, 2000.

Blum, John Morton. *Woodrow Wilson and the Politics of Morality.* Boston: Little, Brown, 1956.

_____. *Years of Disorder: American Politics and Society, 1961-1974.* New York: Norton, 1991.

Bowker, Mike and Cameron Ross, eds. *Russia after the Cold War.* London: Longman, 2000.

Branch, Taylor. *Parting the Waters: America in the King Years 1954-63.* New York: Simon & Schuster, 1988.

Braunstein, Peter and Michael W. Doyle, eds. *Imagine Nation: The American Counterculture of the 1960s and 70s.* New York: Routledge, 2002.

Brownlee, W. Elliot. "The Public Sector." In *Cambridge Economic History of the United States,* 2000.

Bullock, Alan. *A Study in Tyranny.* London: Oldhams, 1952.

Burleigh, Michael. *The Third Reich: A New History.* London: Macmillan, 2000.

Caron, Francois. *An Economic History of Modern France.* Translated by Barbara Bray. New York: Columbia University Press, 1979.

Carosso, Vincent P. *The Morgans: Private International Bankers, 1854-1913.* Cambridge, MA: Harvard University Press, 1987.

Carr, E. H. "A Historical Turning Point: Marx, Lenin, Stalin." In *Revolutionary Russia: A Symposium,* edited by Richard Pipes. Cambridge: Harvard University Press, 1968.

Carroll, E. Malcolm. *Germany and the Great Powers 1866-1914: A Study in Public Opinion and Foreign Policy.* New York: Prentice-Hall, 1938.

Cashman, Sean Dennis. *America in the Gilded Age.* New York: New York University Press, 1993, 3rd ed.

Caute, David. *The Year of the Barricades: A Journey Through 1968.* New York: Harper & Row, 1988.

Cavallo, Dominick. *A Fiction of the Past: The Sixties in American History.* New York: St. Martin's Press, 1999.

Census, Bureau of the. *Statistical Abstract of United States.* Washington, 1930.

_____. *Statistical Abstract of the United States.* Washington, 1940.

_____. *Historical Statistics of the United States, Colonial Times to 1970, part I.* Washington, 1975.

. *Statistical Abstract of the United States.* Washington, 1925.

_____. *Statistical Abstract of the United States. Historical Statistics of the United States: Colonial Times to 1970.* Washington, 1999.

Chandler, Jr, Alfred D. *The Visible Hand: The Managerial Revolution in American Business.* Cambridge: Belknap/Harvard University Press, 1973.

Chandler, Lester V. *Benjamin Strong, Central Banker.* Washington: Brookings Institution, 1958.

Chernow, Ron. *Titan: The Life of John D Rockefeller, Sr.* New York: Random House, 1998.

Cirillo, Renato. *"The 'Socialism' of Leon Walras and His Economic Thinking" Leon Walras: Critical Assessments, 2: Walrasian Economics.* Edited by John Cunningham Wood, London: Routledge, 1993.

Clark, Martin. *Modern Italy 1871-1995.* London: Longman, 1996; 1st ed.: 1984.

Clark, Ronald W. *Edison: The Man Who Made the Future.* London: Macdonald & Jane's, 1977.

Clavin, Patricia, ed. *The Great Depression in Europe, 1929-1939.* New York: St. Martin's Press, 2000.

Clough, Shepard B. *The Economic History of Modern Italy.* New York: Columbia University Press, 1964.

Cohen, Stephen F. *Bukharin and the Bolshevik Revolution.* New York: Vintage, 1975.

Collier, Peter and David Horowitz. *Destructive Generation: Second Thoughts about the Sixties.* New York: Summit Books, 1989.

Commager, Henry Steele. *The American Mind: An Interpretation of American Thought since the 1880s.* New Haven: Yale University Press, 1950.

Commerce, U. S. Department of. *Historical Statistics of the United States: Colonial Times to 1957, Series D 46-47: Unemployment 1900-1957.* Washington, DC 1961.

_____. Gross *Domestic Product, 1929-2003* Bureau of Economic Analysis (*doc.gov*), 2004 [cited].

Conquest, Robert. *The Great Terror: A Reassessment.* Oxford: Oxford University Press, 1990.

Dallek, Robert. *Franklin D. Roosevelt, American Foreign Policy, 1932-1945.* New York: Oxford University Press, 1995; 1st ed.: 1979.

Davis, Kenneth S. *FDR: The New York Years 1928-1933.* New York: Random House, 1985: 1st ed.: 1979.

_____. *FDR: The New Deal Years 1933-1937: A History.* New York: Random House, 1986; 1st ed.: 1979.

_____. *FDR: Into the Storm 1937-1940: A History.* New York: Random House, 1993.

Deutscher, Isaac. *The Prophet Unarmed: Trotsky 1921-1934*. London: Oxford University Press, 1959.

_____.*The Prophet Outcast: Trotsky, 1929-1940*. Oxford: Oxford University Press, 1963.

_____. *The Prophet Armed, Trotsky: 1879-1921*. New York: Vintage, 1965; 1st ed.:1954.

Dormois, Jean-Pierre. *The French Economy in the 20th Century*. Cambridge: Cambridge University Press, 2004.

Dostoevsky, Fyodor. *Devils*. Translated by Michael B. Katz. Oxford: Oxford University Press, 1992; 1st ed.: 1871.

Drake, Richard. *The Aldo Moro Murder Case*. Cambridge, MA: Harvard University Press, 1995.

Dreyfus-Armand, Genevieve. *Les Annees 68: Le temps de la contestation*. Brussels: Editions Complexe, 2000.

Eberhard, Wolfram. *A History of China*. Berkeley: University of California Press, 1987; 1st. German ed.: 1948.

Edwards, Lee, ed. *The Collapse of Communism*. Stanford: Hoover Institution Press, 2000.

Engerman, Stanley L. and Robert E. Gallman, eds. *The Economic History of the United States*. 3 vols. Cambridge: Cambridge University Press, 2000.

Esposito, John L. *Unholy War: Terror in the Name of Islam*. Oxford: Oxford University Press, 2002.

Eyck, Erich. *A History of the Weimar Republic, 2 vols*. Cambridge, MA: Harvard University Press, 1962-63.

Faulkner, Harold U. *Politics, Reform, and Expansion 1890-1900*. New York: Harper & Brothers, 1959.

Fay, Sidney B. *The Origins of the World War, 2 vols*. New York: Macmillan, 1930.

Feis, Herbert. *The Diplomacy of the Dollar*. Baltimore: John Hopkins Press, 1950.

Felix, David. *Protest: Sacco-Vanzetti and the Intellectuals*. Bloomington: Indiana University Press, 1965.

_____. *Walther Rathenau and the Weimar Republic: The Politics of Reparations.*Baltimore: Johns Hopkins Press, 1971.

_____. *Biography of an Idea: John Maynard Keynes and The General Theory*. New Brunswick, NJ: Transaction Publishers, 1995.

_____. *Keynes: A Critical Life*. Westport, CT: Greenwood, 1999.

Ferrell, Robert H. *Peace in Their Time: The Origins of the Kellogg-Briand Peace Pact*. New Haven: Yale University Press, 1952.

_____. *The Presidency of Calvin Coolidge*. Lawrence: University Press of Kansas, 1998.

Fest, Joachim C. *Hitler*. Translated by Richard and Clare Winston. New York: Vintage, 1975; 1st Ger. ed.: 1973.

Fischer, Fritz. *Germany's Aims in the First World War*. New York: Norton, 1967; 1st German ed.: 1961.

Fischer, Klaus P. *America in White, Black, and Gray: The Stormy Sixties*. New York: Continuum, 2006.

Fischer, Louis. *The Life of Lenin.* New York: Harper & Row, 1964.

Floud, Roderick and Paul Johnson, eds. *The Cambridge Economic History of Modern Britain, 3: Structural Change and Growth, 1939-2000.* Cambridge: Cambridge University Press, 2004.

Foreman-Peck, James. *A History of the World Economy: International Economic Relations since 1850.* 2nd ed. Hemel Hempstead: Harvester Wheatsheaf, 1996.

Fourastié, Jean. *Les Trente Glorieuses ou la Révolution invisible de 1946 à 1975.* Paris: Fayard, 1979.

Frady, Marshall. *Martin Luther King, Jr.* New York: Lipper-Viking, 2002.

Frank, Joseph. *Dostoevsky: The Years of Ordeal, 1850-1859.* Princeton: Princeton University Press, 1983.

_____. *Dostoevsky: The Seeds of Revolt, 1821-1849.* Princeton: Princeton University Press, 1976.

Friedan, Betty. *The Feminine Mystique.* New York: Norton, 1997; 1st ed.: 1963.

_____. *Life So Far.* New York: Simon & Schuster, 2000.

Friedman, Milton and Anna Schwartz. *A Monetary History of the United States, 1867-1960.* Princeton: Princeton University Press, 1963.

Gaddis, John Lewis. *We Now Know: Rethinking Cold War History.* Oxford: Clarendon Press, 1997.

_____. *The Cold War: A New History.* New York: Penguin, 2001.

_____. *Strategies of Containment.* New York: Oxford University Press, 2005.

Galbraith, John Kenneth. *The Great Crash.* Boston: Houghton-Mifflin, 1955.

Gamble, Andrew. *The Free Economy and the Strong State: The Politics of Thatcherism.* London: Macmillan, 1994, 2nd ed.

Garraty, John A. *Unemployment in History: Economic Thought and Public Policy.* New York: Harper & Row, 1978.

_____. *The Great Depression.* New York: Harcourt Brace Jovanovich, 1986.

Geiling, Martin. "Germany's Changing Political Landscape." In *The Political Economy of Unification.* Edited by Thomas Lange and J. R. Shakleton. Providence: Berghahn, 1998.

Gelb, Leslie H. and Richard K. Betts. *The Irony of Vietnam: The System Worked.* Washington: Brookings Institution, 1979.

Gildea, Robert. *France since 1945.* Oxford: Oxford University Press, 1996.

Gilley, Bruce. *China's Democratic Future.* New York: Columbia University Press, 2004.

Gitlin, Todd. *The Sixties: Years of Hope, Days of Rage.* New York: Bantam, 1987.

Gittings, John. *The Changing Face of China: From Mao to Market.* Oxford: Oxford University Press, 2005.

Glad, Betty. *Charles Evans Hughes and the Illusions of Innocence.* Urbana, IL: University of Illinois Press, 1966.

Gordon, John Steele. *An Empire of Wealth: The Epic Story of American Economic Power.* New York: HarperCollins, 2004.

Green, E. H. H. *Thatcher.* London: Hodder Arnold, 2006.

Hall, Thomas E. and J. David Ferguson. *The Great Depression: An International Disaster of Perverse Economic Policies.* Ann Arbor: University of Michigan Press, 1998.

Hale, David and Lyric Hughes. "China Takes Off." *Foreign Affairs,* no. 82 November-December (2003).

Hall, Walter Phelps and Robert Greenhalgh Albion. *A History of England and the British Empire.* Boston: Ginn, 1937.

Hannah, Leslie. "A Futile Experiment: The State Ownership of Industry." In *The Cambridge Economic History of Modern Britain.* Cambridge: Cambridge University Press, 2004.

Hardach, Karl. *The Political Economy of Germany in the Twentieth Century.* Berkeley: University of California Press, 1980.

Harrison, Mark. "The Economics of World War II: An Overview." In *The Economics of World War II,* edited by Harrison.

Harrison, Mark, ed. *The Economics of World War II: Six Great Powers in International Comparison.* Cambridge: Cambridge University Press, 1998.

Helbich, Wolfgang J. *Die Reparationen in de Ära Bruning.* Berlin: Colloquium, 1962.

Herzen, Alexander. *My Past and Thoughts, abridged.* Edited by Dwight Mac-Donald. Berkeley: University of California Press, 1982; 1st ed: 1973.

Hitler, Adolf. *Mein Kampf.* Translated by Alan Johnson. New York: Reynal and Hitchcock, 1939.

Hoffman, Walther G. *Das Wachstum der Deutschen Wirtschaft seit der Mitte des 19. Jahrhundert.* Berlin: Springer, 1965.

Holborn, Hajo. *A History of Modern Germany 1840-1945.* Princeton: Princeton University Press, 1969.

Hosking, Geoffrey. *The First Socialist Society: A History of the Soviet Union from Within.* Cambridge, MA: Harvard University Press, 1985.

Hunt, Michael H. *The American Ascendancy.* Chapel Hill: University of North Carolina Press, 2007.

Huntington, Samuel P. *The Clash of Civilizations and the Remaking of the World Order.* New York: Simon & Schuster, 1996.

Hurt, R. Douglas. *American Agriculture: A Brief History.* Ames, Iowa: Iowa State University Press, 1994.

Irving, David. *Hitler's War.* New York: Viking, 1977.

Jalan, Bimal. *The Future of India: Politics, Economics, and Governance.* New York: Penguin/Viking, 2005.

Jaszi, Oscar. *The Dissolution of the Habsburg Monarchy.* Chicago: University of Chicago Press, 1966, 1st ed.: 1929.

Jeffries, Ian. *China: A Guide to Economic and Political Developments.* London: Routledge, 2006.

Jevons, W. Stanley. *The Theory of Political Economy.* New York: Kelly & Millman, 5th ed.: 1957; 1st ed.: 1871.

Johnson, H. Clark. *Gold, France, and the Great Depression.* New Haven: Yale University Press, 1997.

Jonas, Gilbert. *Freedom's Sword: The NAACP and the Struggle against Racism in America, 1909-1969.* New York: Routledge, 2005.

Jones, Joseph M. *Tariff Retaliation: Repercussions of the Hawley-Smoot Bill.* New York: Garland, 1983; 1st ed.: 1934 (University of Pennsylvania Press).

Kanigel, Robert. *The One Best Way: Frederick Winslow Taylor and the Enigma of Efficiency.* New York: Viking, 1997.

Kaplan, Lawrence S. *NATO and the United States.* New York: Twayne, 1994; 1st ed.: 1988.

Karnow, Stanley. *Vietnam: A History.* New York: Penguin, 1984; 1st ed.: 1983.

Katz, Barry. *Herbert Marcuse and the Art of Liberation.* London: Verso, 1982.

Keegan, John. *The Second World War.* New York: Viking Penguin, 1990.

_____. *The First World War.* New York: Knopf, 1999.

Kennan, George F. *American Diplomacy 1900-1955.* Chicago: University of Chicago Press, 1951.

_____. *Memoirs 1925-1950.* Boston: Little, Brown, 1967.

_____. *Memoirs 1950-1963.* New York: Pantheon, 1972.

_____. *The Decline of Bismarck's European Order: Franco-Russian Relations, 1875-1890.* Princeton: Princeton University Press, 1979.

Kennedy, Paul. *The Rise and Fall of the Great Powers: Economic Change and Military Conflict from 1500 to 2000.* New York: Random House, 1987.

Kenwood, A. G. and A. L. Lougheed. *The Growth of the International Economy 1820-1990.* London: Routledge, 1992: 3rd ed.

Keynes, John Maynard. *The General Theory of Employment, Interest, and Money.* London: Macmillan, 1936.

_____. *"The Depression in Trade".* Vol. 17: Activities: 1920-1922: Treaty Revision and Reconstuction, *Collected Writings.* London: Macmillan, 1977.

_____. *"An End to Reparations?" Vol.* 18: Activities: 1922-1932: The End of Reparations, *Collected Writings.* London: Macmillan, 1978.

_____. *Collected Writings, vol. 18: Activities 1922-1932: The End of Reparations.* London, 1978.

_____. *Activities 1931-1939: World Crises and Policies in Britain and America.* Vol. 21, *Collected Writings.* London: Macmillan, 1982.

Kimball, Roger. *The Long March: How the Cultural Revolution of the 1960s Changed America.* San Francisco: Encounter, 2000.

Kindleberger, Charles P. *The World in Depression 1929-1939.* Berkeley: University of California Press, 1973.

_____. *A Financial History of Western Europe.* London: George Allen & Unwin, 1984.

Klein, Eleanor R. *Feminism under Fire.* Amherst, NY: Prometheus, 1996.

Labor, U. S. Department of, Bureau of Labor Statistics. *Compensation of the Civilian Labor Force, 1929-2001* [cited]. Available from *bls.gov.*

Labor, U. S. Department of: Bureau of Labor Statistics, *bls.gov. Composition of the Civilian Labor Force. 1929-2001* 2002 [cited]. Available from *bea.gov.*

Labour Party, Great Britain. "Towards a New World: Being the Reconstruction Programme of the Labour Party." New York, Microform (W. R. Browne): 1918.

Lacey, Robert. *Ford: The Man and the Machine.* Boston: Little Brown, 1986.

LaFeber, Walter. *America, Russia, and the Cold War.* New York: McGraw-Hill, 1993: 7th ed.

Landes, David. *The Wealth and Poverty of Nations: Why Some Are So Rich and Some So Poor.* New York: Norton, 1999.

Langer, William L. *The Diplomacy of Imperialism 1890-1902. 2* vols. New York: Knopf, 1935.

Laue, Theodore von. *Sergei Witte and the Industrialization of Russia.* New York: Columbia University Press, 1963.

Lazar, Marc. *Maisons Rouges: Les partis communistes français et italian de la Libération à nos jours.* Paris: Aubier, 1992.

League of Nations. Memoranda on Public Finance 1921-22. Geneva: League of Nations, 1923.

_____. Secretariat: Economic, Financial and Transit Department. *Industrialization and Foreign Trade.* New York: League of Nations, 1945.

Lekachman, Robert. *The Age of Keynes.* New York: Random House, 1966.

Lenin, Vladimir I. *State and Revolution, Selected Works in One Volume.* New York: International Publishers, 1974.

_____. *Development of Capitalism in Russia: The Process of the Formation of a Home Market of Large-Scale Industry.* Moscow: Foreign Language Publishing House, 1956; 1st ed.: [Russian] 1899.

Leuchtenburg, William E. *The Perils of Prosperity 1914-32.* Chicago: University of Chicago Press, 1958.

_____. *Franklin D. Roosevelt and the New Deal 1932-1940.* New York: Harper & Row, 1963.

Lewin, Moshe. *Russian Peasants and Soviet Power: A Study of Collectivization.* New York: Norton, 1975; 1st [French] ed.: 1966.

Licht, Walter. *Industrializing America: The Nineteenth Century.* Baltimore: Johns Hopkins University Press, 1975.

Liebman, Marcel. *The Russian Revolution.* New York: Vintage, 1970.

Lindert, Peter H. *U.S. Foreign Trade and Tariff Policy.* In *The Cambridge Economic History of the United States.* Cambridge: Cambridge University Press, 2000.

Louria, Margot. *Triumph and Downfall: America's Pursuit of Peace and Prosperity 1921-1933.* Westport, CT: Greenwood, 2001.

Love, Philip H. *Andrew W. Mellon: The Man and His Work.* Baltimore: F. HeathCoggins, 1929.

Lukacs, John. *George Kennan: A Study of Character.* New Haven: Yale University Press, 2007.

Mack Smith, Denis. *Modern Italy: A Political History.* Ann Arbor: University of Michigan Press, 1947.

Maddison, Angus. *The World Economy: Historical Statistics.* Paris: Organization of Economic Cooperation and Development, 2003.

Malia, Martin. *Alexander Herzen and the Birth of Russian Socialism.* Cambridge: Harvard University Press, 1971.

Marcuse, Herbert. *Eros and Civilization: A Philosophical Inquiry into Freud.* Boston: Beacon Press, 1955.

_____. *One-Dimensional Man: Studies in the Ideology of Advanced Industrial Society.* Boston: Beacon Press, 1964.

Marwick, Arthur. *The Sixties: Cultural Revolution in Britain, France, Italy, and the United States, 1958-1974.* Oxford: Oxford University Press, 1998.

Marx, Karl. *Capital.* Translated by Samuel Moore and Edward Aveling. Vol. 1. New York: International Publishers, 1947; reprint of edition of 1889.

_____. *Werke.* Vol. 35. (East) Berlin: Dietz, 1973.

_____. *Collected Works.* Vol. 6. New York: International, 1976.

Matusow, Allan. *Nixon's Economy: Booms, Busts, Dollars, and Votes.* Lawrence: University of Kansas Press, 1998.

McClain, James L. *Japan: A Modern History.* New York: Norton, 2002.

McCullough, David. *John Adams.* New York: Simon & Schuster, 2001.

McFaul, Michael. *Russia's Unfinished Revolution: Political Change from Gorbachev to Putin.* Ithaca: Cornell University Press, 2001.

McNamara, Robert S. *In Retrospect: The Tragedy and Lessons of Vietnam.* New York: Random House, 1995.

McWilliams, John E. *The 1960s Cultural Revolution.* Westport, CT: Greenwood, 2000.

Medlicott, W. N. *Contemporary England 1914-1964.* London: Longman, 1967.

Mee, Charles L., Jr. *The Marshall Plan: The Launching of the Pax Americana.* New York: Simon and Schuster, 1984.

Menger, Carl. *Principles of Economics.* Translated by James Dingwall and Bert F. Hoselitz. New York: New York University Press, 1981; 1st German ed.: 1874.

Michaels, Debra. "From Consciousness Expansion to Consciousness Raising." In *Imagine Nation,* edited by Braunstein and Doyle.

Miller, Timothy. "The Sixties-Era Communes." In *Imagine Nation: The American Counterculture of the 1960s and 70s,* edited by Peter and Michael W. Doyle Braunstein, eds. New York: Routledge, 2002.

Mitchell, B. R. *European Historical Statistics 1750-1970.* New York: Columbia University Press, 1978.

Mitrany, David. *Marx against the Peasant: A Study in Social Dogmatics.* New York: Collier, 1961; 1st. ed: 1951.

Mokyr, Joel. *The Lever of Riches: Technological Creativity and Economic Progress.* Oxford: Oxford University Press, 1990.

Moulton, Harold G. and Leo Pasvolsky. *War Debts and World Prosperity.* Washington: Brookings Institution, 1932.

Nettl, Peter. *Rosa Luxembourg: Abridged Edition.* London: Oxford University Press, 1967; 1st ed.: 1966.

Newell, John, ed. *The Italian General Election of 2001: Berlusconi's Victory.* Manchester: Manchester University Press, 2002.

Olmstead, Alan L. and Paul M. Rhode *"The Transformation of Northern Agriculture."* In the *Cambridge Economic History of the United States.*

Overy, R. J. *War and Economy in the Third Reich.* Oxford: Clarendon Press, 1994.

Park, William. *Defending the West: A History of NATO.* Brighton, UK: Wheatsheaf, 1986.

Perkins, Frances. *The Roosevelt I Knew.* New York: Viking, 1946.

Peterson, Edward N. *Hjalmar Schacht: A Political-Economic Study of Germany 1923-1945.* Boston: Christopher, 1954.

Phillips, Anthony. "Economic Reform." In *Russia after the Cold War,* edited by Bowker & Ross.

Pipes, Richard, ed. *Revolutionary Russia: A Symposium.* Cambridge: Harvard University Press, 1968.

Pisani, Sallie. *The CIA and the Marshall Plan.* Lawrence: University Press of Kansas, 1991.

Pollard, Sidney. *European Integration 1815-1970.* London: Thames and Hudson, 1974.

Ranelagh, John. *CIA: A History.* London: BBC Books, 1991.

Rauch, Basil. *Roosevelt from Munich to Pearl Harbor: A Study in the Creation of a Foreign Policy.* New York: Barnes and Noble, 1967; 1st ed.: 1950.

Reeves, Thomas C. *Twentieth Century America: A Brief History.* New York: Oxford University Press, 2000.

Reitan, Earl A. *The Thatcher Revolution: Margaret Thatcher, John Major, Tony Blair, and the Transformation of Modern Britain, 1979-2001.* London: Rowman & Littlefield, 2003.

Ricardo, David. *On the Principles of Political Economy and Taxation.* Georgetown, DC: Joseph Milligan, 1819: 1st American ed.

Ritter, Gretchen. *Goldbugs and Greenbacks: The Antimonopoly Tradition and the Politics of Finance in America.* Cambridge: Cambridge University Press, 1997.

Robbins, Lionel. *The Great Depression.* London: Macmillan, 1934.

Rockoff, Hugh. "The United States: From Ploughshares to Swords." In *The Economics of World War II: Six Great Powers in International Comparison,* ed, Mark Harrison. Cambridge: Cambridge University Press, 1998.

Romano, Flavio. *Clinton and Blair: The Political Economy of the Third Way.* London: Routledge, 2006.

Rosen, Elliott A. *Roosevelt, the Great Depression, and the Economics of Recovery.* Charlottesville: University of Virginia Press, 2005.

Rosenberg, Arthur. *A History of the German Republic.* London: Methuen, 1936.

Rotberg, Robert A. *The Rise of Nationalism in Central Africa: The Making of Malawi and Zambia 1873-1964.* Cambridge: Harvard University Press, 1972; 1st ed.: 1965.

Russell, Francis. *Tragedy in Dedham.* New York: McGraw-Hill, 1962.

Samuelson, Paul A. "Wages and Interest: A Modern Dissection of Marxian Economic Models." *American Economic Review* 47 (1957): 884-912.

Sauvy, Alfred. *Histoire économique de la France entre les deux guerres.* Paris: Fayard, 1965.

Schapiro, Leonard. *The Communist Party of the Soviet Union.* New York: Vintage,1971; 1st ed.: 1960.

Schmitt, Bernadotte E. *The Coming of the War 1914. 2* vols. New York: Scribner's Sons, 1930.

Schreiner, Samuel A. Jr. *Henry Clay Frick: The Gospel of Greed.* New York: St. Martin's Press, 1995.

Schuker, Stephen A. *The End of French Predominance in Europe: The Financial Crisis of 1924 and the Adoption of the Dawes Plan.* Chapel Hill: University of North Carolina Press, 1976.

Schulzinger, Robert D. *A Time for War: The United States and Vietnam 1941-1975.* New York: Oxford University Press, 1997.

Schumpeter, Joseph A. "Power and Pride." In *The Age of Imperialism,* edited by Robin W. Winks. Englewood Cliffs, NJ: Prentice-Hall, 1969.

Schwartz, Benjamin I. *The World of Thought of Ancient China.* Cambridge, MA: Belknap Press, 1985.

Schwartz, Jordan A. *The New Dealers in the Age of Roosevelt.* New York: Knopf, 1993.

Service, Robert. *Stalin: A Biography.* Cambridge, MA: Belknap Press, 2005.

Shenkar, Oded. *The Chinese Century: The Rising Chinese Economy.* Upper Saddle River, NJ: Wharton School, 2005.

Shub, David. *Lenin.* New York: Doubleday, 1945.

Siebert, Horst. *The German Economy: Beyond the Social Market.* Princeton: Princeton University Press, 2005.

Sloan, John W. *The Reagan Effect: Economics and Presidential Leadership.* Lawrence: University Press of Kansas, 1999.

Smith, Adam. *The Wealth of Nations.* Edited by Andrew Skinner. Baltimore: Penguin Books, 1970; 1st ed.: 1776.

Stern, Jessica. *Terror in the Name of God.* New York: Ecco/HarperCollins, 2003.

Students for a Democratic Society. *The Port Huron Statement.* Chicago: Charles H. Kerr, 1990; 1st ed.: 1962.

Tansill, Charles. *America Goes to War.* Boston: Little, Brown, 1932.

Tarrow, Sydney. *Democracy and Disorder: Protest and Politics in Italy.* Oxford: Clarendon Press, 1989.

Taussig, Frank W. *The Tariff History of the United States.* New York: Johnson Reprint, 1931: 8th ed.; 1st ed.: 1888.

Taylor, A. J. P. *The Struggle for Mastery in Europe 1848-1918.* Oxford: Oxford University Press, 1971; 1st. ed.: 1954.

Temin, Peter. *Lessons from the Great Depression.* Cambridge: MIT Press, 1989.

_____. *"The Great Depression."* 2000: In the *Cambridge Economic History of the United States.*

Tocqueville, Alexis de. *Democracy in America.* Edited by Richard D. Heffner. New York: New American Library, 1956; original French ed.:1835.

Townsend, Mary Evelyn. *The Rise and Fall of Germany's Colonial Empire 1884-1914*. New York: Howard Fertig, 1966; 1st ed.: 1930.

Twain, Mark. *Life on the Mississippi[in] The Favorite Works of Mark Twain*. Garden City, NY: Garden City Publishing Company, 1935; 1st ed.: 1883.

_____. *Adventures of Huckleberry Finn*. Berkeley: University of California Press, 2002; 1st ed.:1884.

Twain, Mark and Charles Dudley Warner. *The Gilded Age: A Tale of Today.* 21st ed. New York: Penguin Putnam, 2001; 1st ed.: 1973.

Ulam, Adam B. *Stalin: The Man and His Era*. New York: Viking, 1973.

_____. *Lenin and the Bolsheviks*. London: Fortuna-Collins, 1973: 1st ed.: 1965 as *The Bolsheviks*.

_____. *In the Name of the People: Prophets and Conspirators in Prerevolutionary Russia*. New York: Viking, 1977.

Urban, Joan Barth. *Moscow and the Italian Communist Party*. Ithaca: Cornell University Press, 1986.

Varshney, Ashutosh. "India's Democratic Challenge." *Foreign Affairs,* no. 86 March/April 2007.

Venturi, Franco. *Roots of Revolution: A History of the Populist and Socialist Movements in 19th-century Russia*. New York: Grossett & Dunlop, Universal Library, 1966; 1st [Italian] ed.: 1952.

Wachhorst, Wyn. *Thomas Alva Edison: An American Myth*. Cambridge, MA: MIT Press, 1981.

Waite, Robert G. L. *Vanguard of Nazism: The Free Corps Movement in Postwar Germany 1918-23*. Cambridge, MA: Harvard University Press, 1952.

Walker, Martin. *The Cold War.* New York: Henry Holt, 1994.

Wall, Joseph Frazier. *Andrew Carnegie*. New York: Oxford University Press, 1970.

Walras, Leon. *Elements of Pure Economics or The Theory of Social Wealth*. Translated by William Jaffe. Fairfield, CT: Augustus M. Kelly, 1977; 1st. French [half] ed.:1874.

_____. *Leon Walras, 1834-1910*. Edited by Mark Blaug. Aldershot: Elgar, 1992.

_____. *Vol. 2: Walrasian Economics*. Edited by John Cunningham Wood, *Critical Assessments*. London: Routledge, 1993.

Weiner, Tim. *Legacy of Ashes: The History of the CIA*. New York: Doubleday, 2007.

Wenger, Andreas, ed. *Transforming NATO in the Cold War.* London: Routledge, 2007.

Wheeler, Mark, ed. *The Economics of the Great Depression*. Kalamazoo, MI: Upjohn Institute, 1998.

Wheeler-Bennett, John. *Brest-Litovsk: The Forgotten Peace, March 1918*. New York: Norton, 1971; 1st ed.: 1938.

White, Eugene N. "Banking and Finance in the 20th Century." In *The Cambridge Economic History of the United States*.

Winock, Michel. *Chronique des Années Soixante*. Paris: Editions du Seuil, 1987.

Wolpert, Stanley. *India.* Berkeley: University of California Press, 2005, 3rd ed.

Woytinsky, Wladimir S. *Die Welt in Zahlen.* Vol. 1. Berlin: R. Mosse, 1925.

Wueschner, Sylvan A. *Charting Twentieth Century Monetary Policy: Herbert Hoover and Benjamin Strong, 1917-1927.* Westport, CT: Greenwood, 1999.

Zamagni, Vera. *The Economic History of Italy 1860-1990.* Oxford: Clarendon Press, 1993.

Zieger, Robert H. *American Workers, American Unions.* Baltimore: Johns Hopkins University Press, 1990; 1st ed.: 1986.

Index

\